Apple Watch™ and iPhone® Fitness
Tips and Tricks

Jason R. Rich

800 East 96th Street,
Indianapolis, Indiana 46240 USA

APPLE WATCH™ AND IPHONE® FITNESS TIPS AND TRICKS

ISBN-13: 978-0-7897-5475-2

ISBN-10: 0-7897-5475-4

Library of Congress Control Number: 2015944239

Second Printing: October 2015

TRADEMARKS

WARNING AND DISCLAIMER

SPECIAL SALES

For information about buying this title in bulk quantities, or for special sales opportunities (which may include electronic versions; custom cover designs; and content particular to your business, training goals, marketing focus, or branding interests), please contact our corporate sales department at corpsales@pearsoned.com or (800) 382-3419.

For government sales inquiries, please contact governmentsales@pearsoned.com.

For questions about sales outside the U.S., please contact international@pearsoned.com.

EDITOR-IN-CHIEF
Greg Wiegand

SENIOR ACQUISITIONS EDITOR
Laura Norman

DEVELOPMENT EDITOR
Todd Brakke

MANAGING EDITOR
Kristy Hart

SENIOR PROJECT EDITOR
Lori Lyons

COPY EDITOR
Paula Lowell

INDEXER
Erika Millen

PROOFREADER
Debbie Williams

TECHNICAL EDITOR
Christian Kenyeres

EDITORIAL ASSISTANT
Kristen Watterson

COMPOSITOR
Trina Wurst

COVER DESIGNER
Mark Shirar

CONTENTS AT A GLANCE

TABLE OF CONTENTS

ABOUT THE AUTHOR

Jason R. Rich (www.jasonrich.com) is an accomplished author, journalist, and photographer, who writes extensively about the iPhone, iPad, and Apple Watch.

Some of his recently published books for Que Publishing include: *iPad and iPhone Tips and Tricks (5th Edition)*, *My Digital Photography for Seniors*, *iPad and iPhone Digital Photography Tips and Tricks*, and *My GoPro Camera*.

He also recently created and produced the *Managing Your Information Using Evernote* and *Using Your GoPro Hero3+: Learn To Shoot Better Photos and Videos* video courses for Que, and has written numerous other books about the iPhone, iPad, interactive entertainment, and the Internet.

To read more than 150 free articles about how to use the iPhone, iPad, and Apple Watch written by Jason R. Rich, visit www.iOSArticles.com (and click on the Articles tab) or www.quepublishing.com.

Through his work as an enrichment lecturer, he often offers workshops and classes about mobile technology, digital photography, and the Internet aboard cruise ships operated by Royal Caribbean, Princess Cruises Lines, and Celebrity Cruise Lines, as well as through Adult Education programs in the New England area.

Please follow Jason R. Rich on Twitter (@JasonRich7) and Instagram (@JasonRich7).

DEDICATION

This book is dedicated to my family and friends, including my niece, Natalie, and my Yorkshire Terrier, named Rusty, who is always by my side as I'm writing.

ACKNOWLEDGMENTS

Thanks once again to Laura Norman and Greg Wiegand at Que for inviting me to work on this project and for their ongoing support. I would also like to thank Todd Brakke, Kristen Watterson, Lori Lyons, and Paula Lowell for their ongoing assistance, and offer my gratitude to everyone else at Que whose talents helped to make this book a reality.

I'd like to convey a special thank you to the fitness models who appear throughout this book, including: Michael Jade Paquette, Andrea Cadigan, Richard Wingert, Tamara von Schmidt-Pauli, and Ksenia Desautels, as well as the fitness experts who are featured within the interviews you'll soon be reading.

Finally, congratulations to the Apple Watch development team and executives at Apple for creating yet another exciting product that is changing the way we interact with technology in our everyday lives.

WE WANT TO HEAR FROM YOU!

As the reader of this book, *you* are our most important critic and commentator. We value your opinion and want to know what we're doing right, what we could do better, what areas you'd like to see us publish in, and any other words of wisdom you're willing to pass our way.

We welcome your comments. You can email or write to let us know what you did or didn't like about this book—as well as what we can do to make our books better.

Please note that we cannot help you with technical problems related to the topic of this book.

When you write, please be sure to include this book's title and author as well as your name and email address. We will carefully review your comments and share them with the author and editors who worked on the book.

Email: feedback@quepublishing.com

Mail: Que Publishing
               ATTN: Reader Feedback
               800 East 96th Street
               Indianapolis, IN 46240 USA

READER SERVICES

Visit our website and register this book at quepublishing.com/register for convenient access to any updates, downloads, or errata that might be available for this book.

1

USE THE IPHONE AS A POWERFUL HEALTH AND FITNESS TOOL

When you look into the mirror, what do you see? Perhaps you think to yourself, "Gee, I need to lose some weight." Maybe you would like to pack on some additional muscle, feel better about your overall physique, more efficiently manage the stress in your life, eat healthier, reduce your cholesterol, become more active, get a better night's sleep, or somehow boost your overall self-esteem and confidence level.

Wouldn't it be great if you could simply install an app onto your iPhone, follow the directions offered by the app, and magically see the results you've only dreamed about become a reality?

Well, guess what? Literally hundreds of apps are available from the App Store that can help you achieve these and other fitness, health, diet, stress management, and sleep-related goals. In fact, the iOS operating system that controls your iPhone now comes with pre-installed apps, such as Health, that can help you start working toward your goals right away. For example, these apps can track your activity-related data

that's collected throughout your day, and/or whenever you engage specifically in fitness-oriented activities.

Combining the power of your iPhone and the available apps with the Apple Watch's capabilities, as well as other equipment and accessories, makes it easier than ever before to create, manage, work toward, and ultimately achieve any or all of your fitness, health, diet, stress management, and/or sleep-related goals.

The key phrase in the preceding sentence is *work toward*. Installing the right apps onto your iPhone or wearing an Apple Watch on your wrist in and of themselves will not generate the results you desire. You will not wake up tomorrow 10 pounds lighter, have a six-pack, be stress free, or no longer crave unhealthy foods. However, if you're willing to carefully define your goals, and then take an active role in achieving them by dedicating the time, energy, and effort that are required, your iPhone and/or Apple Watch could prove to be indispensable tools that can assist with your endeavors. Figure 1.1 shows someone using, his iPhone and Apple Watch as part of his daily fitness routine.

iPhone Armband Case

Apple Watch

FIGURE 1.1

The iPhone and Apple Watch can help you achieve your health, fitness, diet, and sleep-related goals.

When you use them with the right apps, the iPhone and Apple Watch combination can help you set and manage realistic fitness, health, diet, and sleep-related goals.

These tools can track and analyze your progress, help you stay motivated, share your successes with others, and provide you with useful guidance and information, when and where it's needed.

> **! CAUTION** Your iPhone and Apple Watch will *not* do the hard work for you! Depending on your goals, you will still need to exercise, eat right (and in moderation), get enough sleep, and follow the advice and strategies that the experts you opt to work with (such as a personal trainer or nutritionist) provide.

WHAT TO EXPECT FROM THIS BOOK

Apple Watch and iPhone Fitness Tips and Tricks is all about showing you how to use these cutting-edge and customizable tools for a wide range of health, fitness, diet, and sleep-related activities. This is not a how-to diet or how-to workout book. It does not replace the need for following a diet plan, or working with a medical professional, dietitian, personal trainer, or other licensed specialist. It can, however, teach you how to use the iPhone and Apple Watch as additional, powerful, and customizable information resources, as well as tracking and management tools.

This book shows you exactly how to set up and use your iPhone and Apple Watch, and about the wide range of optional apps, accessories, fitness trackers, and other products that you can use with them to help you achieve your fitness goals.

In addition, you'll read a handful of in-depth interviews with fitness and medical experts, starting with A Sweat Life (www.asweatlife.com) founder Jeana Anderson, who share their tips and strategies for using the iPhone and Apple Watch as health, fitness, diet, and/or sleep tools.

What this book does is help you quickly become proficient using the technology that's available to you, so you can more efficiently focus on your health, fitness, diet, and/or sleep-related goals.

WHAT THE IPHONE OFFERS

In addition to being a powerful smartphone with Internet connectivity and a host of diverse apps, your iPhone can wirelessly communicate with other equipment and accessories (via Wi-Fi, Bluetooth, or AirPlay), as well as gather, store, analyze, and process information and data using its built-in tools, technologies, and sensors.

For example, your iPhone has GPS (Location Services) capabilities and a built-in digital compass, so it can determine its exact location at any given moment and use this information in a variety of ways as it's needed. The smartphone also has two built-in cameras, a built-in microphone and speaker, a headphone jack, a backlit multi-touch display, a Lightning port connector, as well as a barometer, accelerometer, proximity sensor, ambient light sensor, and in some models, a Touch ID sensor.

Using these built-in technologies, the features and functions that are built in to the iOS operating system, the apps that come preinstalled on the iPhone, and optional third-party apps that are available from the App Store, your iPhone can automatically acquire, analyze, store, and share information not only from the Internet, but also about itself, its surroundings, and its user.

! CAUTION   Because one of the main focuses of this book is on using the Apple Watch with the iPhone, to benefit from all the information you're about to learn, you need to have an iPhone 5, 5c, 5s, 6, 6 Plus, or one of the newest iPhone models. Your iPhone must also run iOS 8.4 or later.

If you have an older iPhone model, you can still take advantage of many of the apps, and some of the products described in this book, as long as your iPhone can run iOS 8.4 or later. However, your older iPhone is not compatible with the Apple Watch, and might not be compatible with some of the other health, fitness, and sleep-related accessories you'll soon be reading about.

As the iPhone's human user, you can interact with your smartphone in a number of ways. For health, fitness, diet, and sleep-related tasks, your iPhone can handle a wide range of functions automatically, and be used in ways that have never before been possible.

Your iPhone is chock-full of cutting-edge technology and software. The good news is you do not have to be a tech-savvy or highly computer-literate person to take full advantage of what your smartphone offers.

WHAT YOU NEED TO GET STARTED

In terms of equipment, to use the information in this book, you need an iPhone and, ideally, an Apple Watch. However, based on your unique goals, you might also want to acquire other optional equipment, such as a fitness tracker, activity monitor, Bluetooth-compatible scale, and/or other fitness and health-related equipment capable of sharing data and communicating with your iPhone and Apple Watch.

Based on the activities you plan to engage in, you might also need a durable iPhone case that you can comfortably attach to your waist or upper arm, so that you can move freely, yet still have quick access to the smartphone. The Belkin Slim-Fit Plus Armband shown in Figure 1.2 is an example of this type of iPhone case.

This Belkin Slim-Fit Plus Armband contains an iPhone 6

FIGURE 1.2

The Belkin Slim-Fit Plus Armband is an example of an iPhone case that allows you to comfortably wear and access your smartphone while you work out or are active.

Wireless headphones are another useful iPhone accessory for active people. Unlike the corded Apple EarPods that come with the iPhone, you can wear wireless headphones during physical activities and hear all audio generated by your smartphone (including music) without being connected to it via a relatively short cable.

The Beats Powerbeats2 Wireless headphones, for example, are designed to be durable and stay comfortably yet snugly in your ears while you're physically active (see Figure 1.3).

Using these optional headphones ($199.95, www.beatsbydre.com/earphones/beats-powerbeats2-wireless.html), you can listen to music, hear the audio generated by apps, or participate in phone conversations (thanks to the headphone's built-in microphone). Best of all, you can be up to 30 feet away from your iPhone at any given time.

Beats Powerbeats2 Wireless headphones

FIGURE 1.3

The Beats Powerbeats2 Wireless headphones are one option for listening to music from your iPhone.

> **NOTE** Many other companies offer wired and wireless headphones that you can safely and comfortably wear with your iPhone during physical activity, some of which include noise-cancelling technology that can be useful when trying to listen to music in otherwise noisy areas (like your gym or fitness center).

Chapter 2, "Tell More Than the Time with Apple Watch," tells you more about the health and fitness capabilities of the Apple Watch, and some of the ways you can use them with your iPhone.

Chapter 3, "Use Fitness Trackers and Other iPhone and Apple Watch Accessories," covers how to connect and use other optional equipment, like fitness, sleep, and activity monitors, or other medical devices, with your iPhone, either in addition to or instead of using the Apple Watch.

UPDATE YOUR IPHONE'S IOS AND APPS

To use the most current third-party apps and/or link your iPhone with other fitness and health-related equipment, as well as the Apple Watch, your iPhone should be running the latest version of the iOS (iOS 8.4 or later is required).

UPDATE IOS

To determine whether a free iOS update is available, and to install it onto your iPhone, make sure you're connected to the Internet over Wi-Fi and follow these steps:

1. From the Home screen, launch the Settings app (shown in Figure 1.4).

FIGURE 1.4

Launch the Settings app from the Home screen (shown here).

BEFORE YOU BEGIN Before initiating an OS update, creating a backup of your iPhone using iCloud Backup or iTunes Sync is a good idea. This step is optional, but recommended. You should also plug your iPhone into an external power source. This step is also optional, but you do not want the phone's battery dying partway through the iOS upgrade process.

2. Tap on the General option from the main Settings menu (shown in Figure 1.5).

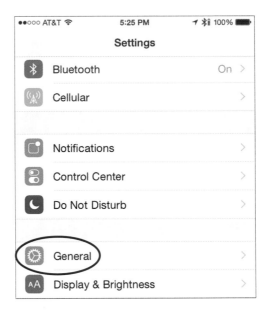

FIGURE 1.5
Access the General menu from Settings.

3. Tap on the Software Update option from the General menu (shown in Figure 1.6).

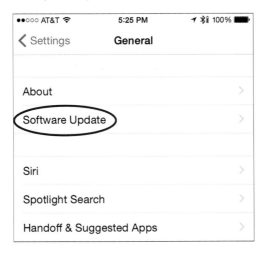

FIGURE 1.6
Tap on the Software Update option.

4. If an iOS update is available, follow the on-screen prompts to download and install it. This process takes between 15 and 30 minutes.

> **TIP** Beyond the Health app that comes preinstalled with iOS 8 (and iOS 9), literally hundreds of optional apps for fitness, health, dieting, and sleep-related tasks are available from the App Store. For example, when you link an Apple Watch to your iPhone wirelessly via Bluetooth, Apple's own Activity app installs onto the iPhone, and also becomes available on your Apple Watch. Learn more about this powerful app in Chapter 5, "Use the Activity, Workout, and Other Fitness Apps."
>
> Chapter 6, "Find and Use Specialized Health Apps," covers how to find, install, and begin using other optional apps.

UPDATE YOUR APPS

In addition to keeping your iPhone and Apple Watch's operating system up-to-date, app developers periodically release updates to individual apps. These updates are typically free, and you can download and install them from the App Store.

To discover whether any of the apps currently installed on your iPhone and/or Apple Watch require updating:

1. From your iPhone's Home screen, open the App Store app.

2. Tap on the Updates icon that appears in the lower-right corner of the App Store screen.

3. The Updates screen lists any apps that require updates. Either tap on the Update button for an app, or tap on the Update All button to update all the apps, assuming your iPhone is connected to the Internet.

Although you can set up your device to automatically download and apply updates, get into the habit of checking for new app updates at least once per week.

> **NOTE** You can do most app updates via a cellular data (3G/4G/LTE) connection. However, if the app update file is massive, you might be prompted to use a Wi-Fi Internet connection to download and install certain app updates.

As you'll learn from the next chapter, you manage all Apple Watch apps from your iPhone. Thus, when an app requires an update, it gets updated through the App Store app on your iPhone, and then wirelessly transfers to your Apple Watch automatically.

> **TIP** To set up your iPhone to automatically download and install app updates as they become available (provided the phone has Internet access), launch Settings, tap on the iTunes & App Store option, and then from below the Automatic Downloads heading, turn on the Updates option.
>
> If you acquire a new app on your iPad, and you want that same app (if it's compatible) to automatically load onto your iPhone, make sure both devices are linked to the same Apple ID account, and then turn on the Apps option switch from the iTunes & App Store menu in Settings.

CUSTOMIZE YOUR IPHONE'S SETTINGS

Based on how you plan to use your iPhone with various third-party apps and accessories, you will most likely need to adjust specific settings in your smartphone. Depending on what you need to do, you can make some of these app-specific adjustments in each app as you're using it. Some, however, require you to launch the Settings app from the Home screen of your iPhone, and then manually adjust specific options.

To adjust a specific app's options from Settings (when applicable), launch the Settings app. From the Settings menu, scroll down to the list of installed apps (see Figure 1.7), and tap on an app to adjust its settings.

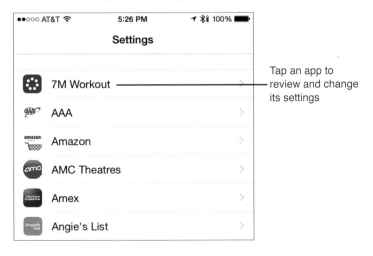

Tap an app to review and change its settings

FIGURE 1.7

You can adjust some app-specific options from the Settings app.

For example, if you have the popular Johnson & Johnson Official 7-Minute Workout app installed (see Chapter 7, "Explore Fitness Solutions for Walkers, Joggers, and Runners"), from Settings, you can adjust the app's Notifications-related settings, as well as the Background App Refresh option (which, when turned on, allows the app to access the Internet on its own to retrieve information and share updated data). See Figure 1.8.

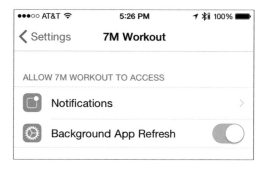

FIGURE 1.8

Adjust settings for the Johnson & Johnson Official 7-Minute Workout app from Settings.

ENABLE LOCATION SERVICES

Built in to your iPhone is the Locations Services feature that allows the iOS and specific apps to determine your exact location, and then use this information for various purposes. The Apple Watch, along with all fitness/activity trackers, and many fitness, health, diet, and even sleep-related apps, takes full advantage of this iPhone feature.

Thus, both turning on the Location Services feature in your iPhone and ensuring that the specific apps you'll be using are granted access to this feature are essential. Typically, when you launch an app that requires Location Services for the first time, you're prompted to turn on this feature by tapping an on-screen button.

However, from the Settings app on your iPhone, you can manually adjust the Location Services feature and how various apps use it. To do this, launch Settings from the Home screen, tap on the Privacy option, and from the Privacy menu, tap on the Location Services option.

Make sure the main Location Services option switch is turned on (see Figure 1.9). Then, scroll down and tap on specific app listings to customize how that particular app can use the iPhone's Location Services function.

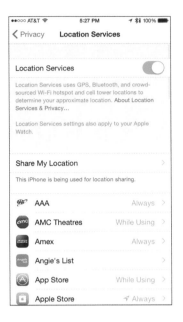

FIGURE 1.9

Turn on and adjust the Location Services feature of your iPhone from the Settings app.

ADJUST NOTIFICATION-RELATED SETTINGS FOR SPECIFIC APPS

If the app you plan to use takes advantage of the iPhone's Notifications feature to generate alerts, alarms, or notifications, you will probably want to customize how the iPhone notifies you by adjusting the Notifications options for the specific app. For example, many fitness, health, diet, or sleep-related apps generate various types of notifications to remind you at specific times to do something.

To adjust Notifications-related settings for a specific app, launch Settings from the Home screen, tap on the Notifications option, and then tap on the app's listing. Tap on the Notifications option for that app. A screen like the one shown in Figure 1.10 appears.

From the Notifications screen you can use the Show in Notification Center option to determine how many app-specific notifications you want Notification Center to track at any given time (No Recent Items, 1 Recent Item, 5 Recent Items, or 10 Recent Items). To keep your Notification Center screen from becoming overly cluttered, choose the 1 or 5 Recent Items option.

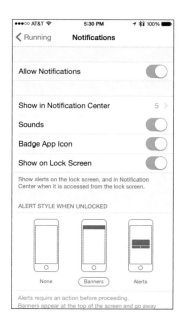

FIGURE 1.10

Many apps allow you to customize how you want to generate, hear, or display app notifications.

WHAT IS NOTIFICATION CENTER? Your iPhone automat-

ically keeps track of all iOS and app-related notifications that occur while you're away from your phone. You can then display all of them on a single screen, called Notification Center.

Regardless of what you're doing, when your iPhone is turned on, to access Notification Center, place your finger at the top of the device's screen and then swipe down. To view missed notifications, tap on the Notifications tab at the top of the screen.

If you want to enable the app you're adjusting Notification settings for to generate audible alarms, turn on the Sound option. If you want to enable that same app to display Badges on your Home screen, then in the upper-right corner of the app's icon, turn on the Badge option's virtual switch.

BADGES Badges are the small, numbered red dots that appear above

some apps. You see them most often on the Mail app, indicating how many unread emails you have.

To enable the app to display alerts and notifications on the iPhone's Lock screen, turn on the Show On Lock Screen option.

For the specific app you're adjusting the Notification settings for, decide how you want those alerts and non-audible notifications to appear onscreen. Your options include None, Banner, or Alerts.

If you tap on the None option, the app can only generate audible alarms (or vibrations if sound is turned off). If you tap on the Banner option, notifications briefly appear as a text-based banner on your iPhone's screen, regardless of what you're doing. That message disappears automatically after a few seconds, but remains listed on the Notification Center screen.

If you select the Alerts option, notifications remain displayed on your iPhone's screen until you tap on the appropriate button on the screen to dismiss or respond to the message.

USE BLUETOOTH DEVICES WITH YOUR IPHONE

If you use your iPhone with an Apple Watch, any other fitness/activity tracker, or with wireless headphones or other wireless accessories, the first time you attempt to establish a wireless connection between your smartphone and each wireless device, you must turn on the iPhone's Bluetooth feature, and then pair each device with the phone.

To turn on Bluetooth, access the Control Center menu by placing your finger at the bottom of the iPhone's screen and swiping up. From the Control Center menu, tap on the Bluetooth icon (see Figure 1.11).

To initially pair a new Bluetooth device with your iPhone:

1. From your iPhone's Home screen, launch Settings.
2. Tap on the Bluetooth option from the Settings menu.
3. Turn on the Bluetooth option (if it's not on already) located at the top of the screen.
4. Follow the pairing directions that came with your Bluetooth device.
5. When that device appears in the Bluetooth menu on your iPhone (see Figure 1.12), tap on its listing to finalize the pairing process.

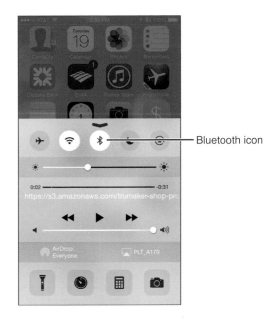

Bluetooth icon

FIGURE 1.11

The iPhone's Control Center menu.

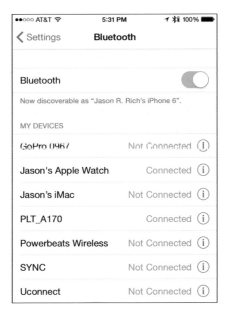

FIGURE 1.12

Manage Bluetooth devices that can link to your iPhone from the phone's Bluetooth screen (in Settings).

After a device has been paired once with your iPhone, any time both the iPhone and the device are turned on, they're within approximately 150 feet from each other, and both have their respective Bluetooth features turned on, the Bluetooth device will automatically establish a connection with your iPhone.

ESTABLISH YOUR HEALTH GOALS

Apple Watch and iPhone Fitness Tips and Tricks shows you exactly how to use your iPhone (and Apple Watch, if you have one), for health, fitness, diet, and sleep-related purposes.

The first five chapters delve into what's possible using the iPhone and Apple Watch (with optional apps and equipment). Subsequent chapters focus on using the iPhone and Apple Watch for specific types of health and fitness-oriented activities.

For example, Chapter 8, "Explore Fitness Strategies for Bicyclers," focuses on how to use the iPhone and Apple Watch for biking (and cycling-related activities), as well as on how to use these tools for working out at a gym (or home gym) using popular fitness equipment, and Chapter 10, "Achieve Your Dieting Goals," focuses specifically on using the iPhone and Apple Watch for diet and nutrition-related tasks and data tracking.

Chapter 11, "Monitor Your Sleep and Sleep Better," explains how to use the iPhone and Apple Watch to help improve your overall quality of sleep, overcome insomnia, and wake up feeling more rested, and Chapter 12, "Getting the Most from General Fitness Apps," focuses on apps and accessories to help you stay motivated, calm, clear-headed, and relaxed throughout your day.

There is no shortage of ways you can use the iPhone and Apple Watch as tools to improve or enhance your life by helping you become healthier, more physically fit, or less stressed out.

THE IPHONE AND APPLE WATCH ARE NOT MAGICAL

No shortcuts, cheats, or magical solutions exist for becoming healthier, more physically fit, or for losing weight. However, to make the process easier, you can follow proven steps, take organized approaches, and use tools (like the iPhone and Apple Watch) to help you gather, track, organize, and understand data and useful information; remind you of important tasks; and motivate you by showcasing your results and displaying uplifting messages.

However, before engaging in any health or medical-related endeavors, consult with your doctor to make sure you're physically fit enough to pursue whatever fitness-oriented activities you're interested in.

Next, consult with a trained professional to help you develop realistic goals and expectations that you can achieve without putting yourself at risk. For example, if you want to start working out and building muscle, consider working with a trainer or taking some fitness classes at a local gym to help you get started. If you're having issues with poor sleep, stress, or anxiety, consult with a sleep specialist or psychologist.

If you want to adopt healthier eating habits, or go on a diet, consult with a nutritionist and/or medical professional.

Then, before you start installing all sorts of health, fitness, diet, or sleep-related apps, or invest money in activity trackers and other equipment, follow these important steps:

- Figure out exactly what you want to accomplish.
- Set a time frame for achieving each goal.
- Make sure each goal and your expectations are realistic.
- Write down your goals and the deadlines for them.
- Understand exactly why you want to achieve each goal.
- Figure out which iPhone and Apple Watch apps and accessories you can use to help you achieve your goals.
- Adopt a well-thought-out and organized approach to achieving each of your goals.
- Add to your schedule the time needed each day to work toward each goal. Set aside specific time in the morning, afternoon, and/or evening for specific tasks, activities, or workouts.
- In addition to using the iPhone and Apple Watch apps to help you stay focused or motivated, consider working with a trained professional. Also, consider recruiting friends or family members with similar goals to partner with you for motivation and companionship.
- When you start something, stick with it! Don't give up after a few days or weeks if you do not initially achieve the results you desire. If something isn't working the way you expected, tweak your approach, or seek out additional advice. Persevere, and keep working toward each of your goals.

TAKE ADVICE FROM EXPERTS

To shed more light on each topic that this book covers, I've tapped experts for their knowledge and shared it in the form of interviews. These interviews provide additional insight into various health, fitness, diet, and sleep-related topics.

Keep in mind that what you read in these interviews is the advice or philosophy of that particular person, whose thoughts and opinions might or might not apply directly to your needs.

The goal is to offer additional information and insight from people who are recognized experts in their field. Chances are that each of these interviews will include at least one or two tidbits of advice or information that you'll deem worthwhile or applicable to your situation.

CHAT WITH AN EXPERT

MEET JEANA ANDERSON, FOUNDER OF ASWEATLIFE.COM

Jeana Anderson is a certified personal trainer who believes in variety when it comes to her workouts. As a result, she began visiting gyms throughout Chicago and participating in the plethora of fitness classes each had to offer. She later founded a website, called ASweatLife.com, which initially served as a forum for her to share details about her favorite fitness classes with others, but has since become an interactive community comprised of fitness fanatics and enthusiasts who share their experiences, fitness class recommendations, advice, and personal success stories.

In this interview, Anderson shares some of her personal experiences and strategies for using the iPhone and Apple Watch as fitness tools with her established daily fitness routine.

"As I became more and more interested in personal fitness and health, I wanted to take my friends and family along this journey with me. However, after I initially joined a gym, I found myself stuck in a rut, because I found myself doing the same thing, over and over, and it became tedious," said Anderson.

To make things more interesting, Anderson vowed to take a different fitness class, at a different gym, every single week, and then choose the ones that she really enjoyed and got the most out of.

"This was where the concept for ASweatLife.com came from. People kept asking me for my opinions and thoughts about the fitness classes I was taking, and were looking for gym recommendations," she added. "The website now offers content for people who want to stay healthy at home, on the road, or in the gym. The site offers a vast array of health and fitness information, including a continuously updated meal preparation guide, which is put together in conjunction with a dietitian."

In terms of using a smartphone and smartwatch in conjunction with someone's fitness activities, Anderson believes these can be valuable tools. "Mobile and wearable technology can be incorporated into someone's fitness routine in a variety of ways. There are apps, for example, that can occasionally replace the need to attend a fitness class at a gym, and provide a guided workout anywhere you happen to be. There are also apps that provide accountability, plus other types of apps that provide valuable information or insight for fitness-minded people."

Anderson recommends the Calorie Counter & Diet Tracker app by MyFitnessPal, for example, to people who are trying to meet fitness or diet-related goals, because it keeps people accountable for the calories in and calories out aspect of fitness. "I also use the ClassPass app to discover new classes and gyms wherever I am, and I use some of the running apps not just to track my activity, but to discover new running trails, for example. Nike+ Running is my favorite running app. I enjoy the simplicity of it, and it works nicely with the Apple Watch as well.

"Another app I use constantly, and that I recommend, is Nike+ Training Club, which is also called NTC. It offers a constantly expanding collection of fitness classes and routines that is accessible right from the iPhone. It's particularly useful when you can't attend an actual class. For runners, the MapMyRun app will help you discover new running routes, and engage with your surroundings, while tracking your progress and achievements."

Anderson believes that fitness tracking is incredibly important, but its necessity depends on your goals and activity level. A fitness or activity tracker can help people who are first starting to become interested in fitness understand how active or inactive they are. This is important for establishing a baseline and an initial understanding of how much activity they need to incorporate in order to achieve their goals.

"The Apple Watch will help people become aware of their own activity level. For amateur athletes, wearable technology is important for tracking and analyzing activity, which makes it easier to understand the results you're achieving. When you're not working with a coach or trainer, but you do have a goal, Apple Watch or another activity tracker can help you monitor your progress in real time. Depending on the types of fitness-oriented activities people engage in, there are very specialized activity monitoring apps being introduced that can become valuable tools for people at all fitness levels," said Anderson.

"Fitness goals need to be clearly defined, and should have a time associated with them. Each goal should be attainable, realistic, and have some type of accountability associated with it. I believe a goal should begin with the words, 'I want to.' For example, a goal might be, 'I want to run a marathon by the end of the summer.' You should also have a clear reason why you want to achieve each fitness goal. Without understanding and believing in the 'why' aspect of a goal, it is very hard to achieve it," said Anderson.

Many fitness-oriented apps are available for iPhone and Apple Watch, some of which can replace the need to attend an in-person fitness class at a gym or studio.

"I believe these apps are a great augmentation to participating in in-person fitness classes, but should not be a total replacement for them. When you take a fitness class, there's a sense of community, plus there's a human who oversees your activity and progress, and who makes sure you're doing things correctly. If you've committed to a fitness routine, but you go on a vacation or business trip and can't attend your regular class, that's when this type of iPhone or Apple Watch app can be most useful," said Anderson.

Anderson believes that everyone should engage in at least 150 minutes of moderate activity every week, or 30 minutes per day. "If you engage in high-intensity activities you can cut this down to 75 minutes per week. If you're willing to commit to this amount of time, and utilize that time in a way that will help you achieve your goals, you'll find that those goals can be attainable. I recommend that you re-evaluate your goals every month."

"The number one thing someone should do, with or without an app, is to write down and document their goals, and then refer back to them regularly," added Anderson.

"I am of the belief that having more data available to you is better. Using the iPhone and the Apple Watch as a fitness tool helps to provide you with plenty of data. Keep in mind, some pieces of fitness equipment, like treadmills or elliptical machines, now wirelessly link with the iPhone via Bluetooth or the Internet in order to share data. Some people find this a useful feature when it comes to tracking what they've done, and keeping tabs on how close they are to achieving their goals. If this is important to you, seek out a gym that offers this type of equipment, or invest in it at home."

TELL MORE THAN THE TIME WITH APPLE WATCH

In April 2015, Apple released the Apple Watch and, like the iPhone before it, it quickly began changing the way people interact with mobile technology and the Internet. In this case, Apple has provided a tool that can be comfortably worn on a wrist (see Figure 2.1).

Like the iPhone and iPad, you can interact with the Apple Watch in several ways, such as by using its touch screen display, pressing its built-in button, turning or pressing its Digital Crown, or by speaking directly to the watch using the Siri feature. Plus, thanks to the technology that's built in to Apple Watch, it has the ability to collect data and wirelessly communicate with your iPhone to access and share information via the Internet.

FIGURE 2.1
The Apple Watch is useful for a wide range of health, fitness, and diet-related tasks.

NOTE   The *Digital Crown* is the dial on the right side of the watch, which is used for several different purposes, depending on the function or app that's being used. For example, the Digital Crown can be pressed to access the watch's Home screen, or it can be turned to scroll up and down or zoom in/out on content being displayed.

Thanks to several of the apps that come preinstalled, as well as a growing selection of optional, third-party apps, Apple Watch is proving to be a powerful tool that can handle a wide range of fitness and health-related tasks, as covered later in this chapter.

Because of its durability, you can wear the Apple Watch comfortably during rigorous activities (shown in Figure 2.2), like during your daily workout. Keep in mind that some Apple Watch models are more durable and weather resistant than others.

FIGURE 2.2
Wear the Apple Watch during your workouts and throughout your day.

DISCOVER THE APPLE WATCH

Three versions of the Apple Watch are available: Apple Watch Sport, Apple Watch, and Apple Watch Edition. Each version of the watch has multiple options, like the size of the watch face and the type(s) of watch bands available. All versions of the Apple Watch include the same built-in processor and technologies, all operate using the same version of the Apple Watch OS (operating system), and all run the same collection of preinstalled and optional apps.

> **NOTE** All versions of the Apple Watch have a built-in heart rate sensor, GPS capabilities, gyroscope, and accelerometer; operate using Apple's proprietary S1 professor chip; and have other technologies built in that allow the watch to be used for a wide range of health and fitness-related tasks. The differences among the various Apple Watch versions are the materials the watch and watch band are constructed from, and the price.

> **TIP** The Apple Watch is sold at Apple Stores and by select authorized Apple resellers. You can also purchase it online directly from Apple's online-based store (www.apple.com).

As someone interested in health and fitness, your best bet is likely the Apple Watch Sport, for which ten configurations are available. These versions of the Apple Watch are designed for activity-oriented people and are the most durable. All versions of Apple Watch are available in two sizes: 42mm and 38mm. Both sizes function exactly the same. As shown in Figure 2.3, the difference is the height and width of the touch screen display (watch face and housing).

42mm Apple Watch Sport   38mm Apple Watch Sport

FIGURE 2.3

Apple's website (www.apple.com) enables you to compare all the various Apple Watch models and styles, as well as the interchangeable watch bands available for them.

> **TIP** If you purchase an Apple Watch with a leather or stainless steel band, but want to use it for fitness-oriented activities without ruining the band, the Apple Watch Sport Band (for non-Apple Watch Sport models) is sold separately (http://store.apple.com/us/watch/bands). It is made from fluoroelastomer and comes in a variety of colors. Apple Watch watch bands can be changed in less than 15 seconds.

Apple Watch Sport's housing is made of an extremely strong, durable, and lightweight anodized aluminum (which is 60 percent stronger than standard aluminum) and is available in silver or space gray. Strengthened, scratch-resistant lon-X glass protects the touch screen display.

The watch band that comes with the Apple Watch Sport is made from waterproof, durable, flexible fluoroelastomer, which is a hybrid plastic and rubber-like substance that's soft and comfortable to wear. The band comes in five colors (white, blue, pink, green, or black).

The 38mm version of Apple Watch Sport costs $349.00, whereas the 42mm version of Apple Watch Sport costs $399.00. More expensive, but less durable, versions of Apple Watch and Apple Watch Edition are available, ranging in price from $549.00 to $17,000.00 (for a version of Apple Watch Edition that's made from 18-karat yellow gold).

> **NOTE** From a fashion standpoint, and depending on your level of activity, you can easily wear the mid-priced Apple Watch ($549.00 to $1,099.00) with formal business attire, or with your favorite workout outfit. However, this version of the watch is a bit less durable. Some of the watch bands (including those made from leather) are water resistant, but not necessarily waterproof. A fluoroelastomer Sport Band, available in black or white, is also available for this version of the Apple Watch (in addition to the Apple Watch Sport models).
>
> The versions of the Apple Watch that comprise the Apple Watch Edition collection are designed to be highly fashionable, are much more expensive, and not really suitable for use during high-intensity activities that might include exposure to harsh climates or water.

> **TIP** Apple Watch watch bands are interchangeable. If you plan to wear your Apple Watch on a daily basis to work and typically dress in business attire, but you also want to wear your watch when engaged in more rigorous activities and workouts, consider choosing the mid-priced Apple Watch (as opposed to the Apple Watch Sport), and purchasing both a more formal (leather or stainless steel) watch band, as well as a fluoroelastomer Sport Band for it.

All versions of the Apple Watch come with the watch, one watch band (which you select), a proprietary magnetic charging cable, and a USB adapter. Each watch also comes with a standard limited warranty, one year of hardware repair coverage, and up to 90 days of free support.

For an additional $49.00 (for all Apple Watch Sport models), the optional AppleCare+ protection plan is available. This extends the coverage for two years, and includes up to two incidents of accidental damage (each of which is subject to a $69.00 service fee). Without AppleCare+, Apple Watch repair costs are rather high.

AppleCare+ does not cover the loss or theft of the watch. For this type of coverage, in addition to coverage for accidental damage, third-party insurance is available, although this insurance does not include Apple's technical support.

Especially if you're active, and will be using the Apple Watch while engaged in high-intensity activities, investing in AppleCare+ or third-party insurance is definitely worthwhile.

> **TIP** One independent company that offers optional Apple Watch insurance is SquareTrade (www.squaretrade.com/smartwatch-warranty). A two-year plan that includes a $75.00 per claim deductible is priced at $69.00. A two-year plan that has no deductible is priced at $159.00. Neither of these plans covers loss or theft of the watch, but do cover repairs due to accidental damage or hardware failure.

INTERACT WITH YOUR APPLE WATCH

Most interaction with the Apple Watch involves using your finger to tap, swipe, drag, or press and hold down (Force Touch) something on the display.

In addition to the usual finger gestures adapted for use on the watch's touch screen, you use the Digital Crown in two ways: by pressing it inward, or turning the crown to scroll or zoom.

You use the button located just below the Digital Crown by pressing it inward. Depending on what you're doing with the watch at any given time, how you use the Digital Crown and the button will vary.

The Apple Watch also responds to specific movements of your wrist. For example, if you move your wrist so you can view the watch face, the display automatically turns on (wakes up) and displays the selected watch face. Likewise, if you have the "Hey Siri" feature turned on, as soon as you wake up the watch by moving your wrist, you can activate Siri by saying "Hey Siri," and then issuing your question, command, or request by speaking to the watch.

> **NOTE** Depending on how you have the watch set up, and which app you're using, the watch responds to you in several ways. For example, it can display information onscreen, activate the haptic engine and tap your wrist or vibrate, and/or generate sound.

PREPARE YOUR APPLE WATCH

You need to do a few things before you can wear and use your new Apple Watch for your favorite health and fitness applications. After you charge the watch's battery, you need to pair it with your iPhone to establish a wireless Bluetooth connection between the two devices.

PAIR YOUR APPLE WATCH WITH YOUR IPHONE

Before using your new Apple Watch, you need to pair it with your iPhone. You only need to do it once. Before you begin, make sure your iPhone model is compatible with Apple Watch, running at least iOS 8.4, and has its Bluetooth mode turned on (refer to Chapter 1, "Use the iPhone as a Powerful Health and Fitness Tool").

To establish the required Bluetooth connection between your Apple Watch and iPhone, follow these steps:

1. Turn on the Wi-Fi feature of your iPhone, and make sure it's connected to the Internet via a Wi-Fi hotspot or wireless home network. Your iPhone's 3G/4G/LTE cellular data connection will not work for this process.

> **NOTE** **Proximity**: During this initial pairing process, place your iPhone and Apple Watch close together. In the future, the Bluetooth connection works when the two devices are up to 150 feet apart.

2. On your iPhone, launch the Apple Watch app. Tap on the My Watch icon that appears in the bottom-left corner of the screen (see Figure 2.4).

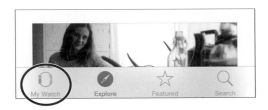

FIGURE 2.4

The My Watch icon appears at the bottom of the Apple Watch app when it's running on the iPhone.

3. On the Apple Watch, after it's on, select your language by rotating the Digital Crown. You can also swipe up or down on the screen to scroll through the menu listings.

4. Tap on the Start Pairing button that appears on your Apple Watch after you choose a language.

5. Tap on the Start Pairing button that appears on your iPhone. At this point, the pairing animation should appear on your Apple Watch's screen.

6. As directed by the watch and iPhone, hold your iPhone directly over the Apple Watch's screen, and center the watch face in the iPhone's viewfinder. Hold the iPhone and Apple Watch in this position until the Apple Watch Is Paired message appears.

7. The Set Up As New option appears on the iPhone's screen. Tap on it.

8. From the Apple Watch app that's running on the iPhone, select on which wrist (left or right) you plan to wear the Apple Watch, and then tap on the Agree button when the Terms and Conditions information appears.

9. When prompted, enter your Apple ID username and password. This activates the Digital Touch, Apple Pay, and Handoff features on your Apple Watch.

10. As the setup process continues, a prompt appears for you to create a passcode for your Apple Watch. You do this, too, from the Apple Watch app on your iPhone. This passcode is used for security purposes later, when you use Apple Pay, for example.

11. Toward the end of the initial pairing process, your iPhone will sync all of your compatible (and optional) apps to your Apple Watch, including the fitness apps you have installed on the iPhone that have an Apple Watch counterpart. You can also install additional fitness apps later—for example, on both your iPhone and Apple Watch. Tap on the Install All option to transfer all of these compatible apps. At the same time, applicable app-specific data that's stored on your iPhone will transfer as well.

> **TIP**   During the pairing process between the Apple Watch and iPhone, be sure to keep the two devices close together.

The Apple Watch chimes when the pairing and syncing process is complete. You're now ready to customize your Apple Watch for wearing and using it.

CUSTOMIZE YOUR APPLE WATCH

You can customize your experience wearing and using the Apple Watch in several ways, many of which are relevant to using your watch as a health and fitness device. Some of your options include:

- Choosing and then customizing the watch face
- Adjusting the Apple Watch's Notifications options
- Customizing the Glances screens
- Personalizing the App Layout on the watch's App screen
- Selecting personalized settings for the sound, haptics, text size, and screen brightness
- Adding additional apps to the Apple Watch to expand its capabilities

With the exception of choosing and customizing a watch face, you handle the majority of these customization and personalization options via the Apple Watch app on your iPhone, after you pair the iPhone and Apple Watch.

CUSTOMIZE YOUR WATCH FACE

To customize your Apple Watch's watch face, tap on the screen to wake it up, and then press and hold down your finger on the screen while viewing the currently active watch face. Tap on the Customize button (shown in Figure 2.5), and then follow the directions offered on Apple's website (https://help.apple.com/watch/#/apdb0c5fb937).

When customizing your Apple Watch, one of the first things you'll do is select a watch face, and then you are able to customize that watch face with what Apple calls "Complications," which are specific pieces of data that can display on the watchface, such as your heart rate, details from the watch's Activity app, the date, or the current weather.

FIGURE 2.5
Choose your favorite watch face, and then customize it directly from the Apple Watch.

> **✓ TIP**   Choose a watch face that appeals to you visually, but keep in mind that certain watch face options offer more flexibility regarding the information displayed. For example, some of the watch faces always display and make details accessible from the Activity app (shown in Figure 2.6) and/or the stopwatch functionality that's built in to the watch.
>
> Chapter 5, "Use the Activity, Workout, and Other Fitness Apps," covers more about the Activity app that comes preinstalled on the Apple Watch (and that's available for the iPhone).

> **✎ NOTE**   In addition to Watch OS2 (which is an operating system update for the Apple Watch released in Fall 2015), it's widely believed that in early 2016, Apple will begin releasing "smart bands" for Apple Watch. These optional bands will have additional sensors built into them, which will allow the watch to monitor or track additional information such as blood pressure, respiratory rate, blood oxygen levels, and body temperature. Smart bands will greatly expand the health and fitness tracking capabilities of Apple Watch, without the need to replace the watch itself with a newer model.

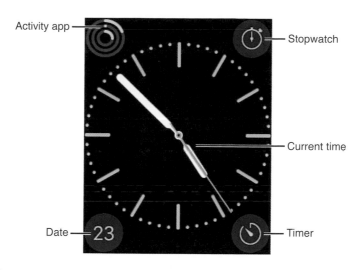

Activity app — Stopwatch

Current time

Date — 23 — Timer

FIGURE 2.6

Details from the Activity app and other information display on your selected watch face. Tap on an app's icon to launch it right from the watch face.

USE THE APPLE WATCH APP ON THE IPHONE TO CUSTOMIZE OTHER WATCH SETTINGS

When you're ready to customize other Apple Watch options and settings, after pairing your iPhone with the Apple Watch, launch the Apple Watch app on your iPhone, and tap on the My Watch icon that appears in the bottom-left corner of the screen.

As you can see in Figure 2.7, the My Watch menu screen offers a variety of options for customizing your Apple Watch. Tap on one option at a time to adjust specific settings.

FIGURE 2.7

Make customizations via the My Watch menu screen of the Apple Watch app.

PERSONALIZE THE APPEARANCE OF THE APP SCREEN

Tap the App Layout option, the first option on the My Watch menu screen. On the iPhone's screen, the App screen of the Apple Watch appears. The app icons represent the apps currently installed on your Apple Watch.

To move the app icons around, one at a time, place your finger on an app icon and drag it to the desired location. The changes you make to the appearance of the App screen transfer to your Apple Watch almost instantly.

Figure 2.8 shows the Layout screen being customized on the iPhone, and Figure 2.9 shows the App screen on the Apple Watch. To exit out of this screen and save your changes, tap on the "< My Watch" option at the top-left corner of the screen; you return to the My Watch menu of the Apple Watch app on your iPhone.

FIGURE 2.8

This Layout screen is being customized on the iPhone from the Apple Watch app. This watch already has several third-party apps installed.

FIGURE 2.9

At any time, press the Digital Crown to reveal the App screen on the Apple Watch to launch and use an installed app.

> **✓ TIP** Use the App screen on your Apple Watch to launch apps. To access this screen at anytime, gently press the Digital Crown. Then, to launch an app, tap on its icon. To navigate around the watch's App screen, place your finger on the display and drag it around. Rotate the Digital Crown to zoom in or out as you're looking at this screen.

Any time you install an app onto the Apple Watch, an app icon for it appears on the App screen in a location determined by the watch. To change this location at any time, access the App Layout screen of the Apple Watch app on your iPhone, place your finger on the app icon you want to move, and drag it to a different location on the watch's Home screen. The changes you make will be reflected within seconds on the watch automatically.

ENABLE AIRPLANE MODE

Just like the iPhone, you can put the Apple Watch in Airplane mode. When enabled, Airplane mode restricts the watch from sending or receiving information via Bluetooth.

Instead of having to turn on or off Airplane mode separately on your iPhone and Apple Watch each time you board an airplane, from the Apple Watch app, tap on the Airplane Mode option, and then turn on the Mirror iPhone virtual switch (shown in Figure 2.10).

FIGURE 2.10

From the Apple Watch app on the iPhone, tap on the My Watch icon, followed by the Airplane Mode option, and then turn on the virtual switch associated with the Mirror iPhone option.

By turning on this virtual switch, any time you enable Airplane mode on your iPhone, Airplane mode turns on automatically on your Apple Watch (and vice versa).

To manually enable or disable Airplane mode from your Apple Watch:

1. Tap on the display to wake up the watch face screen, place your finger near the bottom of the watch's display, and swipe up.

2. Swipe horizontally to access the watch's Connected glance screen.

3. Tap on the Airplane icon to turn Airplane mode on or off (see Figure 2.11).

Tap on the Do Not Disturb icon to turn this feature on or off. Tap on the Silent icon to turn the Apple Watch's speaker on or off, and tap on the Pinging option to generate an audible alarm on your iPhone to help you locate it quickly, assuming it's within about 150 feet of your Apple Watch.

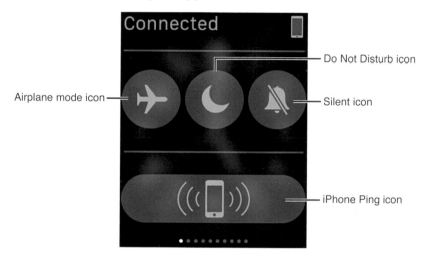

FIGURE 2.11

Tap on the Airplane mode icon on the Apple Watch's Connected screen to turn this feature on or off.

CUSTOMIZE THE GLANCE SCREENS

Glance screens not only display the watch face and provide access to the various apps on your Apple Watch, they also give you quick access to specific information. Many of the watch's built-in features (such as the heart rate sensor), as well as preinstalled apps and some third-party apps, have glance screens.

A glance screen offers a way to view summarized app-specific information quickly, without your launching a specific app on your Apple Watch. For example, the Heart Rate glance screen (shown in Figure 2.12) displays your current heart rate, whereas the Activity app glance screen (shown in Figure 2.13) shows a multi-colored graphic depicting the current day's Movement, Exercise, and Standing data (more about that in Chapter 5).

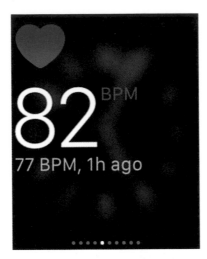

FIGURE 2.12

The Heart Rate glance screen.

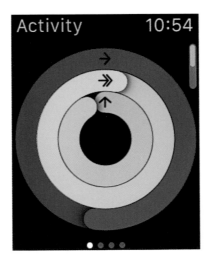

FIGURE 2.13

The Activity app's glance screen.

To access the glance screens, make the watch face screen appear by tapping on the display or moving your wrist to look at the watch. Place your finger near the bottom of the display and swipe up. The last-viewed glance screen appears. Swipe sideways to scroll between the various glance screens.

To determine what glance screens display and in what order, launch the Apple Watch app on your iPhone, tap on the My Watch option, and from the My Watch menu, tap on the Glances option (refer to Figure 2.7).

The apps listed at the top of the screen and below the Settings heading are the ones currently set up to display glances (see Figure 2.14). Tap on an app's red-and-white negative sign icon to deactivate that app's glance screen.

To change the order of the active glance screens, place and hold your finger on an app's move icon and drag It up or down to the desired location.

FIGURE 2.14

You decide what app or feature-related glance screens appear, and in what order.

Toward the bottom of the Glances menu screen of the Apple Watch app (shown in Figure 2.15), under the Do Not Include heading, are the apps and Apple Watch functions that have an inactive glance option. To include any of these app-specific glance screens as part of your glance display, tap on an app's green-and-white plus-sign icon. That listing disappears from its current location on the Glances screen and reappears below the Settings heading.

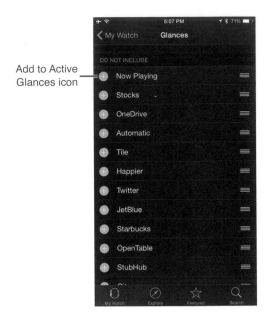

Add to Active Glances icon

FIGURE 2.15

All apps and Apple Watch features that have a glance screen appear under the Settings or Do Not Include heading.

ADJUST SCREEN, SOUND, AND HAPTIC ENGINE–RELATED SETTINGS

Being able to see information the Apple Watch's screen displays and hearing any audio the watch generates is important. You also want to be able to feel the watch's haptic engine feedback.

The My Watch menu screen of the Apple Watch app on the iPhone contains options for customizing screen brightness, text size, sound, and haptics (see Figure 2.16).

FIGURE 2.16

Adjust the screen brightness, text size, and other options from the My Watch menu screen of the Apple Watch app on the iPhone.

Tap on the Brightness & Text Size option to manually adjust the screen brightness and text display size sliders. To make text easier to read, turn on the Bold Text option (shown in Figure 2.17).

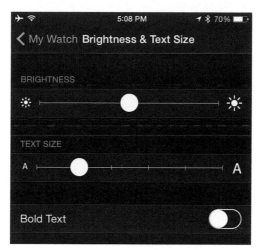

FIGURE 2.17

The Brightness & Text Size menu screen of the Apple Watch app (running on the iPhone).

Tap on the Sound & Haptics menu option to access the sound and haptics settings (shown in Figure 2.18). Use the slider to adjust the volume of the watch's built-in speaker, turn the Mute feature on and off, and adjust the intensity of the haptic engine.

FIGURE 2.18

Make adjustments on the Sound & Haptics menu screen.

> **☑ TIP** To be able to quickly mute the watch if an audible alert, alarm, or notification goes off in the future (while you're in a meeting, for example), enable the Cover to Mute option.
>
> This option lets you quickly activate the watch's Silent feature by simply covering the watch's display with your palm for two to three seconds. When the Silent feature is on, the watch immediately stops generating any sound through its speaker until you manually turn off the feature.
>
> To turn the Silent feature on or off, with the watch face displayed, swipe up to view the Glance screen, and then swipe sideways to access the Connected screen. Tap on the Silent icon to toggle it between the on and off position. (When the icon is red, Silent mode is on.)

CUSTOMIZE THE WATCH'S NOTIFICATIONS OPTIONS

Just like your iPhone, the Apple Watch has a Notifications function and a Notification Center screen. This functionality allows the watch to monitor all the compatible apps running on your watch and display alerts, alarms, and notifications related to those apps on a single screen.

To customize the Notifications options of the Apple Watch, and choose the apps you want the watch to continuously monitor, from the My Watch menu screen (on the iPhone), tap on the Notifications option. From the app's Notifications screen (see Figure 2.19), turn the Notifications option on or off, and adjust Notifications-specific settings for each compatible app by tapping its listing.

> **☑ TIP** When you're wearing the watch, you access the Notification Center screen by activating the watch face, placing your finger near the top of the screen, and then swiping down.
>
> As you view the listing of alerts, alarms, or notifications generated by specific apps, tap on any listing to launch that app and see the relevant content.

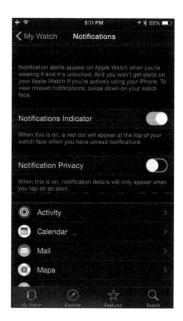

FIGURE 2.19

Decide how you want specific Apple Watch apps to generate and display alerts, alarms, and notifications.

ADJUST THE REST OF THE WATCH'S SETTINGS

Also displayed on the My Watch menu screen of the Apple Watch app (on the iPhone) are a handful of other menu options for customizing specific settings or options. Tap on one option at a time to display a relevant submenu.

> **TIP** To learn what each of these additional options does and how to use them, consult the interactive *Apple Watch User Guide* that's available online (http://help.apple.com/watch/#/) or read a how-to book, like *My Apple Watch* (Que), that focuses more on how to use the watch's general options, as opposed to the health, fitness, diet, and sleep-related watch applications.

KEEP THE APPLE WATCH'S OPERATING SYSTEM UP TO DATE

Periodically, Apple releases updates to the Apple Watch OS, which is the operating system that controls the smartwatch. To continue getting the most out of your

Apple Watch, and ensure full compatibility with all apps, you definitely want to make sure your watch has the most recent version of the operating system installed.

You upgrade the Apple Watch's operating system via the Apple Watch app on the iPhone. Follow these steps to download and install Apple Watch OS updates as they become available:

1. Make sure your Apple Watch and iPhone are paired, and the wireless (Bluetooth) link is active.

2. Make sure your iPhone is connected to the Internet via a Wi-Fi connection. (A cellular data connection will not work.)

3. Plug the Apple Watch into an external power source via its supplied magnetic charging cable, and make sure the battery is at least 50 percent charged before proceeding.

4. From the iPhone's Home screen, launch the Apple Watch app.

5. Tap on the My Watch icon located in the lower-left corner of the screen.

6. Tap on the General option that appears on the My Watch menu screen.

7. Tap on the Software Update option (shown in Figure 2.20).

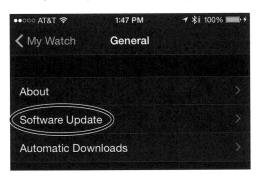

FIGURE 2.20

From this General menu screen, tap on the Software Update option.

8. If a software update is available, a message stating this appears on the screen, as shown in Figure 2.21. (If no update is available, a message saying, "Your software is up to date" appears. In this case, exit out of the Apple Watch app by pressing the Home button.)

FIGURE 2.21

This message appears only if an Apple Watch OS update is available.

9. Tap on the Download and Install option. The operating system update file(s) download to your iPhone, and then wirelessly and automatically transfer to your Apple Watch. This process takes between 3 and 10 minutes.

After the new operating system software transfers to the Apple Watch, the watch automatically resets. When the OS update process completes, your selected watch face displays, and the watch is again ready to use.

> **NOTE** Most Apple Watch OS updates are released to fix known bugs and add performance improvements to the watch and the apps that come preinstalled with it. Apple also uses Apple Watch OS updates to introduce new features and functions to the watch.

> ☑ **TIP** When applicable, preinstalled Apple Watch apps automatically get updated during an Apple Watch OS update. However, all apps that you install yourself onto the watch might require periodic updates as well. The App Store app on the iPhone handles these updates in exactly the same way as an iPhone app update described in Chapter 1.
>
> When an app updates on your iPhone edition of the app, the Apple Watch edition automatically updates as well.

DISCOVER THE ACTIVITY AND WORKOUT APPS THAT COME PREINSTALLED WITH APPLE WATCH

Right out of the box, Apple Watch is designed to be a powerful health and fitness tool. Activity and Workout are two apps that come preinstalled on the Apple Watch, and that work with the iPhone. Chapter 5 covers how to use these apps in more detail.

> ☑ **NOTE** You can also use Stopwatch, Timer, and the Music app as fitness tools.

USE THE ACTIVITY APP

Activity, shown in Figure 2.22, is designed for use on an ongoing basis, throughout your day. The app takes advantage of the watch's built-in sensors and continuously monitors your level of movement, exercise, and periods of inactivity (as long as you're wearing the watch).

As you'll discover, this information displays in several ways, and syncs automatically with the Activity and Health apps running on your iPhone. The Activity app also shares data with other health and fitness apps, as needed.

The Activity app can help you become more active throughout your day via three daily fitness goals, Move, Exercise, and Stand, which you set up the first time you activate the app. For example, the watch can tap your wrist using its haptic engine and display a message to remind you to stand up for at least one minute every hour (see Figure 2.23).

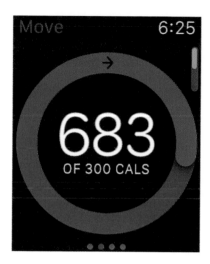

FIGURE 2.22

As you wear the watch, the Activity app tracks all of your movement all day and helps you achieve pre-set goals.

FIGURE 2.23

The Activity app reminds you to stand up and move around for at least one minute every hour.

The Activity app also encourages you to Move more throughout your day to burn a pre-determined number of calories, whereas the app's Exercise component encourages you to be active for at least 30 minutes per day. (This means participating in the equivalent of a brisk walk, or more intense activities.)

> **☑ TIP** As soon as you activate the Activity app on your Apple Watch, the iPhone edition of the app automatically installs itself on your phone, so you can better view and utilize the data the Apple Watch collects. On the Apple Watch, the Activity app displays data only from the current day. The iPhone edition of Activity, however, enables you to see and analyze all the Activity data collected for every day you've worn the watch.

USE THE WORKOUT APP

You use the Workout app, shown in Figure 2.24, for whenever you engage in any type of cardio fitness workout session, such as jogging, running, bike riding, or using an elliptical machine (or treadmill). The Workout app collects and displays real-time stats, such as time, distance, calories, pace, and speed.

FIGURE 2.24

The Workout app can help you set fitness goals, track your workouts, and view your progress in real time.

Like in the Activity app, the data the watch collects and displays automatically syncs with the iPhone, and a growing selection of other health- and fitness-oriented apps, including the Health app that comes preinstalled with iOS 8.2 on the iPhone, can use this data.

The Health app on the iPhone collects real-time health and fitness-related data from the iPhone, Apple Watch, and other compatible equipment (such as a Bluetooth scale, for example), as well as data you manually input, and then monitors, analyzes, stores, and potentially shares that information from the one, centralized Health app.

> ☑ **TIP** Chapter 4," Work with the iPhone's Health App," focuses exclusively on how to utilize the Health app with the iPhone, Apple Watch, and other health and fitness-related apps and equipment you might use.

Just as Notification Center monitors apps and keeps track of all alerts, alarms, and notifications, and then displays this information in one centralized place, the Health app serves a similar purpose, but deals exclusively with health, fitness, nutrition/diet, and sleep-related data and information.

> ☑ **TIP** Chapter 5 covers in full detail how to set up and use the Activity and Workout apps.

FIND AND INSTALL ADDITIONAL HEALTH AND FITNESS-RELATED APPS

The Apple Watch comes with a handful of apps preinstalled. In addition to these apps, however, you can download and install an ever-growing selection of Apple and third-party apps from the App Store.

Two of the ways to find, download, and install these apps include the following:

■ Launch the App Store app on your iPhone, and locate apps that have an Apple Watch component to them. Installing one of these apps onto your iPhone installs the Apple Watch component automatically as well. An app's description in the App Store highlights compatibility with the Apple Watch, as you can see in Figure 2.25.

■ From the Apple Watch app on the iPhone, tap on the Featured or Search icons at the bottom of the screen to find, browse, download, and install only iPhone apps that have an Apple Watch component.

FIGURE 2.25
In the App Store, all iPhone apps that are also compatible with the Apple Watch are clearly labeled with the message, "Offers Apple Watch App."

THE COST OF APPS

The App Store allows app developers to release iPhone and Apple Watch apps using a variety of pricing options, which include

- **Free apps**—These apps you can download and install for free.
- **Paid apps**—These apps have a one-time purchase price. After you buy the app, you can download and install it on your iPhone and Apple Watch, as well as any other compatible iOS mobile devices that are linked to your Apple ID account. Paid apps range in price from $0.99 to $9.99 or higher. The app developer sets the one-time purchase price.
- **In-app purchases**—A free or paid app can offer in-app purchases. Making the purchase while using the app (via the credit or debit card that's linked to your Apple ID, or a pre-paid iTunes gift card) unlocks various features, functions, or components of the app that are otherwise not available.

> **☑ TIP**   The App Store indicates any apps listed as free, but that have in-app purchases associated with them. Scroll down to the bottom of the app's Details screen, and look for the In-App option. Tap on it for details about what paid options are available for the app, and discover how much they cost before you install and use the app. This also applies to subscription-based apps.

- **Advertiser-supported apps**—These apps are typically free, but as you use the app, display ads (typically in the form of small banners) appear on the screen.

- **Subscription-based apps**—These apps are typically offered for free, but to fully utilize the app or access information related to the app, you must pay for and acquire an ongoing daily, weekly, monthly, or annually paid subscription while using the app. As covered later in this book, a variety of fitness, diet, and nutrition-related apps that allow you to communicate with a coach, trainer, or specialist via text message or video call from the app are among the types of apps that use a subscription-based payment model.

> **NOTE** You acquire Apple Watch and iPhone apps together. Currently, all the optional apps that you can download and install onto the Apple Watch also have a corresponding iPhone app. Thus, when you acquire and install the iPhone edition of an app, the Apple Watch version automatically gets installed onto the watch. If the app has a fee, you only pay for it once for access to it on all iOS mobile devices (including your Apple Watch) that are linked to the same Apple ID account.

USE THE APPLE WATCH APP TO FIND AND INSTALL APPS ONTO YOUR WATCH

The only way to find, download, and install apps onto your Apple Watch is to use the Apple Watch app on your Internet-connected iPhone. If you already know the name of the app you're looking for, such as one of the third-party apps you'll be reading about in subsequent chapters of this book, tap on the Search icon in the lower-right corner of the Apple Watch app, and then enter what you're looking for within the Search field (see Figure 2.26).

In the Search field, enter the title of the app, such as "Nike+ Running" or "Lose It." A list of related apps appears. Tap on a search result listing to display more detailed information about an app.

From one of the more detailed listings (shown in Figure 2.27), you can either acquire the app by tapping on the Get or Price button, or tap on the app's title or app icon to display the Details screen for the app. This functionality works just as it does for other iOS App Store purchases you're likely already familiar with.

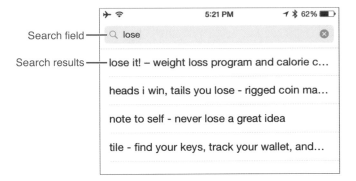

Search field

Search results

FIGURE 2.26

In the Apple Watch app on the iPhone, tap on the Search icon and enter a keyword or search phrase in the Search field to find Apple Watch apps.

FIGURE 2.27

Search results appear as condensed app listings. (Only one relevant result is shown here.) Tap on the app's name or icon to display more information, or tap on the Get or Price button to acquire, download, and install it onto your iPhone and Apple Watch simultaneously.

> **✓ TIP** In the Search field, enter a relevant keyword or search phrase for the type of app you're looking for, instead of an app's title. For example, if you were looking for the Nike+ Running app, but didn't know the exact name of it, you could enter the keyword "Nike," or "running" in the Search field to find listings for all related apps.

> ### NOTE
> For free apps, the Get button appears as part of an app's listing and description in the App Store. For apps you have to purchase, the price appears in the button, instead of "Get." Tap on this button to acquire the app.
>
> When prompted, enter your Apple ID password (or use the iPhone's TouchID sensor, if applicable) to confirm your purchase and, if necessary, pay for the app using the credit/debit card that's linked with your Apple ID account (or part of your iTunes gift card's available balance).
>
> If, however, you have already downloaded and installed the app, you will see the Open button. If you have the app, but it's not currently installed on your iPhone/ Apple Watch, an iCloud logo appears. Tap on this cloud-shaped logo to download and install the already-acquired app onto your device.

This book introduces you to many popular third-party apps that are available from the App Store that you can use on your Apple Watch (with your iPhone). New apps, however, are continuously released.

To learn more about the latest Apple Watch apps, launch the Apple Watch app on your iPhone, and tap on the Featured icon at the bottom of the screen (shown in Figure 2.28). This Apple Watch App Store screen lists apps based on categories Apple is showcasing. For example, under the Get Started heading is a collection of apps that Apple recommends to new Apple Watch users.

Featured icon

FIGURE 2.28

From the Apple Watch app, tap on the Featured icon to browse the Apple Watch App Store.

If you want to focus your search for apps based on a particular category, tap on the Categories option in the top-left corner of the screen, and then tap on a particular category. The majority of apps featured in this book fall under the Health & Fitness category.

Tapping on the Health & Fitness category option displays the available apps, starting with those that Apple opts to feature or showcase. To the right of the Get Started or More to Explore heading, tap on the See All option (shown in Figure 2.29) to view a more comprehensive listing of apps (shown in Figure 2.30).

See All options

FIGURE 2.29

To see a listing of all apps in a particular category, tap on the See All option.

Remember, you can tap on any app's icon or title to view more details about the app, or tap on the Get or Price button to acquire the app. Installing additional apps onto your Apple Watch (and iPhone) can greatly expand the health and fitness-related tasks that these devices can handle.

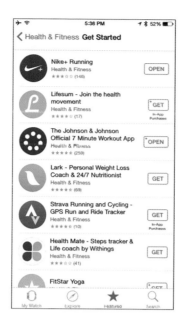

FIGURE 2.30

Tap on the See All option to see a comprehensive app listing. Scroll down to view all apps.

> ☑ **TIP** New health, fitness, diet, nutrition, and sleep-related apps are introduced via the App Store literally every day. In addition to brand-new apps, many more popular and existing iPhone apps are continuously being redesigned to include Apple Watch compatibility. Thus, to stay current and ensure access to the latest selection of Apple Watch apps to assist you in achieving your health, fitness, and/or dieting goals, be sure to check out the Featured section of the App Store (via the Apple Watch app) often.

PEBBLE TIME AS A VIABLE APPLE WATCH ALTERNATIVE

Although the Apple Watch is still a relatively new piece of wearable technology that can handle many of the same tasks as popular fitness and activity trackers from companies like Jawbone, Fitbit, and Garmin, the Apple Watch can also handle a wide range of other health and fitness-related tasks that are unique to the watch. This functionality is based on which app(s) you utilize with your Apple Watch and iPhone.

However, other smartwatches on the market can do most of what the Apple Watch is capable of. For example, just weeks after the release of Apple Watch, Pebble released its iPhone-compatible, second-generation Pebble Time watch.

Released in late-May 2015, the Pebble Time (shown in Figure 2.31) is priced at just $199.00, has a battery that lasts for a full week, and offers a full-color display. The display, however, is not a touch screen, and this watch has fewer built-in sensors than the Apple Watch. Yet, with some of the optional apps available for it, it's designed to work with several different fitness and activity trackers currently on the market.

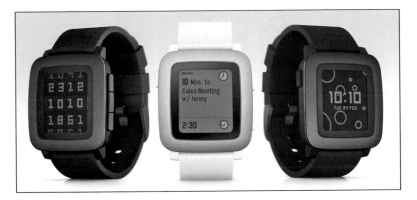

FIGURE 2.31

The Pebble Time smartwatch is a lower-cost alternative to the Apple Watch. It, too, works with an iPhone, and has optional health and fitness apps available for it. Photo courtesy of Pebble ©2015.

If you already own an activity or fitness tracker that's compatible with the Pebble Time watch, and the price of this watch is more appealing to you than the Apple Watch, you might discover that the Pebble Time watch can meet your needs and serve you well as a wearable health and fitness tool.

> **TIP** To learn more about the Pebble Time smartwatch, visit www.getpebble.com. Optional apps for the Pebble Time watch are available from the Pebble App Store, which you can access via your iPhone by first installing the free Pebble Smartwatch app.

Along with the Apple Watch and Pebble Time smartwatch, a handful of less popular smartwatches are available that you can use for health and fitness-related purposes, but that do not necessarily rely heavily on a connection with the iPhone.

These watches are available from companies such as LG Electronics, Sony, Motorola, Samsung, Garmin, and TomTom, and are typically sold by consumer electronics stores, such as Best Buy, as well as sporting goods stores, such as REI or Eastern Mountain Sports.

> **NOTE** Some smartwatches, like those from Garmin and TomTom, are designed specifically for hikers, bikers, golfers, and people who utilize GPS information to navigate with precision during their activities.

Although many of these watches can be used for health and fitness-related tasks, covering them is beyond the scope of this book, which primarily focuses on the Apple Watch and iPhone, as well as activity/fitness trackers (and other accessories) that you can use with the iPhone.

> **NOTE** In addition to full-featured smartwatches that offer a viable and often lower-cost alternative to the Apple Watch, fitness enthusiasts can invest in an activity/fitness tracker that wirelessly links with the iPhone.
>
> As discussed in Chapter 3, "Use Fitness Trackers and Other iPhone and Apple Watch Accessories," you can get these wearable devices from companies such as Fitbit and Jawbone, and use them to easily collect, analyze, and share different types of movement, location, and fitness-related data.

3

USE FITNESS TRACKERS AND OTHER IPHONE AND APPLE WATCH ACCESSORIES

As you know, on its own, the iPhone is chock-full of technologies you can use to help gather, analyze, display, and store useful information about your health and fitness activities. When combined with the Apple Watch, these capabilities significantly increase.

However, if you don't want to invest in an optional Apple Watch, less expensive, but powerful fitness and activity trackers are available from a variety of different companies, such as Jawbone (see Figure 3.1) and Fitbit. These offer some of the same health and fitness-related data-gathering functionality as the Apple Watch.

UP MOVE device

FIGURE 3.1

The Jawbone UP MOVE is one of the least expensive and compact fitness/activity trackers on the market.

You can wear these wireless fitness/activity trackers during your workouts or activities, during which they gather information and wirelessly transmit the relevant data to your iPhone. The Health app, a proprietary app specifically for the fitness/activity tracker you're using, or an independent app that can share data with these devices, can then collect and utilize the data.

> **NOTE** Every fitness/activity tracker, Bluetooth scale, or other health/fitness-oriented device this chapter covers offers its own proprietary app for the iPhone that collects, analyzes, displays, and stores data collected from that device. Virtually all the devices are also compatible with the iPhone's own Health app, which comes preinstalled with iOS 8 and iOS 9. More often than not, the proprietary app designed for a specific device can do more with the collected data than the Health app.

Meanwhile, in addition to the iPhone and Apple Watch (or a fitness/activity tracker), other consumer and medical devices can collect and share different types of data with the iPhone using wireless Bluetooth technology. One of the most popular and widely used of these optional tools is a Bluetooth weight scale, which works just like any other weight scale, but it also transmits its data to your iPhone so that you can track your weight.

This chapter covers some of the more popular fitness/activity trackers from Jawbone and Fitbit, as well as strategies for utilizing the proprietary apps available for these devices. It then introduces you to some of the Bluetooth scale options, as well as other health and fitness tools you can use with your iPhone.

> ### ✓ TIP
> You can train yourself to get a better night's sleep. Some of the fitness/activity trackers covered in this chapter can also serve as sleep monitors that track how much sleep you get per night.
>
> The stand-alone S+ Sleep Better device from ResMed is a consumer-oriented, but cutting-edge product that does much more than track your sleep patterns. You can use it to help you achieve a better night's sleep and overcome many common sleep-related problems.
>
> Chapter 11, "Monitor Your Sleep and Sleep Better" covers more about this optional device that works with your iPhone.

JAWBONE FITNESS/ACTIVITY TRACKERS

Jawbone (www.jawbone.com) offers a robust selection of optional Bluetooth accessories for the iPhone, including a line of Bluetooth headsets, wireless speakers, and several different fitness/activity trackers.

The company's UP fitness trackers are currently comprised of several devices (sold separately), including the least expensive UP MOVE ($49.99), as well as the UP2 ($99.99), UP3 ($179.99), and UP4 (released in Summer 2015). You can use the majority of these devices (with the proprietary UP app) to track activity, monitor sleep, log food consumption, help maintain heart health, and serve as a virtual coach during various fitness activities.

You can wear the UP MOVE in several different ways, whereas you wear the UP2, UP3, and UP4 around your wrist. A device collects the data and wirelessly transmits it to your iPhone where one of two Jawbone apps analyzes and displays it. You can also import this same data into the iPhone's Health app.

> **NOTE** Like the Health app that displays data collected by the Apple Watch or other devices on the Dashboard in the form of graphic "snapshots" of specific types of data, the optional UP apps do this, but also incorporate a Smart Coach feature that analyzes your data and offers personalized health and fitness advice. This advice can help you make better life choices, and discover timely information about your health, fitness, sleep, and nutrition-related activities or patterns that can help you better understand and achieve your goals.

These devices come in a variety of colors, are water-resistant (not waterproof), and utilize a battery that lasts anywhere from seven days to six months, depending on the device. In terms of just their fitness/activity monitoring functions, the various UP devices offer much the same functionality as the Apple Watch, but at a lower cost.

The Jawbone UP fitness/activity trackers are available directly from the company's website and from many consumer electronics and mass-market retailers.

DIFFERENCES BETWEEN UP DEVICES

Aside from the price difference, each of the UP devices offers a slightly different assortment of features and functions. The UP MOVE, for example, is the company's most basic device. It is a small plastic disc about the size of a quarter that you can either clip onto your clothing or wear on your wrist like a watch (if you purchase an optional wrist strap accessory).

The UP MOVE works with the UP iPhone app, and includes the Smart Coach feature, along with the ability to track your movement during fitness-related activities. You can also use it to measure calories burned, to time yourself when engaged in specific activities, track sleep, and log meals.

The UP2, UP3, and UP4 have a bracelet design that you wear around your wrist either all day or as you participate in specific fitness activities. The UP2 has all the capabilities of the UP MOVE, but also offers a Smart Alarm and Idle Alert feature. The UP3 does all of this as well, and includes Heart Health Monitoring and Advanced Sleep Tracking features.

Announced in April 2015 and released in Summer 2015, the UP4 includes the additional feature of linking the bracelet to an American Express credit card account, and you can then use the bracelet to make retail purchases in the United States at participating businesses or restaurants that accept American Express.

You can learn more about the UP fitness trackers from the Jawbone company's website (see Figure 3.2).

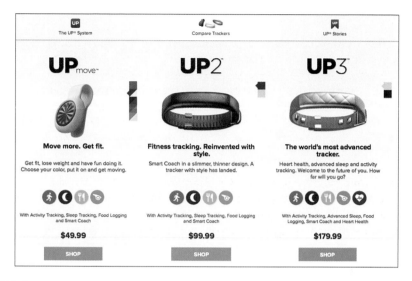

FIGURE 3.2

Jawbone's website offers a feature-by-feature comparison among its various devices.

You set up and control the UP device features via the UP app on the iPhone. Many additional third-party apps, including the RunKeeper, MyFitnessPal, MapMyFitness, and Fitt apps, for example, also work seamlessly with the UP devices.

> **TIP** To learn more about the additional, third-party fitness and health-related apps that work with the UP fitness/activity trackers, visit https://jawbone.com/marketplace.
>
> These devices also work with the Health o meter Lose It! scale, which you'll learn more about later in this chapter.

GET THE LOWDOWN ON THE UP APPS

Jawbone offers two different UP apps for the iPhone, which at first glance can be confusing because they don't look all that different (see Figure 3.3). Which one you should download and install onto your smartphone depends on which model fitness/activity tracker you purchase.

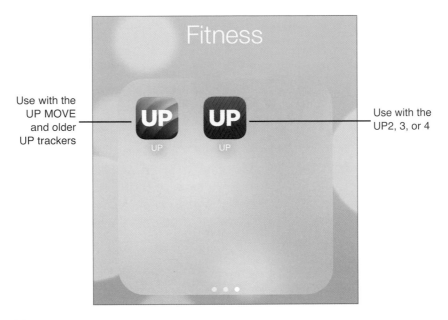

FIGURE 3.3

Here are the two UP apps installed on an iPhone, and stored in a Fitness folder on the Home screen.

After you purchase an UP device, you need to download and install either the blue or purple UP app. The blue edition of the app is for use with the UP MOVE and older versions of the UP fitness/activity trackers, including the UP and UP24. You use the purple edition of the app with the UP2, UP3, or UP4, or use it as a stand-alone fitness app without an UP device.

> 📝 **NOTE**   This chapter offers detailed directions for using the UP app with an UP fitness/activity tracker. Other apps, for competing fitness/activity trackers, offer similar functionality, although the look of the screens, menus, and on-screen icons vary. After you understand the basics of using the UP app, however, you can easily navigate and utilize any proprietary app for a specific fitness/activity tracker.

After downloading and installing the appropriate app, launch the app on your iPhone. The app's introductory screen (shown in Figure 3.4) offers three options:

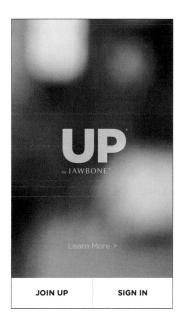

FIGURE 3.4

The Introductory screen of the UP app offers three options.

- **Learn More:** Tap on this option to go online and learn more about what's possible using the app with a compatible UP fitness/activity tracker.

- **Join Up:** Tap on this button to set up an account online. This is necessary to upload and sync data collected by the UP tracker to your online-based account, and to take advantage of the online-based tools offered by Jawbone.

- **Sign In:** Tap on this button to log in to your UP online-based account that you've previously set up.

SET UP YOUR UP ACCOUNT

Make sure your iPhone has Internet access, and then from the app's opening screen, tap on the Join Up button the first time you attempt to use the UP app with your UP tracker.

The app prompts you to tap on the UP device you'll use with the app (see Figure 3.5). This demonstration focuses on the UP MOVE:

FIGURE 3.5

You must pair your UP device with your iPhone.

1. Follow the on-screen directions to install the battery into the UP MOVE device, or if you're using a different UP tracker, to learn how to charge its battery. Tap on the Next option to continue.

2. On your iPhone, turn on the Bluetooth feature, and then "wake up" the tracker by pressing and holding the main button on the device until the lights flash. The UP device establishes a wireless connection with your iPhone via Bluetooth.

3. Give permission for the UP app to exchange data with the iPhone's Health app (see Figure 3.6). Turn on the Sleep Analysis and Steps switches if you want your UP device to send (write) data to the Health app, and turn on the two other switches to allow the UP app to access (read) data from the Health app. Tap on the Done option to continue.

4. Create a profile for yourself. This involves providing your Gender, Height, Weight, and Birthdate, which you enter by tapping on the appropriate icons (see Figure 3.7). Tap on the Done option to continue. Confirm your entries, and then tap on the Next option.

5. Set your goals. Based on the information you entered about yourself, the UP app recommends how many steps per day you should be taking on average, as well as how much sleep you should be getting per night. Tap on the Next option to continue.

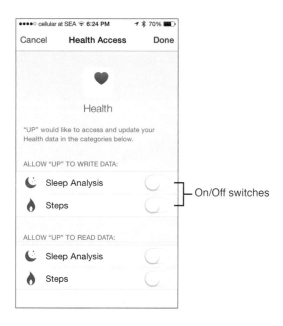

FIGURE 3.6

Any time a third-party app requires access to other apps or iPhone functions to access or exchange data, you must grant permission.

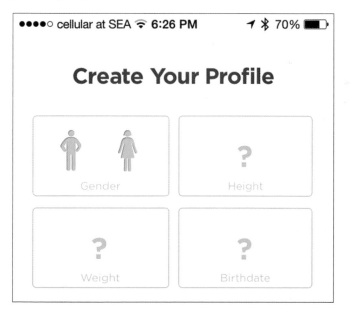

FIGURE 3.7

Create a profile for your online-based account that you use with the UP app.

6. Set up notifications. Tap on the Enable feature to set up this function now and determine what types of notifications the app will generate and how often, or tap on the Not Now option to continue and set up Notifications at a later time.

> **TIP** Keep in mind, you can always adjust Notifications by launching Settings, and then tapping on the Notifications option.

7. To have the UP app provide you with location-specific insight and information as appropriate, tap on the Enable option, or tap on Not Now to deactivate this feature for the time being.

8. From the Create Your Account screen, enter your First and Last Name and Email Address. Also, create an account-specific password.

9. Tap on the camera icon if you want to import a photo of yourself into the app, which you could later share with the UP online community and/or your designated fitness buddies.

10. Select the "I acknowledge and agree to the: Jawbone Terms of Service and Jawbone Privacy Policy" checkbox. Tap on Agree & Finish to continue (shown in Figure 3.8).

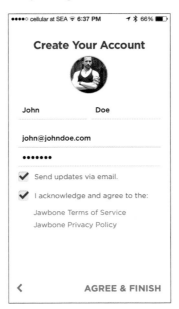

FIGURE 3.8

Enter the required information on the Create Your Account screen.

11. At the prompt that appears, sign in to the app and UP online service (via the app). This initial setup only needs to be done once.

MANAGE YOUR HEALTH WITH THE UP APP

After you sign in to the UP app on your iPhone, the app's main screen appears. This screen shows your daily activity on the current day, if any, using a colorful graphic (see Figure 3.9). Tap on it to display detailed text-based information and a graph depicting your activity-related data collected from your UP device and/or other compatible equipment, as well as relevant data the Health app imported (see Figure 3.10).

FIGURE 3.9

Here is the main screen of the UP app.

FIGURE 3.10

View detailed information about your activities on the iPhone's screen.

Tap on the Menu icon in the top-left corner of the screen to manage the app or adjust your goals. Tap on the iPhone-shaped icon in the top-right corner of the screen to set up or edit app-specific notifications.

To work with each of the app's modules—Fitness, Mood, Food, Weight, or Sleep—tap on the "+" icon near the bottom-center of the screen, and then tap on one of the color-coded module icons shown in Figure 3.11. The following sections outline what you use each of the app's modules for.

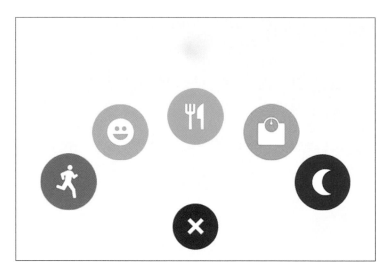

FIGURE 3.11

Tap on a colored icon to choose among the app's Fitness, Mood, Food, Weight, and Sleep modules.

TRACK YOUR WORKOUTS AND ACTIVITY

When you're about to begin any type of activity or workout, tap on the Fitness Tracker (orange) icon. From the Log Workout screen (see Figure 3.12), tap on the Activity Type option to select a specific type of fitness/workout activity (see Figure 3.13).

FIGURE 3.12

The UP app's Log Workout screen offers several tracking options.

FIGURE 3.13

Choose the type of activity you plan to engage in.

You can choose from 19 options, including Walk, Run, Weights, Cross Train, Bike, Stationary Bike, Elliptical Machine, Cardio, Zumba, Yoga, Pilates, Dance, Tennis, Soccer, Basketball, Swim, Hike, Ski, or Other.

Next, tap on the Effort Level. A graphic of a person appears. Using your finger, swipe up on this graphic (starting at its feet) to increase the intensity or difficulty level of the upcoming workout/activity.

Tap on the Start Time option to enter the time and date the workout or activity will begin (the default is the current time and date), and if you want, tap on the Duration option to set a time for how long you plan to engage in the workout/activity.

After you enter all the requested information, tap on the checkmark icon in the top-right corner of the screen to begin that workout/activity. Your UP device (or other compatible equipment) then collects your information and imports it into the UP app and the Health app, as appropriate.

TRACK YOUR MOOD

Your emotional state and your physical state are undeniably interrelated, with each having an impact on the other. Throughout each day, and from day to day, your mood changes. To keep a record of your mood, especially if you suffer from depression, for example, use the UP app's Mood tracking feature. Tap on the Mood (yellow) icon, and then swipe up or down on the Happy Face graphic to rate your current mood (see Figure 3.14).

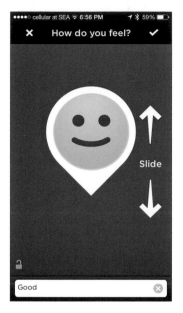

FIGURE 3.14

Choose this mood graphic setting when you're having an average day.

The UP app automatically records the time and date of each Mood input. You can also tap on the text field at the bottom of the screen if you want to manually add a description or keyword related to your mood. For example, you can document any trigger or cause for a change in mood.

> **TIP** After adding or editing any information in the UP app, including your mood, be sure to tap on the checkmark icon in the top-right corner of the screen to update the app and save your information.

TRACK YOUR FOOD INTAKE

The UP app allows you to keep track of what and how much you eat. It then automatically analyzes the related nutritional information. Each time you tap on the Food (green) icon to log a meal, snack, or drink, you can also take a photo of the food (using the camera built in to your iPhone), scan the barcode on the food's packaging, input information about where you're dining and what you ordered, and track your water intake (see Figure 3.15).

FIGURE 3.15
Input your consumed snacks, meals, and drinks information.

Based on the type of meal you enter, common food and drink items for that meal appear, along with their caloric information. Tap on all applicable food items as you eat them to keep tabs on your consumption. The app then calculates caloric intake and other nutrition-related data.

TRACK YOUR WEIGHT

The UP app can monitor your weight and track weight fluctuations on an ongoing basis (see Figure 3.16). You can weigh on a compatible Bluetooth scale and have the information automatically import into the app, or tap on the Weight option to manually enter your weight if you use a scale that's not paired with your iPhone. Tap on the blue Weight icon to use this function of the UP app.

FIGURE 3.16
Use the UP app with a Bluetooth scale, or manually enter your weight-related data.

> **TIP** Maintaining a log of your weight from day to day, particularly when working toward a specific fitness goal or while on a diet, helps you more clearly see the impact of what you eat on your weight and overall health.

TRACK YOUR SLEEP

Either by collecting data from your UP tracker or by your manually inputting the data (see Figure 3.17), the UP app's Sleep module tracks what time you go to bed each night, when you wake up, and how much sleep you got during the night. In addition to monitoring your sleep patterns, the UP app also offers a Smart Coach feature that uses this data with all the other information you enter into the app to provide you with personalized feedback and advice. For example, it recommends the optimum amount of sleep you should get, based on your personal information. To use this function, tap on the purple Sleep icon.

FIGURE 3.17
The UP app can keep track of your sleeping habits and show you how much sleep you're getting.

> 📝 **TIP**   As with any fitness/activity tracking app, the only way for it to pro-
> vide you with ongoing, accurate, and insightful information and feedback is if you
> use it on a consistent basis over an extended period of time. Just putting on an UP
> tracker once per week or month, or randomly entering various pieces of data into
> the UP app on an inconsistent basis, prevents the app from truly helping you reach
> your fitness goals because the long-term data that's needed for analysis will be
> unavailable.

FITBIT FITNESS/ACTIVITY TRACKERS

Another industry leader in smartphone-compatible fitness and activity trackers is
Fitbit (www.fitbit.com). As you can see in Figure 3.18, which shows the company's
website, Fitbit offers a plethora of solutions for fitness-minded people who want to
use technology to track, manage, and analyze their activities.

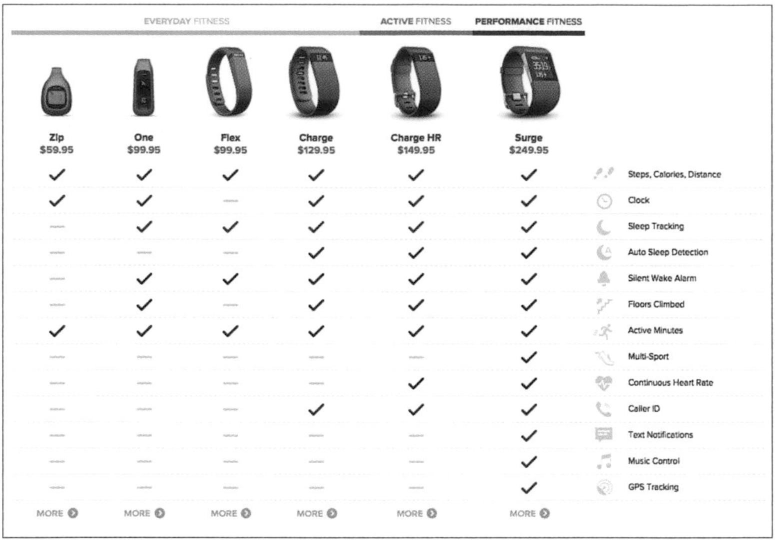

EVERYDAY FITNESS				ACTIVE FITNESS	PERFORMANCE FITNESS		
Zip $59.95	One $99.95	Flex $99.95	Charge $129.95	Charge HR $149.95	Surge $249.95		
✓	✓	✓	✓	✓	✓		Steps, Calories, Distance
✓	✓	—	✓	✓	✓		Clock
—	✓	✓	✓	✓	✓		Sleep Tracking
—	—	—	✓	✓	✓		Auto Sleep Detection
—	✓	✓	✓	✓	✓		Silent Wake Alarm
—	✓	—	✓	✓	✓		Floors Climbed
✓	✓	✓	✓	✓	✓		Active Minutes
—	—	—	—	—	✓		Multi-Sport
—	—	—	—	✓	✓		Continuous Heart Rate
—	—	—	✓	✓	✓		Caller ID
—	—	—	—	—	✓		Text Notifications
—	—	—	—	—	✓		Music Control
—	—	—	—	—	✓		GPS Tracking
MORE ❯	MORE ❯	MORE ❯	MORE ❯	MORE ❯	MORE ❯		

FIGURE 3.18

The company's website showcases a line-up of Fitbit fitness/activity trackers.

Along with the Fitbit Zip ($59.95), among the company's other offerings are the Fitbit One ($99.95), Flex ($99.95), Charge ($129.95), Charge HR ($149.95), and the Surge (a $249.95 smartwatch). As you can see from the company's website, the Zip and One are small, clip-on trackers, whereas the Flex, Charge, Charge HR, and top-of-the-line Surge are bracelets.

You can find Fitbit products at consumer electronics stores such as Best Buy, as well as mass-market retailers, including Target and Walmart.

> **NOTE** The Fitbit company also offers its own Bluetooth weight scale, called the Aria, that's compatible with its fitness/activity trackers and the iPhone.

All of these Fitbit devices track steps, calories burned, and distance throughout the wearer's day (including when they're involved in workouts or fitness-oriented activities). These devices can monitor "active minutes" versus time when the wearer is stationary.

Depending on the Fitbit model, some also display a clock, handle sleep tracking, track the number of floors climbed, and allow the user to set various types of alarms.

The Charge HD and Surge also include some of the broader functionality of a full-featured smartwatch. For example, the Surge offers GPS tracking, the ability to remotely control the iPhone's Music app, the ability to display incoming text messages and Caller ID information from the iPhone, and it has a built-in heart rate monitor.

> **TIP** The Fitbit app for the iPhone can collect data from multiple Fitbit devices that are linked to a single account. When used with the Aria scale, the app also monitors the user's weight, body fat percentage, and BMI.

After purchasing one of the Fitbit tracker devices and/or the Aria scale, you need to download and install the free Fitbit app, which is available from the App Store. This proprietary app can handle a variety of tasks, including:

- **Tracking activity throughout the day**—Depending on which Fitbit tracker the app is wirelessly linked with, the app tracks and maintains details about steps taken, floors climbed, active minutes, and calories burned. In addition to displaying data from a single day, the app makes it easy to view progress over time by enabling you to look at and compare data from the past.

- **Logging meals and caloric intake**—Via a variety of food logging tools, the app makes it easy to track the foods you eat and what you drink, calculate your caloric intake, and determine other nutrition-related information with minimal manual data entry. For example, you can use the camera built in to your iPhone to scan a food or drink product's barcode (shown in Figure 3.19).

- **Set and monitor personalized goals**—The app allows you to set and work toward step, weight, and activity-related goals. Based on data collected, the app suggests ways to improve the results you're achieving while working toward each goal.

- **Interact with friends to share achievements**—Using communication tools built in to your iPhone, including email and Facebook connectivity, you can easily share your fitness-related achievements with your online friends, as well as the Fitbit online community (if you choose to).

- **Track a runner's progress via the MobileRun feature**—Instead of using a stand-alone app for runners, the Fitbit app has specific tools available for runners that allow you to track your pace, time, and distance, and differentiate between runs, walks, and hikes. The app can also utilize GPS data either from the iPhone or one of the higher-end Fitbit trackers to map routes.

FIGURE 3.19

One way to track food and drink consumption is to scan barcodes for food and drink products using the camera built in to your iPhone.

- **Maintain a sleep record**—On an ongoing basis, the app (working with a Fitbit tracker) keeps tabs on how much sleep you get each night, allows you to set alarms, and lets you view your sleep patterns over time in the form of colorful charts.

- **Monitor weight**—Whether you use the Aria scale, or manually enter data, the Fitbit app allows you to track your weight, BMI, lean muscle, and body fat percentage over time.

- **Stay highly motivated over time**—Like with many fitness apps, when you achieve specific goals or milestones, the Fitbit app offers virtual awards that you can display, collect, and showcase online. The app can also display messages as reminders or motivators to keep you active.

- **Import data from Fitbit trackers and scales**—Although you can manually enter data for any category that the Fitbit app can track, what makes the app truly useful is its ability to automatically obtain, analyze, store, and display data collected from one or more Fitbit trackers and/or the Aria Bluetooth scale. However, no tracker is required to use the free app.

After you set up a Fitbit account via the app, the Dashboard screen displays a graphic-based summary of all information tracked and stored by the app, including the app's analysis of activity, fitness, sleep, and weight data, as well as the raw numbers.

FITBIT AND THE HEALTH APP As of Summer 2015, Fitbit fitness/activity trackers and Bluetooth scale work with the iPhone when used with the proprietary Fitbit app, or a handful of other third-party fitness apps. These fitness/activity trackers do not support Apple's Health app (which comes preinstalled on the iPhone with iOS 8 and iOS 9). As a result, data collected by the Fitbit devices does not sync or share with the Health app. This could change in the future, perhaps by the time you read this. For now, however, if you want data from any Fitbit device to be shared with the Health app, you'll need to use another app, called Sync Solver ($1.99, https://itunes.apple.com/us/app/sync-solver-for-fitbit/id935306292), which is available from the App Store.

WEIGHING IN ON BLUETOOTH WEIGHT SCALES

The great thing about a Bluetooth scale is that it doesn't forget. In addition to telling you your weight, percentage of body fat, BMI, and other information every time you step on it, the scale sends this data to your iPhone for analysis and storage. All the Bluetooth scales have proprietary apps associated with them, but they also work with the Health app, and a variety of third-party health and fitness apps.

☑ **TIP** The various Bluetooth scales and their associated apps can keep track of multiple family members and store each person's data separately. How to set this up varies based on which scale you have and the proprietary app you're using it with.

Choose a Bluetooth scale based on the features you need. Most fall within the $50.00 and $150.00 price range, and most are available online or from retail chains (such as Bed, Bath & Beyond), consumer electronics stores (such as Best Buy), or mass-market retailers (such as Target, Costco, or Walmart).

☑ **TIP** Amazon.com sells most of the popular Bluetooth scales, often at a discount. Several models are also available directly from the Apple website (www.apple.com).

The following sections include information about a few of the more popular Bluetooth scales currently available. To find more, enter the search phrase "Bluetooth Scale" into your favorite Internet search engine, or visit an online store such as Amazon.com.

HEALTH O METER LOSE IT! SCALE

Available from the developers of the Lose It! app, which you'll learn more about in Chapter 10, "Achieve Your Dieting Goals," this $69.95 Bluetooth scale is one of the least expensive on the market, but it offers many of the same features as the pricier models.

When used with the Lose It! app, the iPhone and scale combination allow you to more easily track and then view exactly how your diet and exercise program impact your weight on a day-to-day basis. The whole concept of tracking your food might seem like a daunting task, but the Lose It! app includes a variety of built-in tools to make it easier, and when you use it with the scale, you don't need to manually enter your weight data into your iPhone on a daily basis, because the app gathers this information directly from the scale.

> **TIP** When shopping for any Bluetooth scale, select one that not only measures your weight, but also other information that your other health, diet, and/or fitness apps can use. For example, many scales, including the Health o meter Lose It! scale, measures body fat, hydration levels, BMI, and other data each time you simply step on the scale.
>
> Another feature to look for in a scale is its ability to automatically detect the different people in your family, so the data collected can be recorded accurately, without the need for excessive manual data entry.

WITHINGS SMART BODY ANALYZER

Priced at $149.95, the Withings Smart Body Analyzer scale can track your weight and body composition in a way that presents you with accurate data you can use to more easily understand and, if necessary, alter your lifestyle to achieve a more optimum weight or fitness level.

In addition to all the standard types of measurements a Bluetooth scale takes, this one calculates your fat-lean ratio and your heart rate to give you a better representation of your current situation.

To give you an even broader picture of your overall health and well-being, the scale monitors indoor air quality and temperature. For example, it tracks the carbon dioxide levels in your home, and notifies you if you need to take steps so you can breathe cleaner and healthier air.

The scale can share this information with the proprietary Withings app, or any of more than 60 compatible iPhone apps, including RunKeeper, MyFitnessPal, and LoseIt!, all of which you'll learn more about elsewhere in this book.

> **TIP** One unique feature of the Withings Smart Body Analyzer scale is that each time you step on the scale and stand there for a few seconds, the device measures your heart rate through your feet, and along with the other data it collects, sends this information to the scale's proprietary app, the Health app, or any other compatible app you're using for health, diet, or fitness purposes.

> **TIP** The Withings Smart Body scale utilizes Bluetooth or Wi-Fi to transmit data (wirelessly) from the scale to the iPhone. This enables you to place the scale almost anywhere in your home and have your smartphone collect data from it even if the two devices are in separate rooms.

Using the proprietary Withings Health Body Analyzer app (available for free from the App Store), you can view weight fluctuations and other data collected over time, set weight-related goals, receive useful tips for achieving them, and automatically break down your larger goals into more achievable weekly goals that the app sets and guides you toward.

FITBIT ARIA SCALE

If you're already using a Fitbit fitness/activity tracker, you might also want to invest in the Aria Bluetooth scale ($129.95), which when used on a regular basis, collects more information about your body as you engage in health, fitness, or dieting activities. This additional information includes body fat percentage, BMI (Body Mass Index), and lean mass.

> **TIP** Although the Aria scale is designed for use with the Fitbit fitness/ activity trackers, you can use any compatible Bluetooth scale to accomplish the same data collection objectives. This scale also works with Apple Watch, other fitness/ activity trackers, and a wide range of optional health, fitness, and diet-related apps.

As you would expect, the Aria automatically measures your weight, body mass index (BMI), lean mass, and body fat percentage each time you step on the scale. It automatically recognizes up to eight different users, and can keep each person's results private.

Using the proprietary app designed specifically for use with the scale on your iPhone, you can view weight stats and progress trends displayed in text and easy-to-understand charts and colorful graphs.

When used with a Fitbit fitness/activity tracker, the scale can help you more accurately calculate calories and determine how caloric intake impacts your weight, for example, based on the level of activity you engage in.

> **NOTE** *Lean Body Weight* is calculated by taking your total body weight and subtracting your body fat weight.
>
> *Body Mass Index (BMI)* is a calculation done in an effort to quantify someone's amount of tissue mass (muscle, fat, and bone), and determine whether he or she is underweight, normal weight, overweight, or obese. On the BMI scale, anyone who scores 25 or higher is considered overweight. Calculating BMI requires height and weight data.
>
> Most Bluetooth scales can automatically handle these calculations, and then store and track the data as it changes over time.

OTHER BLUETOOTH HEALTH AND FITNESS TOOLS THAT WORK WITH YOUR IPHONE

Beyond fitness/activity trackers and Bluetooth scales, a growing selection of other consumer-oriented health and fitness tools are available that can work with the iPhone and specialized apps.

For example, the Withings Wireless Blood Pressure Monitor ($129.95) includes everything needed to accurately monitor your systolic and diastolic blood pressure, as well as your heart rate. Monitoring blood pressure is not a function offered by the Apple Watch, or other fitness/activity trackers, but this is useful information for people with high blood pressure, suffering from hypertension, who have a heart condition, or who are serious about fitness.

Each time the Withings Wireless Blood Pressure Monitor acquires data, it transfers it to the Health app and other compatible apps capable of analyzing, displaying, and archiving the data. The device (with the help of your iPhone's Internet connection) utilizes data acquired from the National Health Institute and other data from the Health app (or Withings own Health Mate app) to quickly gauge the state of your health.

iHealth Labs (www.ihealthlabs.com) also offers its own Wireless Blood Pressure Wrist Monitor ($79.95), which measures and tracks your systolic/diastolic numbers, heart rate, and pulse wave, using a device that's smaller than a traditional arm cuff (see Figure 3.20). It then transmits data to the free iHealth MyVitals app (available from the App Store), as well as to the Health app.

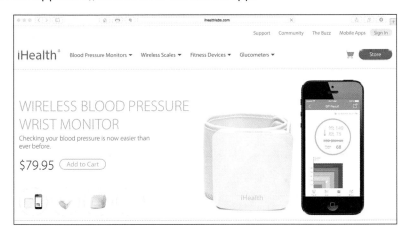

FIGURE 3.20

Learn more about the iHealth Wireless Blood Pressure Wrist Monitor from the company's website.

> ☑ **TIP**   An app can analyze data collected by a blood pressure monitor over time, and you can easily share that data with a doctor. You can use these monitors with a fitness/activity tracker and/or Bluetooth scale, allowing your iPhone to gather more data about you on a regular basis, as compared to using the iPhone with just a fitness/activity tracker, for example.

Sold separately, iHealth Labs offers two different model Bluetooth scales, including the iHealth Wireless Body Analysis scale ($99.95). It also offers two different glucometers (starting at $29.95) that can obtain and track blood glucose levels and link with the iPhone (see Figure 3.21).

The device can get your glucose readings within five seconds, and you can view the data on the device itself, or on the iPhone's screen when you use the company's proprietary iHealth Gluco-Smart app. (iHealth Test Strips are sold separately from the company's website.)

FIGURE 3.21
Measure blood sugar level with the Wireless Smart Gluco-Monitoring System.

If you need to check or monitor your body temperature, the Kinsa Smart Thermometer ($29.95, www.kinsahealth.com) connects directly to the iPhone (via the smartphone's headphone jack), and works with the proprietary Kinsa SmartHealth app, as well as the Health app. The thermometer can achieve professional-level accuracy within 10 seconds, whether the thermometer is used orally, under the arm, or rectally.

In addition, some stand-alone home workout equipment, such as treadmills, elliptical machines, rowing machines, or stationary bikes, now offer Bluetooth and/or Internet functionality, allowing data from each one of your workouts to automatically transfer (wirelessly) from the workout equipment to your iPhone. In some cases, this data is more extensive than what the Apple Watch or another independent fitness/activity tracker can collect.

> **TIP** If you're planning on joining a gym, look for one that's equipped with the latest Bluetooth-compatible fitness equipment, or that links with an iPhone (directly or via the Internet).

For example, some of the more recently released pieces of home fitness equipment from Bowflex (www.bowflex.com), including the Bowflex Max Trainer M5, offer a proprietary iPhone app (in this case, the Max Trainer app) that tracks total calories burned, time, watts, and other data in real time, and allows you to analyze and store this data.

Some of the latest fitness equipment from Nordic Track (www.nordictrack.com) and ProForm (www.sears.com/proform-power-995-c/p-00664148000P) is iFit-compatible, meaning that it offers wireless data syncing between the equipment, the Internet, and a proprietary app running on the iPhone.

TIP One place to learn about new iPhone-compatible fitness accessories is by visiting any Apple Store, or Apple's own website, which now has a health and fitness section (http://store.apple.com/us/accessories/all-accessories/fitness).

IN THIS CHAPTER

- Set up the Health app on your iPhone
- Use the app's Medical ID feature
- Track your activity, health, and fitness data using Health
- Share your health data or keep it private

4

WORK WITH THE IPHONE'S HEALTH APP

The Health app comes preinstalled with iOS 8 and iOS 9. On its own, this app doesn't do a whole lot. However, when used with other iPhone health, medical, and fitness-related apps, the Apple Watch, and/or other health and fitness-oriented devices that can link wirelessly to the iPhone (such as a scale, blood pressure monitor, or a treadmill), the Health app becomes a centralized place for collecting, viewing, analyzing, storing, and potentially sharing a wide range of personal health, medical, and fitness-related data and information.

Included in iOS 8 and iOS 9 is a collection of specialized app programming tools, known as HealthKit, that allows app developers to utilize the sensors and tools built in to the iPhone and Apple Watch to collect a lot of different types of health, medical, and fitness-related information about the user. As this information is gathered, it can be automatically imported into the Health app, allowing you to access crucial data (see Figure 4.1).

In addition, you can manually enter personal information and data into the app as needed, allowing you to create a highly personalized database that stores specific types of health, medical, and/or fitness-related information that's collected over time.

FIGURE 4.1

The sharing of activity, fitness, or health-related data collected by the Apple Watch, for example, can automatically happen in real time with the Health app on your iPhone while you're on the go.

Data collected from the Activity and Workout apps on an Apple Watch, as well as heart rate data and data collected by some third-party apps, can automatically be sent to, shared with, and stored in the Health app for analysis, viewing, and archiving.

NOTE Just as Notification Center serves as a centralized place to collect and view alerts, alarms, and notifications the iPhone and the apps running on it generate, the Health app serves as a centralized place for collecting, viewing, analyzing, storing, and sharing health, medical, and fitness-related data.

This data can include everything from your movement throughout the day (step count), to your heart rate, blood pressure, weight, caloric intake, respiratory rate, body temperature, and/or other information that the iPhone, Apple Watch, apps, and any other equipment that's linked to your iPhone collect in real time and on an ongoing basis.

You can set up virtually all the medical, health, fitness, nutrition, and sleep-related apps you'll ultimately be using (some of which the later chapters of this book cover) to work with the Health app. However, you can also opt to keep data collected by other stand-alone apps, or the specialized apps associated with a fitness/activity tracker (or other equipment), totally separate from the Health app. This gives you a lot of flexibility in terms of how you utilize the Health app in your everyday life.

> **✓ TIP** If you want, you can forego using the Health app altogether so that the app does not collect, track, or store any health, medical, activity, or fitness-related data.
>
> For example, Jawbone activity and fitness trackers have their own proprietary app to collect and manage data. You can share this data automatically with the Health app, or not, based on how you have each set up on your smartphone.
>
> To deactivate the Health app, launch Settings on your iPhone, tap on the Privacy option, and then tap on the Health option. If the Health menu screen lists any apps, tap on each one, and turn off all their virtual switches.
>
> Next, return to the Privacy menu in Settings, and tap on the Motion & Fitness option. Turn off the virtual switches for Fitness Tracking and Health.
>
> In the future, if you install any Health-compatible apps onto your iPhone, when prompted, deny permission to share information and data with the Health app. This option typically appears when you launch a Health-compatible app for the first time.

After adjusting the privacy-related settings for the Health app, you might need to adjust additional app-specific settings for other apps, first to establish a link between those other apps and the Health app, and then to properly manage app-specific data.

> **❗CAUTION** As an iPhone user, you have 100 percent control over what information the Health app collects, as well as how, when, and with whom to share this information or data.
>
> You learn how to set up the private and sharing features in the Health app on the iPhone later in this chapter. How you ultimately want to share and utilize each type of data is up to you, though.
>
> For example, you might opt to share your caloric intake and weight data with your dietitian or personal trainer, but share other medical-related data exclusively with your physician or another medical professional. At the same time, you might opt to share details about your fitness-related activities, such as milestones you've achieved, with your friends on social media, such as Facebook, but keep everything else private. You can do all this with the Health app, provided you set up the privacy settings correctly.

Many health and fitness experts, including several you'll be reading interviews with throughout this book, believe that one of the best ways to help yourself achieve your goals is to track your progress along the way so you can see firsthand how you're doing.

The Health app collects specific data that's directly relevant to your goal(s), and displays this information in a graphical, "snapshot" way that enables you to see the cause-and-effect relationship between your actions and their impact on your goals.

SET UP THE HEALTH APP

Any time you launch the Health app, four command icons appear along the bottom of the screen (see Figure 4.2): Dashboard, Health Data, Sources, and Medical ID.

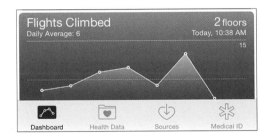

FIGURE 4.2

The Health app's four main command icons appear along the bottom of the screen.

Tap on the Dashboard icon to display the data collected by the Health app in a somewhat customizable format. You decide what information appears, and by tapping on the Day, Week, Month, or Year tab (see Figure 4.3), you determine over what time period specific data covers using a graphical, easy-to-understand, "snapshot" format.

Tap on the Health Data icon to determine what data you want to collect and how and what information to share, and what to display on the app's Dashboard.

Tap on the Sources tab, to see from where the Health app gathers information and real-time data. This can include from the iPhone itself, from the Apple Watch, from specific apps (running on the iPhone), or from equipment that's linked with your iPhone (such as a Bluetooth scale, or a compatible piece of medical or fitness equipment).

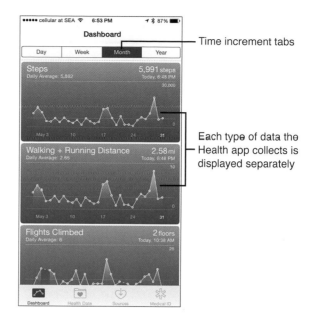

Time increment tabs

Each type of data the Health app collects is displayed separately

FIGURE 4.3

Tap on the Dashboard icon to choose the time increment in which you want to view your data. Options include Day, Week, Month, or Year.

Tapping on the Medical ID icon reveals personal details about yourself and medical history (after you've set it up). This feature is particularly useful to a doctor or emergency first responders to quickly get them up to speed about you and your medical condition(s) and history, if you experience an emergency and require treatment.

> **TIP** A doctor or emergency medical personnel can access the informa-tion you provide in the Medical ID feature of the Health app from your iPhone's Lock screen, so they can view this content even if you're not conscious, or unable to unlock the phone yourself.
>
> To turn on the feature that allows someone to view Medical ID information from the Lock screen, tap on the Medical ID icon when running the Health app, tap on the Edit option in the top-right corner of the screen, and then turn on the virtual switch for the Show When Locked option.
>
> To view Medical ID information from your iPhone's Lock screen, turn on or wake up the iPhone. From the Lock screen, swipe from left to right to access the Touch ID or Enter Passcode screen. Tap on the Emergency option in the bottom-left corner of the screen (see Figure 4.4), and then tap on the Medical ID option.
>
> Only the data you opt to include in the Medical ID portion of the Health app appears.

FIGURE 4.4

Tap on this Emergency option, followed by the Medical ID option, to reveal the app's Medical ID screen from the Lock screen.

CUSTOMIZE THE DASHBOARD'S DISPLAY

To set what information appears on the Health app's Dashboard (refer to Figure 4.3), tap on the Health Data icon. A menu appears that divides the types of data the app can collect and track into categories (see Figure 4.5). Each menu option has a submenu that you can access by tapping on a specific listing.

> ✓ **TIP** To see this comprehensive listing of the types of data the Health app can track, tap on the All option at the top of the Health Data screen (see Figure 4.6).

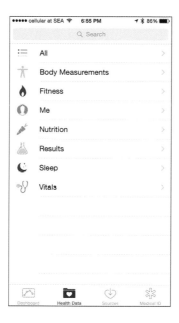

FIGURE 4.5

Select the information you want to display on the Dashboard screen from any of these main categories, each of which has submenu options.

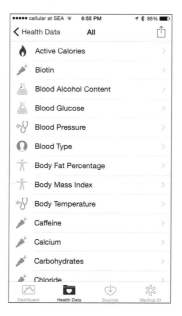

FIGURE 4.6

Tap on the Health Data icon, and then tap on the All option to view all the different types of data that the Health app can monitor and track.

You can manually enter certain types of information into your iPhone, have the iPhone (or Apple Watch) collect it automatically, or have optional equipment linked to the iPhone collect specialized data, and then transfer it to the Health app automatically.

For example, if you have a Bluetooth scale linked to your iPhone, then each time you weigh yourself, the iPhone records the time, date, and your exact weight. This information transfers to the Health app, where you can view the data as it's collected, or refer to the data collected in the past.

So, by tapping on the Dashboard icon, followed by the Day, Week, Month, or Year tab, you can view how your weight fluctuates over a specific time period, and then compare that data with corresponding activity and caloric intake data, for example, for that same period, to see the positive or negative impact of your actions over time.

Some data, however, remains constant, such as your height and birthday (which the app uses to determine your age), and you can manually enter it into the app.

Tap a main menu option and its submenu options to determine whether the Health app collects and monitors a particular data type, and set how to display and share that data.

For example, tap on the Health Data icon and Body Measurements option (see Figure 4.7); from the resulting submenu, tap on the Weight option to see its submenu (see Figure 4.8).

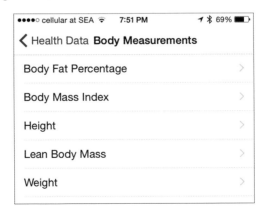

FIGURE 4.7

From the Body Measurements submenu, tap each option to customize its settings and to determine whether to have the Health app track this type of data.

FIGURE 4.8

Tap the Add Data Point option to manually input information.

From this submenu, to see collected weight-related data and display it on the Dashboard, turn on the Show On Dashboard option. At any time, to see what weight-related data the app has collected thus far, tap on the Show All Data option.

To manually add your weight data, tap on the Add Data Point option. For example, if you typically use a Bluetooth scale at home, but you're traveling and weigh yourself in your hotel room or at a gym, tap on the Add Data Point option (refer to Figure 4.8), and fill in the prompts on the Add Data screen (shown in Figure 4.9). Tap on the Add option (in the top-right corner of the screen) to add the information to the Health app.

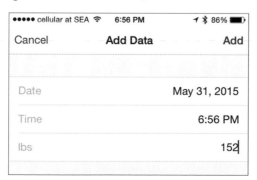

FIGURE 4.9

You can manually enter any type of data the Health app can monitor. This is called a Data Point. This figure shows the Add Data screen for the Weight option.

To enable the Heath app to share your Weight data, tap on the Share Data option (see Figure 4.10) on the Weight screen. Any other apps installed on your iPhone that can utilize your weight data appear below the Share Data With heading. Tap on one listing at a time, if applicable, to grant or deny permission for the listed app to access, utilize, and potentially share that specific data, which in this case is weight-related data.

FIGURE 4.10

You determine what information the Health app monitors from other apps and equipment, and how to use and potentially share it.

Also from the Share Data screen, you can set the sources from which you want data collected, such as your iPhone, Apple Watch, or your Bluetooth scale. For example, for the Weight option, to enable your Bluetooth scale to send your weight to the iPhone's Health app automatically each time you weigh yourself, you must grant permission once from this Share Data submenu, after you've paired the iPhone and scale.

> **NOTE** For directions on how to pair optional Bluetooth-compatible equipment with your iPhone, refer to the instruction manual provided with that equipment; the steps for Bluetooth pairing vary.

The Health app requires you to select units of measurement for certain types of data. Unit options for Weight, for example, include pounds (lbs), kilograms (kgs), or stones (st).

> ✅ **TIP** For each Health Data menu option, tap on only the submenu items that are relevant to your own health, fitness, nutrition, diet, or sleep-related goals. Unless you manually activate tracking for a specific item or type of data, it will remain inactive, and the Health app will not automatically collect or track it.
>
> You only need to adjust each setting once, or when you want to alter what information the Health app collects and monitors.

The main Health Data menu options include:

- **Body measurements**—Submenu listings for this option include Body Fat Percentage, Body Mass Index, Height, Lean Body Mass, and Weight. Tap on each option, one at a time, to set whether the Health app collects, tracks, displays, and shares this type of data.

- **Fitness**—Submenu listings for this option include Active Calories, Cycling Distance, Flights Climbed, NikeFuel, Resting Calories, Steps, Walking+Running Distance, and Workouts.

- **Me**—From this submenu, manually enter details about yourself, including your birthdate (used for calculating your age), Sex, and Blood Type.

- **Nutrition**—This submenu has more than three dozen options that enable you to track your intake of specific nutrition-related items, such as Caffeine, Fiber, Protein, Sodium, or Sugar. If you're sticking to a specific diet and using a diet or nutrition app, collecting and tracking this type of information can be extremely useful.

- **Results**—This submenu enables you to collect data from specialized pieces of medical equipment that are linked to your iPhone. You can also manually enter data related to things such as Blood Alcohol Content, Blood Glucose level, Inhaler Usage, or Oxygen Saturation, for example.

- **Sleep**—When used with specialized apps and equipment (such as the S+ Sleep Better device or a Jawbone Up tracker), the iPhone (and the Health app) can monitor and track your sleep patterns and habits. See Chapter 11, "Monitor Your Sleep and Sleep Better."

- **Vitals**—The Health app can monitor your Blood Pressure, Body Temperature, Heart Rate, and Respiratory Rate using data collected by your iPhone, Apple Watch, and other equipment that's linked to your iPhone.

> **NOTE** To track and analyze specific types of data, it will either need to be collected by the iPhone, Apple Watch, an optional fitness/activity tracker, or an optional piece of equipment that wirelessly links with the iPhone, such as a Bluetooth scale or sleep monitor. Nutrition data, for example, typically needs to be entered manually, although there are specific third-party apps (which you'll learn about later) that make this a very easy process.

> **TIP** If you're an Apple Watch user and want the Health app to track your Heart Rate, after your iPhone and Apple Watch are paired, launch the Health app, tap on the Health Data icon, select the Vitals option, and then tap on the Heart Rate option. From the Heart Rate submenu, turn on the Show On Dashboard option, and then tap on the Share Data option to make sure your Apple Watch is listed (which should happen automatically).

The information for which you turn on the Show On Dashboard feature determines the appearance of your Dashboard. You can set up the Health app to track certain types of data, but not display them on the Dashboard.

> **TIP** On the Dashboard display, tap on any data's graph to return to the Health Data menu and further customize that type of data's options. To switch between the Day, Week, Month, or Year view, simply tap on the appropriate tab. All data the Dashboard screen displays is in real time, or represents the most current information collected by the Health app.

At any time, if you want to discontinue the type of data another app or device gathers, launch the Health app, tap on the Sources icon, and then tap on the applicable app or equipment listed in the Sources menu. Turn off the virtual switches for the type(s) of data you no longer want tracked.

For example, if you were using the Nike+ Running app to track your runs, but choose to stop using the app, or don't want the Health app to track your running data, tap on the Running app listed in the Health app's Sources menu, and then turn off the NikeFuel, Workouts, and Heart Rate options.

Remember, you must adjust each type of data that the Health app can monitor separately.

ADJUST HEALTH-RELATED OPTIONS FROM THE SETTINGS MENU

Before you begin to fully utilize the Health app, be sure to launch Settings, tap on the Privacy option, and then tap on the Health option to make adjustments to third-party apps that can share information with the Health app. Only apps that are compatible with the Health app display. Tap an app's listing on the Health screen to adjust what data flows between it and the Health app.

Figure 4.11 shows the options available in Settings for the popular Nike+ Running app. Based on how the options on this screen are set up, the Nike+ Running app can send NikeFuel and Workouts-related data to the Health app to be monitored and collected, and at the same time, the Nike+ Running app can access Heart Rate data from the Health app (that may be collected from the Apple Watch or another activity/fitness tracker or manually entered into the Health app).

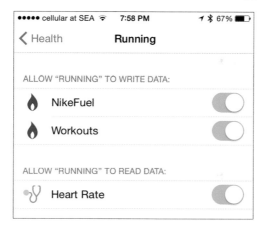

FIGURE 4.11

To adjust the Health app-related options for specific third-party apps, tap the Privacy option in Settings, and then tap on the app's listing.

Also from the Privacy menu in Settings, tap on the Motion & Fitness option. From this submenu you can turn on the iPhone's ability to track fitness-related data using its built-in sensors and equipment, plus allow the Health app to access this data as the iPhone collects it.

ADD PERSONAL INFORMATION TO THE HEALTH APP'S MEDICAL ID FEATURE

Nobody wants to experience a medical emergency, but in the event something does happen, your iPhone and the Health app can help you be prepared, and provide the doctors and/or emergency first responders with valuable information about you, your medical history, allergies, and other data that can help potentially save your life.

The Medical ID feature of the Health app is simply a database that stores personal information about you, your emergency contacts, and important aspects of your medical history, and then makes it available to someone in the event of an emergency.

To set up the Medical ID feature, launch the Health app and tap on the Medical ID icon. The first time you use this feature, tap on the Create Medical ID option (see Figure 4.12), and then fill in each field on the resulting screen (see Figure 4.13). The Health app pulls some information, such as your profile picture, name, and birthday, from your own entry in the Contacts app to save you time entering information.

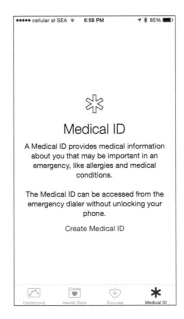

FIGURE 4.12

The first time you launch the Health app and tap on the Medical ID icon, you need to tap on the Create Medical ID option to continue.

FIGURE 4.13
Manually fill in each Medical ID data field in the Health app.

> **TIP** When creating or editing your Medical ID information, make sure that the Show When Locked option is turned on. This allows emergency responders or doctors to quickly access potentially vital information about you if you can't communicate yourself in an emergency situation.
>
> Even if you opt to use the Health app for no other purpose, turn on the Medical ID feature, and be sure to include the information the app requests. Doing this could someday help save your life.

Some of the data fields in the Medical ID menu screen might already be populated with personal information you have already entered into your iPhone via the Health or other compatible apps. Tap any field that's populated with data to update it manually, or tap an empty field to enter the requested information.

If your profile photo has not already been imported into the Health app, then as you fill in the Medical ID information, tap the Photo icon, and select a recent photo of yourself that nicely showcases your face. The Medical ID screen displays a thumbnail of the selected photo to help health workers verify that the data they see applies to you.

Fill in the following data fields with up-to-date information:

■ **Name**—Type in your full name as it appears on your driver's license or in your medical records.

- **Birthdate**—Enter your complete birthdate, including month, day, and year. This allows the app to calculate how old you are, and makes it easier for an emergency responder or doctor to access your medical records and ensure the records match up with you.

- **Medical Conditions**—Use the iPhone's virtual keyboard to describe any medical conditions you have, whether it's high blood pressure or anything else that a doctor should know about.

- **Medical Notes**—Add any additional information you would want a doctor to know about you, your medical history, and your current medical condition(s). Be as detailed as possible.

- **Allergies and Reactions**—Create a list of your allergies, including those to medications.

- **Medications**—Create a detailed list of the prescription medications you currently take. Include the name of the medication, the dose, and the frequency you take it. Again, the more information you provide, the better.

Tap on the Add Emergency Contact field (see Figure 4.14), and select a contact from your Contacts database. You can include separate listings for multiple people, such as a spouse, relative, or close friend whom you would want contacted in the event of an emergency.

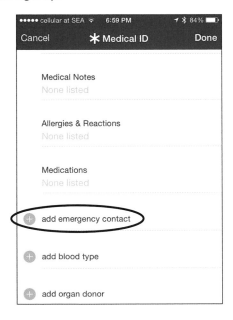

FIGURE 4.14

Add one or more emergency contacts, such as your spouse, a relative, a friend, and your primary care physician. If you work with a specialist for a particular medical issue, list that person as well.

After selecting a contact, from the Relationship screen, tap on the person's relationship to you. Choose one of the dozen or so options listed, such as Mother, Brother, Friend, Spouse, or Doctor.

> **✓ TIP** Use the Add Emergency Contact feature to list your primary care physician, along with any other doctors or specialists you work with, based on who you would want contacted in an emergency. For example, if you have a heart condition, be sure to list your cardiologist.

Tap on the Add Blood Type field to enter your blood type, if you know it. If you don't know it, consider calling your primary care physician and asking. Also, if you're an organ donor, tap on the Organ Donor option, and select the Yes option.

If the Health app has not already imported this information, enter your Weight and Height in the fields provided.

After entering all the information on the Medical ID screen, tap on the Done option (in the upper-right corner of the screen) to save your information.

Figure 4.15 shows what the Medical ID screen might look like if someone were to access it from the Lock screen of your iPhone.

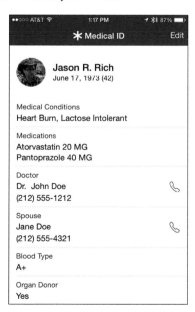

FIGURE 4.15

This is what the Medical ID screen might look like if a doctor were to access it from your iPhone's Lock screen.

TIP At any time, if you want to delete all information stored in the Medical ID portion of the Health app, launch the app, tap on the Medical ID icon, tap on the Edit option, and then scroll down to the bottom of the screen. Tap on the Delete Medical ID option.

Instead, if you want to edit or update any of the Medical ID fields, launch the app, tap on the Medical ID icon, tap on the Edit option, and then tap on the field you want to modify. Tap the Done option after updating your information to save your changes.

! CAUTION In addition to medical professionals, anyone who picks up your iPhone can potentially access your Medical ID information, even if the phone is locked (assuming you've turned on the Show When Locked feature). You can turn off this feature, but doing this also prevents medical professionals from accessing the information in an emergency situation. Using this feature, and the personal details you share with it, is a matter of personal preference.

USE THE ACTIVITY, WORKOUT, AND OTHER FITNESS APPS

Activity and Workout are two apps that come preinstalled on the Apple Watch. The first is designed for anyone, whether you're fitness-minded or not, to help you adopt and maintain a slightly more active lifestyle by tracking your movements throughout the day, and showing you how much activity you've participated in on an hour-by-hour basis.

Many fitness experts believe that one of the easiest ways to begin pursuing a healthier lifestyle is simply to move—stand up and walk around (see Figure 5.1). The Activity app reminds you to do this, and helps you achieve basic activity goals for yourself on a daily basis.

FIGURE 5.1

Whether you enjoy walking, running, or engaging in other activities, simply moving around during your day will help you stay healthy.

> **NOTE** The Activity app does not come preinstalled on the iPhone, but as soon as you begin using it on your Apple Watch, the iPhone edition of the app automatically installs itself onto your smartphone. The Apple Watch and iPhone editions of the Activity app are similar and fully compatible.
>
> The Apple Watch tracks your movement data, imports it into the Activity app on the Apple Watch, and then automatically transfers it to the iPhone edition. Although the Apple Watch edition of the app stores only the current day's data, the iPhone edition begins storing data the moment you put on the watch for the very first time, and then maintains a daily log of your movement on an ongoing basis.

The second app, Workout, is a more versatile app designed for people who are fitness minded, and who engage in specific types of fitness-oriented activities. This app uses the technologies built in to the Apple Watch to monitor movement, speed, heart rate, and other data, and tracks this information in real time during activities. The app then compiles this data, so you can view your accomplishments over time.

> ☑ **TIP** Workout is a comprehensive app with features for tracking a wide range of activities. However, if you're serious about one particular activity, such as running, cycling, using an elliptical machine (or other workout equipment), weight lifting, circuit training, rowing, or engaging in various other types of fitness classes, check out the wide range of specialized apps available from the App Store that you can use with any one of these fitness-oriented activities.
>
> You will probably find that some of these more specialized apps are more powerful, accurate, and comprehensive because they relate to a particular fitness-oriented activity. For example, as its name implies, the popular Nike+ Running app is designed exclusively for running enthusiasts.

GET ACQUAINTED WITH THE ACTIVITY APP ON THE APPLE WATCH

The Activity app is designed for one thing: to make measuring your daily activity easy and automatic. Then at any time, with a quick glance at your Apple Watch's screen, you can gauge your activity level throughout the day via three colored activity rings (see Figure 5.2).

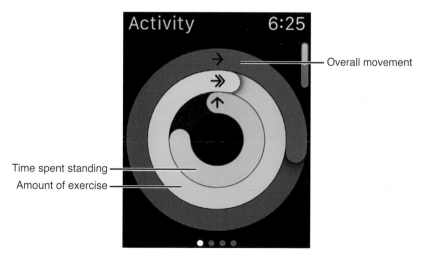

FIGURE 5.2

The Activity app displays three "activity rings" to help you quickly gauge your level of activity within the past 12 hours.

The red ring (Move) displays your overall movement and shows approximately how many *active calories* you've burned thus far during the day. The green ring

(Exercise) represents your exercise for the day (that is, any movement more rigorous than a regular walk). The blue ring (Stand) displays how often throughout a 12-hour period you stood up to move around for at least one minute per hour.

> **NOTE** An *active calorie* is one that gets burned as a result of your participating in any type of physical activity. This is different from calories your body burns by default, just by functioning when you're at rest or not actively moving.

The first time you launch the Activity app, it prompts you to establish daily goals for yourself. Based on these goals, the app determines how much activity you must do on a daily basis to achieve them. You can easily set up your watch to display reminders to be more active throughout your day.

In addition, using a message on the screen and the watch's haptic engine (which gives you a tap on the wrist), the app automatically reminds you every hour you are stationary to stand up and move around for at least one minute.

As you move and engage in activities throughout your day, each of the app's three activity rings expand and fill in accordingly. Your ultimate goal is to have all three activity rings complete their circles at least once during each 12-hour period that you're wearing the watch (see Figure 5.3). If you exceed a daily goal, the appropriate ring(s) begin to overlap (see Figure 5.4).

FIGURE 5.3

Each day, your goal when using the Activity app is to have all three colored activity rings form complete circles.

FIGURE 5.4

An activity ring overlaps on itself if you exceed your daily goal for what that ring is tracking.

> **TIP** If you find yourself continuously exceeding your daily activity goals, it's time to increase those goals. To update your daily Move goal, press and hold down your finger on your watch's activity rings screen for about two seconds. The message Change Move Goal appears over a silver disc. Tap on this icon, and then use the "+" or "-" icon below the Change Your Daily Goal heading to create a new goal for yourself for burning active calories. Tap on the Update button to save your changes.

As you make your way through each day, the Activity app displays the three activity rings via a glance screen, but also shows slightly more detailed progress reports each day or week (depending on how you have the app set up), so you can monitor your movement and activities in each 12-hour period directly from the watch. When you achieve a daily goal, the app displays a reward screen. If you exceed your goals, the app awards you with Achievements. An Achievement is a virtual trophy that's presented by the app and displayed on the screen. There are many different types of Achievements you can earn using the app.

SET UP THE ACTIVITY APP

The first time you launch the Activity app on your Apple Watch, the app asks you to enter your age and weight. With this information and the sensors and technologies built into the watch, the app begins to measure your overall activity level and caloric burn automatically and continuously.

Beyond answering the initial questions the first time you launch the app on your Apple Watch, you can further customize your goals, as well as how and when you receive notifications and reminders from the app. You do this from the Apple Watch app on your iPhone.

When you open the app, tap on the My Watch icon. Next, tap on the Notifications option, and turn on the Notifications Indicator option (see Figure 5.5).

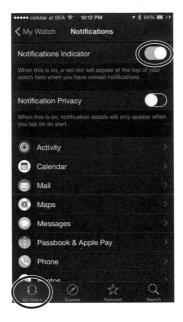

FIGURE 5.5

This is the Notifications menu screen found in the Apple Watch app.

Tap on the Activity app listing on the Notifications screen. Turn on the four switches you see there (see Figure 5.6) as you deem appropriate to activate the following features:

■ **Stand Reminders**—Be reminded to stand up and move for at least one minute every hour. A text message and a tap on the wrist alert you if you've been stationary for the first 50 minutes of an hour that you have been wearing the watch.

■ **Goal Completions**—Turn on this option to receive a notification each day as soon as you meet or exceed your Move, Exercise, or Stand goals.

■ **Achievements**—Each time you achieve a specific Move, Exercise, or Stand milestone or exceed your personal best, you receive an Achievement, which is a virtual award or medal of honor to commemorate your accomplishment (see Figure 5.7).

FIGURE 5.6

Customize the notifications you want to receive on your Apple Watch from the Activity app.

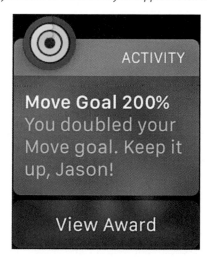

FIGURE 5.7

Reach your goals and earn Achievements when using the Activity app with the Apple Watch.

■ **Weekly Summary**—Every Monday, the Activity app prepares a brief summary report outlining your previous week's performance for your Move, Exercise, and Stand goals. To automatically display this report on your watch's screen, be sure to turn on this feature. Otherwise, you can review your long-term performance history anytime via the iPhone edition of the Activity app.

> **TIP** You can use the Progress Updates option on the Activity screen to display periodic updates on the watch's screen related to show your progress toward reaching your daily goals. From the Progress Updates menu, shown in Figure 5.8, you can opt to receive these reminders every four, six, or eight hours. To turn off this feature, select the None option. There is no virtual switch associated with it.

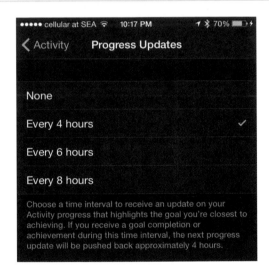

FIGURE 5.8

Choose how often you want to view a Progress Update for your activity when wearing the Apple Watch.

To adjust the placement of the Activity app's icon on the watch's Home screen, launch the Apple Watch app on your iPhone, tap on the My Watch icon, and then tap on the App Layout option. When viewing a mirror image of your Apple Watch's Home screen on your iPhone (via the Layout screen), place your finger on the Activity app's icon, and drag it to the desired location (see Figure 5.9).

Exit out of the Layout screen to save your changes. Within a few seconds, the changes you made to the Home screen's layout on your iPhone appear on your Apple Watch's Home screen automatically (see Figure 5.10).

Activity app icon ——

FIGURE 5.9

The Apple Watch's Home screen is mirrored on the iPhone when you launch the Apple Watch app and choose the Layout option.

Activity app icon

FIGURE 5.10

When you rearrange the app icons on your iPhone with the Apple Watch's Layout option, the changes go into effect on your watch almost immediately.

> **☑ TIP**   To set up and adjust the placement of the Activity app's glance screen on your watch, launch the Apple Watch app on your iPhone, tap on the My Watch icon, and then tap on the Glances option.
>
> Next, under the Settings heading, make sure the Activity app is listed (shown in Figure 5.11). To change the order in which the Activity app's glance screen displays, place your finger on the app's Move icon and drag it up or down. Exit out of the Glances menu to save your changes. To do this, either tap on the <My Watch option in the top-left corner of the screen, or press the Home button on the iPhone.

FIGURE 5.11
Change the order of the glance screens on your Apple Watch to access the Activity app's glance screen faster.

LAUNCH THE ACTIVITY APP

While wearing your Apple Watch, you can launch the Activity app in three easy ways, including:

- From the Home screen, which displays all the watch's installed apps, tap on the Activity app's icon (refer to Figure 5.10).

- On your selected watch face (which displays the time and potentially other information), swipe your finger up on the screen to display the glance screen, and then swipe sideways to reveal the Activity glance screen.

- You can customize some of the watch faces to display the Activity icon in addition to the time and other information you opt to display. This offers a miniature view of the Activity app's rings. However, you can launch the Activity app quickly by tapping on this tiny Activity icon (shown in Figure 5.12) that displays as part of a watch face.

Activity app icon ———

FIGURE 5.12

Customize a watch face to display the Activity app icon.

> ☑ **TIP** To launch the iPhone edition of the Activity app, access your
> phone's Home screen and tap on the Activity app icon. If the app is already run-
> ning in the background, as you're using your iPhone, quickly press the Home but-
> ton on your phone twice to access multi-tasking mode, and then swipe sideways
> until the Activity app appears in the center. Relaunch the app by tapping on its
> icon or the Activity app thumbnail. As long as your iPhone and Apple Watch are
> paired and wirelessly connected, all of your real-time Activity app data automati-
> cally and wirelessly transfers from the Apple Watch and displays in the iPhone edi-
> tion of the Activity app.

DISCOVER WHAT INFORMATION THE ACTIVITY APP GATHERS AND HOW TO VIEW IT

Each of the three colored activity rings has a corresponding information screen
that you can access from the Apple Watch app. These screens offer more detailed
information.

To access each of these screens, launch the Activity app on your Apple Watch so
that the three activity rings appear. Tap once on this display screen. The first of
three sub-screens appears. Swipe from right to left to see each activity ring's sub-
screen and its additional information.

For example, on the first activity ring sub-screen, in addition to seeing the red (Move) ring, you also see a message that says, "## out of ### Cals." This message tells you how many calories you've burned thus far, based on your daily goal (shown in Figure 5.13).

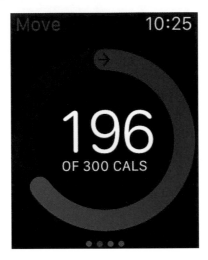

FIGURE 5.13

This screen shows your movement details during the current day.

The Exercise activity ring sub-screen includes the green ring and a message indicating how many minutes you've engaged in a more vigorous activity (compared to a normal walk) during the past 12 hours.

Swipe from right to left again to view the blue Stand activity ring sub-screen. This shows how many times within the past 12 hours you've stood up and moved around for one minute each hour (shown in Figure 5.14).

In addition to these three screens, a text-based summary screen and individual graph displays are available to present your daily activity information.

From the main Activity app three-ring display, swipe up to view the text-based summary screen (shown in Figure 5.15). This displays the total number of active calories you've burned, the total number of steps you've taken, and the total distance you've traveled within the past 12 hours.

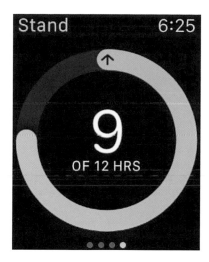

FIGURE 5.14

Have you been sitting still for too many hours today? The blue Stand activity ring lets you know.

FIGURE 5.15

The Activity app offers this text-based summary screen, in addition to displaying the three color-coded activity rings.

From this screen, swipe from right to left to see each of the activity ring sub-screens. Then, from a sub-screen, swipe up to see the same information in a colorful graph format.

Figure 5.16 shows the graph screen for the red Move ring. Figure 5.17 shows the graph screen for the green Exercise ring, and Figure 5.18 shows the graph screen for the blue Stand ring.

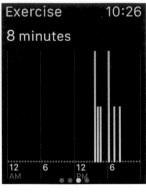

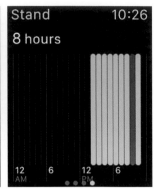

FIGURE 5.16

The red Move ring graph.

FIGURE 5.17

The green Exercise ring graph.

FIGURE 5.18

The blue Stand ring graph.

GET ACQUAINTED WITH THE ACTIVITY APP ON THE IPHONE

The Apple Watch edition of the Activity app displays information about your movement and activity within a 12-hour period, but does not store information from past periods in the watch. To retrieve and review this information, you must use the iPhone edition of the app, which stores information as soon as you start wearing your Apple Watch, and then stores all information on a daily basis, so you can review it in one day, one week, or monthly increments.

The iPhone edition of the Activity app automatically installs onto your iPhone as soon as you begin using the Apple Watch edition. You don't need to manually install it from the App Store.

> **NOTE** Without an Apple Watch feeding data into the iPhone edition of the Activity app, this smartphone edition of the app serves little purpose on its own.

After the Activity app icon appears on your iPhone's Home screen, all you need to do is tap on that icon to launch the app. The current day's activity data, in the form of the three colored activity rings, appears (see Figure 5.19). Either tap on the History icon at the bottom of the screen, or tap on one of the smaller activity ring icons along the top of the screen, each of which corresponds to a day of the week, to view that day's data.

FIGURE 5.19

View the current day's activity data via the activity rings in the center of the screen. The current week's data appears one day at a time along the top of the screen.

To see a Month view, tap on the "<" icon in the top-left corner of the screen (see Figure 5.20). You can then scroll up or down to see past or upcoming months. An activity ring icon appears for each day of the month (that's already occurred). Tap on it to view that day's Activity app data in detail.

As you're viewing Activity data for a single day, the three colored activity rings display rather largely on the screen, along with the date. Scroll down on this screen to view individual activity ring data, and its corresponding graph for that day (see Figure 5.21).

From any of these graphics, swipe your finger from right to left across the chart to view the same information using text and numbers (see Figure 5.22). Swipe from left to right to return to the graphic view, or simply scroll up or down to view additional information collected for that day.

For example, if you look at the text data for the Move graph (and red activity ring), the number of active calories burned, along with your daily calorie burn goal, appears first, followed by the number of Active Calories burned again, the number of Resting Calories burned, and the Total Calories burned.

FIGURE 5.20

The Month at-a-glance view of the Activity app (iPhone edition).

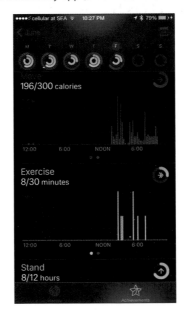

FIGURE 5.21

View details about each activity ring for any given day from your iPhone.

FIGURE 5.22

View Activity app information as a chart, or using text and numbers.

Look at the bottom of each day's screen to see the total number of steps taken and the distance traveled (in text and number format, instead of graphics).

To view a separate graphics-based screen that shows the Achievements you've earned since day one of using the Activity app, tap on the Achievements icon at the bottom of the screen.

> **! CAUTION** Although the Apple Watch's built-in sensors are designed for accuracy, the watch itself (and the technology in it) is classified as a consumer-oriented product, and not a medical device. Don't rely on the watch's built-in sensors to offer 100 percent accurate activity-related data collection.
>
> In the early weeks after the Apple Watch's release, many fitness-savvy people who compared the results collected by the Apple Watch with data collected by other pieces of equipment did find discrepancies and inaccuracies, which Apple had begun to address through Apple Watch OS updates. At the time this book was being written, these issues had not been fully resolved.
>
> Other optional devices, including fitness/activity trackers and heart rate monitors, are available from third parties, some of which are also classified as consumer-oriented products, whereas others are considered extremely accurate medical devices. If you require better data accuracy than what the Apple Watch can currently offer, consider using one of these other devices in addition to or instead of the Apple Watch.

GET STARTED USING THE WORKOUT APP ON THE APPLE WATCH

The Workout app is somewhat similar to the Activity app, but instead of being designed for use at all times while you're wearing the watch, this app allows you to collect and analyze data related to actual workouts.

To use this app, launch it from the Home screen of the Apple Watch (see Figure 5.23), and from the main menu, select the fitness-related activity you're about to participate it. Options include Outdoor Walk, Outdoor Run, Outdoor Cycle, Indoor Run, Indoor Walk, Indoor Cycle, Elliptical, Rower, Stair Stepper, or Other.

Workout app icon

FIGURE 5.23

Launch the Workout app from the Apple Watch's Home screen.

Based on which option you select, for each workout, typically you can set a Caloric, Distance, or Time goal, and then have the watch display real-time data it collects as you pursue that goal during your workout.

> **NOTE** The Workout app automatically shares certain applicable data with the Activity and Health apps, so anything you do during a workout helps you reach your daily goals set in the Activity app.

When you're ready to begin a workout, follow these steps to activate the Workout app on your watch:

1. From any watch face you've selected to be displayed on the watch's screen, press the Digital Crown to access the watch's Home screen.

2. Tap on the Workout app icon to launch the Workout app.

3. When the main menu appears, tap on the type of workout you plan to engage in.

4. Depending on the activity you select, a submenu screen enables you to Set Calories, Set Time, or Set Miles, or select Open (if you have no goal in mind, but simply want to track your workout-related data). If you select the Set Time screen, a timer appears, showing 0:00, with a negative sign (–) icon on the left and a plus sign (+) icon on the right. Tap the + icon to set the desired duration for your workout. Press the Start button, shown in Figure 5.24, to begin your workout.

> **NOTE** If you select Outdoor Walk, for example, the Set Calories, Set Time, Set Miles, and Open options are available. However, for other activities, like Elliptical, only the applicable Set Calories, Set Time, and Open options are available.

> **TIP** Instead of setting the default Set Calories screen (shown in Figure 5.25), swipe from right to left to scroll between Set Calories, Set Time, Set Miles (shown in Figure 5.26) or Open.

FIGURE 5.24
Adjust Set Time or Set Miles options by tapping on the + icon or – icon.

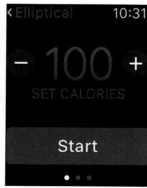

FIGURE 5.25
The Set Calories screen of the Workout app.

FIGURE 5.26
The Set Miles screen of the Workout app.

5. As soon as you press the Start button, begin your workout. Obviously, make sure you're wearing the Apple Watch comfortably on your wrist. You'll be given a three-second countdown before the app begins collecting real-time data.

> **TIP** If you're planning an extended workout, such as a several-hour walk or hike, consider putting your Apple Watch into Power Saving mode to conserve battery life.
>
> To do this, access the watch's selected watch face, swipe up to access the glance screen, and then swipe sideways until the Battery Life glance screen appears (see Figure 5.27). Tap on the Power Reserve button to turn on this feature.
>
> When you turn on Power Reserve mode, the Heart Rate monitor deactivates and does not collect heart rate data.

FIGURE 5.27
The Battery Life glance screen on the Apple Watch.

6. During your workout, you can adjust what information appears on the watch's screen (see Figure 5.28). By default, the Elapsed Time displays. Scroll sideways (right to left) to view real-time Pace, Distance, Calories, and Heart Rate data. The screen to the extreme left allows you to End or Pause/Resume your workout.

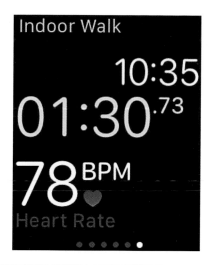

FIGURE 5.28

View real-time data being collected on your Apple Watch's screen during a workout.

TIP If you want the Workout app on your Apple Watch to display color-coded activity rings that represent Distance, Calories, and Time, you must turn on this feature.

To do this, launch the Apple Watch app on your iPhone, tap on the My Watch icon, scroll down and select the Workout option, and then from the Workout menu screen (see Figure 5.29), turn on the Show Goal Metric option.

From this menu, you can also have Apple Watch enter into Power Saving Mode each time you launch the Workout app. To do this, turn on the Power Saving Mode option.

FIGURE 5.29

The Workout menu screen found in the Apple Watch app.

7. After you end your workout, all data transfers to the iPhone and gets stored in the Health app that comes preinstalled with iOS 8.3 or later. Certain other third-party apps can also import this information, provided you grant those apps permission to do this. A workout summary screen showcasing your accomplishments appears on the Apple Watch's screen at the conclusion of every workout (see Figure 5.30). Choose whether to delete or store that workout's data by scrolling down on this screen to view the applicable command buttons.

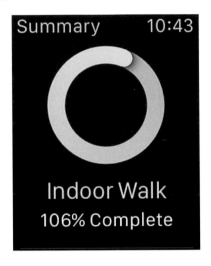

FIGURE 5.30

Scroll down the Workout Summary screen to view all collected data pertaining to that workout, and then choose whether to save it. If you save it, relevant data transfers to the Activity and Health apps.

> **NOTE** According to Apple, to improve the accuracy of the Workout app's data collection, wear the Apple Watch regularly, not just when you work out. Also, select the workout activity from the app's main menu that is closest to what you're actually doing.
>
> To track GPS-related data during your outdoor workouts, you need to also carry your iPhone with you. However, you can keep it in a pocket, wear it in a case strapped to your arm or waist, or attach it to your bike, for example.
>
> To obtain accurate heart rate data, the back of the watch must touch the skin on your wrist. You can't wear it over a long-sleeve shirt, for example. Also, the fit around your wrist should be snug.

HOW TO USE THE HEART RATE APP

As you know, the Apple Watch has a built-in heart rate monitor that tracks your heart rate and records this data on an ongoing basis while you wear the watch. This data automatically transmits to the Health app on your iPhone, where it is stored. Thus, if you want to refer to your changing heart rate over time, you can find this information in the Health app, or use a third-party app that imports the data (with your permission).

The easiest way to launch the Heart Rate feature on the Apple Watch (while you're wearing it) is to wake up the watch, display the selected watch face, and then swipe up on the screen to reveal the glance screen. Swipe horizontally until the Heart Rate screen appears (see Figure 5.31).

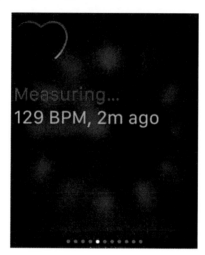

FIGURE 5.31

The initial Heart Rate screen on the Apple Watch.

When you activate the Heart Rate screen, the last recorded heart rate appears for a few seconds, until the watch can get and display a current heart rate, measured in beats per minute or BPM (see Figure 5.32). On the Apple Watch, this is the only information that appears for this feature.

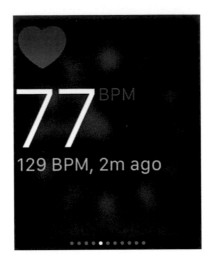

FIGURE 5.32

It takes a few seconds for the Heart Rate monitor to display your current BPM rate.

> ☑ **TIP**   To see additional heart rate–related data, launch the Health app on the iPhone, and view the Dashboard. Refer to Chapter 4, "Work with the iPhone's Health App," to customize the app's Dashboard to display Heart Rate data.

APP OPTIONS FOR FITNESS-MINDED PEOPLE

Because the apps that come preinstalled on your Apple Watch work seamlessly with the Health app (or in the case of the Activity app, with the iPhone edition of the app as well), using either or both of these apps is convenient.

That said, if you want to participate in a specific fitness-oriented or workout activity, the Apple Watch and iPhone App Stores offer a vast and ever-growing selection of viable alternatives to using the Activity and/or Workout apps, and/or the watch's Heart Rate monitor feature.

You'll learn more about specialized apps for specific workout and fitness-related activities in future chapters, as well as from the expert interviews that are scattered throughout the book.

CHAT WITH AN EXPERT

LEARN ABOUT THE OPTIONAL FITNET APP FROM ITS CREATOR

Fitnet is a mobile fitness application for the iPhone (see Figure 5.33) and Apple Watch from Fitnet Corporation (www.fit.net) that delivers video-based exercise introduction and workout routines in five-minute increments. It also provides a variety of different intensities, based on the user's needs. The app's workouts combine yoga, strength, and cardio workouts that are tailored to the user's fitness level.

FIGURE 5.33

The Fitnet app, shown here on the iPhone, features video-based workouts for users to follow.

Bob Summers, the app's creator, is a fitness enthusiast, as well as an entrepreneur with a computer engineering degree from Virginia Tech and an MBA from MIT.

Summers said he designed Fitnet for himself, but made it so that it would appeal to any iPhone user who wants to move more and/or supplement an existing exercise plan.

"Thanks to the technologies being built into the latest iPhones and now the Apple Watch, including higher speed processors, easier to read displays, more sensors, and network connectivity, it is becoming easier to achieve accurate assessment delivery and monitoring, which are key elements in fitness tools," said Summers.

Although the Activity app monitors and reports a user's daily activity, the Fitnet app goes a step further. "For example, if you determine you want or need 30 more minutes of exercise, and want to know how to efficiently get it, that's where the Fitnet app comes in," added Summers. "Convenience is critical to someone keeping up with a fitness goal. Convenience reduces excuses. Apple Watch is a convenience tool that brings fitness applications that would otherwise be running on iPhones closer to the individual."

Of course, wearing an Apple Watch or installing Fitnet onto your iPhone won't cause you to achieve your fitness goals by themselves. "There is still hard work to do, which must become a personal and long-term commitment. My best advice is just to get started. Install the Fitnet app, for example, and exercise for just 10 minutes today. Then do it again tomorrow. Get yourself into a daily routine. Before you know it, a habit will be formed, and a fitness routine will be established."

The Fitnet app helps users focus on the current day's goals, and then looks ahead to the upcoming week. One of the features that sets Fitnet apart from other fitness apps is that in addition to including a virtual trainer, the app can also connect users to real-life human trainers, who will help keep the users on track and accountable (see Figure 5.34).

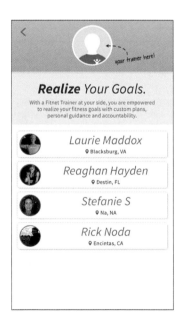

FIGURE 5.34

For a flat monthly fee, the Fitnet app allows you to communicate with a professional and accredited fitness trainer.

"It's this accountability that helps people achieve success in achieving their fitness goals. We help users find the right fitness plan, and then offer hundreds of varied fitness routines in the app," stated Summers.

Fitnet is a free download. It includes more than 200 five-minute video-based workouts for users to follow and participate in. Various menus, like the one shown in Figure 5.35, offer details about each workout offering. You can purchase additional weekly fitness challenges (via in-app purchases) for $0.99, and users can subscribe to have access to their own personal trainer for $19.00 per month.

FIGURE 5.35

Based on your fitness goals, choose which workouts you want to experience from a menu like this one.

Aside from the iPhone, no special equipment is needed to participate in the app's workouts, although Summers does recommend having an Apple TV, so users can watch the iPhone app's videos on a television instead of the iPhone's screen via AirPlay. "The Fitnet app offers deep integration with the Health app, as well as Apple TV and the Apple Watch," he added.

Although Summers initially created the Fitnet app for himself, one of the app's first success stories came from a stay-at-home mother in Texas, who lost 12 pounds in eight weeks using the app. Since then, Summers stated he has heard hundreds of similar success stories.

He explained, "Whether someone uses Fitnet or not, when you adopt a new fitness routine, to help yourself get started and then stay motivated, I recommend working with a personal trainer, plus getting yourself a fitness buddy. In addition to a personal trainer subscription option, Fitnet offers a social interaction element, so you can have a virtual fitness buddy, as opposed to someone being right next to you during each workout."

Fitnet is just one of many general fitness-related apps available for the iPhone and Apple Watch. You can find this popular app in the App Store.

FIND AND USE SPECIALIZED HEALTH APPS

In addition to the collection of apps that come preinstalled with iOS 8 and iOS 9 for the iPhone (as well as preinstalled Apple Watch apps), an ever-growing selection of optional apps are available via the App Store from Apple and third-party app developers. These apps allow you to add specific and customized functionality to your smartphone or smartwatch.

Although you can surf the Web to learn about optional iPhone and Apple Watch apps, the only place to actually acquire them is from Apple's online-based App Store.

The easiest way to access the App Store to learn about and acquire iPhone apps is to launch the App Store app by tapping its icon on your iPhone's Home screen.

This chapter covers how to find, download, and install a wide range of highly specialized health, fitness, medical, nutrition, and sleep-related iPhone apps from the App Store.

In addition to the iPhone App Store, Apple operates a separate but related store that caters exclusively to the Apple Watch. The easiest way to access it is to launch the Apple Watch app on your iPhone, and then tap on the Featured or Search icons that appear at the bottom of the screen (see Figure 6.1).

FIGURE 6.1
You can find, download, and install Apple Watch apps to the Apple Watch via the Apple Watch app running on the iPhone.

> **NOTE** When the Apple Watch was first launched, all optional watch apps had an iPhone counterpart. Starting in late 2015, in addition to these apps, stand-alone Apple Watch apps became available.

What you'll discover when you begin exploring the App Store are literally hundreds of specialized apps that can assist you in setting, managing, and achieving any or all of your fitness, health, medical, nutrition, dieting, and sleep management-related goals using your iPhone (and an Apple Watch, if you own one).

You'll also find proprietary apps designed for the iPhone and Apple Watch that work with third-party activity and fitness trackers, Bluetooth scales, and various other types of medical and/or fitness equipment. Figure 6.2 shows the App Store listing for the official UP app that works with Jawbone's popular UP fitness/activity trackers.

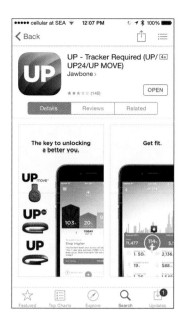

FIGURE 6.2

Specialized pieces of fitness equipment, for example, that can transmit data to the iPhone, all have proprietary apps available for them. This figure shows the UP app for use with Jawbone's UP fitness/activity trackers.

Each category of optional apps contains cutting-edge and innovative approaches developers have taken that allow you to inexpensively transform your iPhone and Apple Watch into powerful tools that you can use in many different ways related to your health, well-being, and fitness.

> **NOTE** Refer to Chapter 2, "Tell More Than the Time with Apple Watch," to learn more about using the Apple Watch app on your iPhone to find, download, and install apps onto your smartwatch.

DISCOVER THE TYPES OF APPS AVAILABLE FROM THE APP STORE

The easiest way to discover what health apps are available is to launch the App Store app, and tap on the Featured icon near the bottom-left corner of the screen.

From the Featured screen, tap on the Categories option in the top-left corner and then select the Health & Fitness or Medical category. The following sections cover information about the types of apps available in each category.

HEALTH & FITNESS APPS

The Health & Fitness category includes many different types of fitness-related apps, as well as nutrition, weight loss (dieting), and sleep-related apps. In terms of the focus of *Apple Watch and iPhone Fitness Tips and Tricks,* the majority of apps you will use come from this app category.

If you're a runner or cyclist; participate in meditation, yoga, interval training; enjoy walking; are looking for fitness-related apps that can teach you how to exercise; or help you monitor and track your progress, these types of apps are available in the Health & Fitness app category (see Figure 6.3).

FIGURE 6.3

Whether you enjoy cycling or any other type of fitness-related activity, specialized apps can help you achieve your goals.

The Health & Fitness subcategories include Classes & Trainers, Food & Nutrition, Apps for Health, Better Sleep, Stay On Track, Apps for Runners, Apps for Cyclists, Interval Trainers, and Meditation & Mindfulness. Below each of these subheadings are app icons representing a handful of featured apps. To see all "featured" apps in a subcategory, tap on the See All option appearing to the right of the heading with the App Store.

> [NOTE icon] **NOTE** A "Featured" app is a third-party app that Apple has chosen to showcase in the App Store. It's typically one of the better apps in its category.

Examples of popular health and fitness-related apps include:

- **Couch to 5K**—A virtual trainer designed to help you prepare for a 5K race/run.

- **Full Fitness: Exercise Workout Trainer**—An interactive app that teaches you how to properly do exercises, and then offers customized training/workout sessions, based on your goals.

- **Map My Run+**—A full-featured app for runners that allows users to plan routes, and then track and analyze all aspects of their runs.

- **Nike+ Running**—A full-featured iPhone and Apple Watch app, designed by Nike's top fitness coaches, that offers a wide range of tools for tracking data associated with running.

- **Yoga Studio**—An iPhone-based interactive Yoga class.

MEDICAL APPS

You can use the apps in the Medical category to help diagnose and/or manage various medical issues or conditions, and some can be used in the process of conducting medical research. This category also contains many specialized medical references apps, as well as apps for learning about medications or keeping track of when to take prescribed medications.

Subcategories under the Medical apps category include: Medical Reference, Medical News & Journals, Apps for Doctors, Medical Education and CME, Apps for Patients, and Personal Care Apps.

In addition to apps you'll be learning more about later in this book, some examples of medical-oriented apps available for the iPhone include:

- **Drugs.com Medication Guide**—This interactive app allows users to learn about their medications, their side effects, and check for interactions between medications.

- **MyQuest for Patients**—This app helps users understand medical test results processed by Quest Diagnostics.
- **ZocDoc - Doctor Appointments Online**—This app allows patients to easily research information about doctors, make appointments online, and keep track of their various doctor appointments.

> **TIP** Apps that allow the iPhone (or Apple Watch) to monitor some type of medical device appear in the Medical Apps category. However, apps that work with fitness equipment and consumer-oriented devices, such as activity trackers, Bluetooth scales, or the S+ Sleep Better monitor, appear under the Health & Fitness category, because these are not considered medical devices.

FOOD & DRINK APPS

From digital, interactive, and specialty recipe and cookbooks, to calorie counters, diet programs, and weight management apps, this is just a sampling of what the Food & Drink App Store category contains.

Because a well-balanced and healthy diet should be part of everyone's fitness routine, these apps can make it easier to plan meals, help control your consumption of food, and assist you in measuring the impact that what you eat has on your weight, energy level, and overall well-being.

You can also find instructional apps that teach you how to prepare various types of foods and meals using step-by-step instructions and video, and apps for finding new restaurants that cater to your specialized dietary needs.

Many apps are designed to help you track your food and drink intake, count calories, and provide healthy recipes based on your unique dietary restrictions. Some popular apps in this category include:

- **Calorie Counter & Diet Tracker by MyFitnessPal**—This iPhone and Apple Watch app offers a variety of tools for easily tracking food and drink intake, counting calories, and monitoring calories burned. It includes access to a detailed food database that contains more than five million entries. More information about this app is covered in Chapter 10, "Achieve Your Dieting Goals."
- **Diabetic Food & Recipes**—This interactive cookbook and healthy eating guide is designed exclusively for diabetics.
- **My Daily Plate**—This interactive app makes it easier to understand the basics of nutrition and plan healthy meals.

■ **Yummly Recipes & Grocery Shopping List**—This app makes finding recipes for virtually any type of food easy. It then allows users to customize the recipe based on how many servings they want to prepare, and also create a fully itemized shopping list. More information about this app is covered in Chapter 10.

SEARCH FOR SPECIFIC TYPES OF APPS IN THE APP STORE

Whether you know the exact title of the app you want, or want to find a specific type of app, the easiest way to find it is to launch the App Store app, tap on the Search icon at the bottom of the screen, and then type an app's title, or a key word or search phrase that describes the app you want (see Figure 6.4).

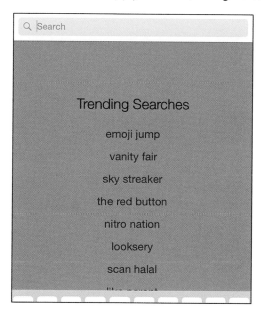

FIGURE 6.4

In the Search field, enter an app's title, or any keyword or phrase that describes the type of app you want to find.

For example, to find apps catering to a specific activity, enter a search word or phrase such as, "running," "cycling," "Zumba," "yoga," "weight loss," "dieting," "meditation," "sleep," "walking," "weight training," "exercise," or "fitness."

CHECK OUT THE APP STORE'S TOP CHARTS LISTS

The App Store creates a continuously updated series of Top Charts lists based on the popularity, sales, and ratings of apps. Each app category, including Health & Fitness or Medical, has multiple Top Charts lists that can help you quickly discover the most popular apps in those categories.

To access specific Top Charts listings, launch the App Store app on the iPhone, tap on the Top Charts icon at the bottom of the screen, and then tap on the Categories option in the top-left corner of the screen.

When viewing the Categories list (see Figure 6.5), tap on your chosen category, such as Health & Fitness, Medical, or Food & Drink. Along the top of the screen are three tabs labeled Paid, Free, and Top Grossing (see Figure 6.6), and each displays a different list.

FIGURE 6.5
Find the best apps in a specific category using the App Store's Top Charts feature.

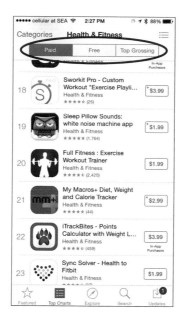

FIGURE 6.6

Each category of apps has three Top Charts listings, including Paid, Free, and Top Grossing apps.

Tap on the Paid tab to see a Top Charts listing of paid apps. These apps have a one-time purchase price associated with them. (Some Paid apps might also have in-app purchases available.)

Tap on the Free tab to discover the most popular free apps in a specific category, such as Health & Fitness. (Many free apps also have optional in-app purchases associated with them.)

> **TIP** When viewing a Top Charts app listing, be sure to scroll down the screen to view listings for up to 150 apps, in order of their popularity.

Tap on the Top Grossing tab to discover the most popular apps in the selected category that generate the highest amount of revenue for the app's developer, based on an app's initial purchase price, in-app purchases, and/or subscription fees associated with the app.

FIND AND INSTALL OPTIONAL IPHONE APPS

Whether you discover an app from the App Store's Featured section, use the Search field, or see a listing within a Top Chart, what you initially see is an app's icon, title, average star-based rating, and its Price button (refer to Figure 6.6). The Price button is labeled "Get" if the app is free.

To view more detailed information about the app, while viewing one of these abbreviated listings, tap on the app's icon or title. If you want to acquire the app straight away, instead tap on the Price or Get button. Then, when prompted, enter your Apple ID password, or place your finger on the iPhone's Touch ID sensor (if applicable) to confirm your decision, and begin the automatic app download and installation process.

An app's main description in the App Store, shown in Figure 6.7, offers several screens' worth of useful information about that app to help you make the decision about acquiring it. At the top of the screen, for example, are the app's icon, title, publisher, star-based rating, age appropriateness rating, and Price button.

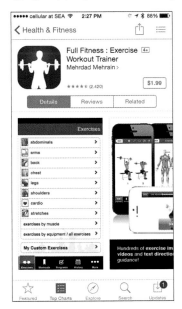

FIGURE 6.7

An app's description screen displays more comprehensive information about the app, including a text-based description and sample screenshots.

Below this basic information about the app are three command tabs, labeled Details, Reviews, and Related. Tap on the Details tab to view sample screenshots from the iPhone, iPad, and/or Apple Watch versions of the app, and then scroll down on this screen to view a detailed, text-based description of the app. Keep in mind that the app's creator or publisher composes the app's Description (found below the Description heading), not Apple.

Under the Information heading found further down an app's Details screen is information about the app's publisher, category, when it was last updated, the most recent version number released, the file size of the app, information about whether the app supports Family Sharing, the app's compatibility with various iPhone and iPad models, and details about the versions of the iOS it's compatible with, whether the app supports the Apple Watch, and information about the languages in which you can display text in the app (see Figure 6.8).

FIGURE 6.8

Displayed under the Information heading are additional details about the app.

Back near the top of the screen, tap on the Reviews tab to view the app's detailed Ratings and Reviews chart. This allows you to see how many one- to five-star ratings an app has received as well as written reviews from other users. If you want to write your own review you can tap the Write a Review option.

From this page, you can also "Like" the app on Facebook, which means you can join the online user's group for that app on this popular social media service by tapping on the "Like" button.

Tap on the Related tab near the top of the screen to learn about similar apps to the one you're looking at that are available from the App Store, as well as apps from the same app publisher/developer.

> **TIP** At any time, tap on the app's Price or Get button to acquire, purchase (if applicable), download, and install the app onto the device you're using. If you're using an iPhone, but the app is also iPad compatible, you can set up the App Store to automatically download and install the app onto your iPad as well. To set up this feature, launch Settings, tap on the iTunes & App Store option, and then turn on the Apps option switch under the Automatic Downloads heading. You need to do this on each of your mobile devices that are linked to the same iCloud (Apple ID) account.

DELETE AND REINSTALL IPHONE APPS

After you acquire an app from the App Store, it is also automatically saved in your online-based iCloud account. Then at any time, you can delete it from your iPhone, iPad, and/or Apple Watch, and later reinstall it for free.

To delete an app from your iPhone, from the Home screen (or from a folder), place your finger on the app icon and hold it down for about two seconds. When all the app icons on the Home screen (or in a folder) start to shake, tap on the "X" icon that appears in the upper-left corner of the app icon you want to delete (see Figure 6.9), and then confirm your decision by tapping the Delete button.

If specialized fitness or health-related data is associated with the app you're about to delete, a prompt appears asking whether you want to keep storing that app-specific data on your iPhone, but delete the app, or delete the data as well as the app.

Later, to reinstall an already-acquired app that is not currently stored on your iPhone, launch the App Store app, locate the listing for that app, and then tap on the iCloud icon, which automatically displays instead of the Price or Get button.

FIGURE 6.9

You can only delete apps you've installed onto the iPhone. You cannot delete preinstalled apps that come with the iOS.

To reinstall a deleted app, re-download it from the App Store. Alternatively, tap on the Updates option at the bottom of the App Store screen, and then tap on the Purchased option near the top of the Updates screen. Either tap on the All or Not On This iPhone tab, and then locate the listing for the app you want to reinstall.

> **! CAUTION**   When you delete an iPhone app that also has an Apple Watch component, the Apple Watch app is also deleted automatically and simultaneously. However, a stand-alone Apple Watch app remains installed and functional on your watch.

> **☑ TIP**   Just about every optional device, such as activity/fitness trackers, Bluetooth scales, and other equipment that you can wirelessly link with your iPhone, has its own proprietary iPhone (and potentially Apple Watch) app available for it. When you purchase an optional device, such as a fitness/activity tracker from Fitbit or Jawbone, for example, you'll be instructed to download the (free) app specifically for use with that device.

USE APP PURCHASES ON MULTIPLE DEVICES

If in addition to an iPhone you have an iPad, keep in mind that all iPhone apps also function on the iPad, and after you acquire an app, you can install it on multiple iOS mobile devices without your having to repurchase it, as long as those devices are linked to the same Apple ID account. However, some iPad-specific apps do not function on an iPhone.

At least initially, all apps that are also compatible with the Apple Watch are also for use on an iPhone, and if a fee applies to acquire the app, it includes both the smartphone and watch versions. This might change in late 2015, after the Apple Watch can have stand-alone apps installed onto it. You will likely eventually need to purchase some stand-alone Apple Watch apps separately from related apps that are also available for the iPhone and/or iPad.

> **!CAUTION** A growing selection of health and fitness-related apps are either initially offered for free, or for a purchase price, but also require in-app purchases to unlock content or features. In some cases, an ongoing subscription fee is required if you want to maintain contact with some type of expert, such as a fitness coach, dietitian, nutritionist, or psychologist, for example.
>
> The app's description in the App Store lists when either in-app purchases or an ongoing paid subscription is required to get full use out of an app. To avoid disappointment or frustration, prior to installing an app, access its description screen in the App Store, tap on the Details tab, scroll down the Details screen, and tap on the In-App Purchases option to see whether it has additional fees associated with it.

ALWAYS PAY ATTENTION TO APP RATINGS AND REVIEWS

A lot of apps are available, and many offer similar titles or descriptions, but differ in how they function. For example, trying to ride on the coattails of the immensely popular Johnson & Johnson Official 7-Minute Workout app for the iPhone and Apple Watch, at least a dozen other apps exist with "7-minute workout" in the title that are not published or endorsed by Johnson & Johnson, and that don't have the research, content, or functionality offered by the official app.

Some apps in the App Store have misleading descriptions, some contain bugs or have compatibility issues with iOS, and some have another type of technical problem that prevents them from functioning properly.

App developers write and publish the descriptions you read in the App Store and their goal is to make their app stand out and sound appealing, so you'll acquire it.

To find the best possible apps to help you achieve your specific goals, try to get a reliable referral from an expert you work with. For example, ask your fitness coach or personal trainer for a recommendation, based on the app(s) he or she personally uses. If you belong to a gym, ask other people you see using an iPhone or Apple Watch which app(s) they recommend.

Also, pay careful attention to the star-based ratings and text-based descriptions offered for each app in the App Store. The star-based rating chart that accompanies each app description shows how many one, two, three, four, and five star ratings the app has received, as well as its average star-based rating. So, if you see an app that has hundreds or thousands of four- or five-star ratings, chances are it's a useful app that functions as described.

Typically, by investing just two or three minutes to reading a handful of reviews for an app written by your fellow iPhone or Apple Watch users, you can quickly ascertain whether it has any problems, and whether it functions as advertised. This can save you time and frustration by helping you avoid apps that just aren't any good.

> ☑ **TIP**   Many cutting-edge, well-designed, highly functional, and powerful health, fitness, medical, nutrition, diet, and sleep-related apps are available. The apps mentioned in this book have proven track records, but you can gauge other apps by looking at their star ratings and reading a few of their reviews.

🔍 CHAT WITH AN EXPERT

LEARN ABOUT THE JOHNSON & JOHNSON OFFICIAL 7-MINUTE WORKOUT APP FROM ITS CREATOR

Out of all the general fitness apps available that can teach you how to exercise, and then track your progress toward achieving specific goals, one stands out. The Johnson & Johnson Official 7-Minute Workout app, shown in Figure 6.10 on the iPhone and Figure 6.11 on the Apple Watch, is available for free from the App Store. As you're about to discover, it offers an easy way for anyone to begin exercising. You can also use it to supplement your existing home or gym fitness routine.

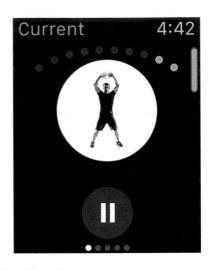

FIGURE 6.10

The Johnson & Johnson Official 7-Minute Workout app is one of the most popular fitness apps for the iPhone.

FIGURE 6.11

The Johnson & Johnson Official 7-Minute Workout app also runs on the Apple Watch.

Unlike some other fitness apps, this one was created based on several decades' worth of research by experts. iPhone users downloaded it more than 1.5 million times within the first three months of its availability.

Chris Jordan is the Director of Exercise Physiology at the Johnson & Johnson Human Performance Institute and is the creator of the Johnson & Johnson Official 7-Minute Workout app. Jordan has held his current position for more than 12 years, but previously served with the British Army and United States Air Force doing high-level research related to exercise physiology.

"The development of the 7-minute workout began more than 12 years ago, long before the iPhone or Apple Watch ever existed. My goal with this program was to make exercise simple, fast and extremely accessible, while keeping it science based," explained Jordan.

"Before the iPhone and Apple Watch, the 7-Minute Workout was printed and distributed on laminated cards that people could easily carry with them. Today, using the iPhone, this same information is presented with photos and videos, and on the Apple Watch, photos, graphics, and audio are currently used."

The Johnson & Johnson Official 7-Minute Workout transforms your iPhone and Apple Watch into an intelligent personal trainer that you can take anywhere. You can work out at home, at your office, in a hotel room, or in a park, and the app provides everything you need to participate in an organized fitness routine. No special gear or equipment is required.

"Our iPhone app, for example, offers a detailed video demonstration of each exercise, so you get a very clear view of what you should be doing, as you learn how to do everything safely and correctly. The iPhone also offers audio prompts related to workout technique that helps to provide an interactive workout experience," explained Jordan. Figure 6.12 shows an exercise demonstration on the Apple Watch's screen.

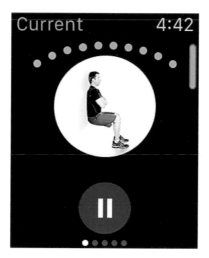

FIGURE 6.12

The Johnson & Johnson Official 7-Minute Workout app demonstrates each exercise using a photo on the Apple Watch (shown) or video on an iPhone.

Using tools built in to the iPhone and the app, the Johnson & Johnson Official 7-Minute Workout app requests information about users and their goals, and then develops a personalized fitness routine, that as the app's title suggests, takes just seven minutes per session to complete.

"The app tracks your progression, so as you get fitter, the workouts get harder over time. When you're using the Apple Watch, it's possible to increase or decrease the exercise intensity during a workout to best fit your current energy level and needs. The app truly offers a virtual trainer in your pocket or on your wrist."

The Johnson & Johnson 7-Minute Workout is for people who are constantly on the go, such as executives, whose biggest obstacles to staying fit are lack of time and the inability to visit a gym on a regular basis. The workout routines incorporate aerobic as well as resistance exercises.

"This is a combined, high-intensity, circuit training program that has over a decade's worth of research and fine tuning behind it. In 7 minutes, you can complete one circuit. The app itself incorporates 22 pre-programmed workouts that range in length from 7 to 32 minutes, as well as the option for creating customized workouts. We have found that consistently doing our 7-minute workout is a great starting point for staying healthy and fit," said Jordan. "The workouts can be done in very limited space. If you can lie down in a flat position, you have the space available to do this workout wherever you happen to be."

When asked whether this workout app completely replaces the need to join a gym or work with a professional trainer, Jordon replied, "If you do have access to other equipment and options, and you have the time, it should be encouraged that you engage in those options as well. For example, if in addition to using the app each day, you also opt to go for a run or go to the gym, that's a great complement to what you will accomplish with the app. But, if you're a single parent at home, or you're traveling for work, and don't have access to a gym, this fitness app is designed to be a comprehensive workout and fitness solution."

One of the biggest mistakes Jordan sees most often among people who opt to use their iPhone or Apple Watch as a fitness tool is that they don't utilize the tools available to them on a consistent basis.

"Don't keep switching fitness apps or fitness routines every time something new piques your interest. Find something that works for you and stick with it. If you jump from one fitness app to another, you lose having a well-balanced and regular routine. Give a selected app or fitness routine a chance to work, before you decide to move on to a new one," said Jordan.

"My biggest tip for people first starting to use the 7-Minute Workout app is to take advantage of all the app's features. The 7-Minute Workout is really many different workouts that are combined into one app, and that are designed to give you a well-rounded and complete exercise experience." Figure 6.13 shows some of these features.

"Other apps that claim to be a 7-minute workout are literally just one workout routine that never changes. Every aspect of our app is based on extensive research and science. In reality, it offers more than 1,000 exercise combinations in order to create comprehensive workouts that change based on your needs and progression.

"It's very helpful for someone to utilize an activity monitor or fitness tracker with their fitness routine. This can be the Apple Watch, or another device that works in conjunction with the app. Any equipment that transmits data to the Health app can become very useful when it comes to making you well aware of your current state. You can use the information collected as a motivator, as well as a way to track your progress accurately," said Jordan.

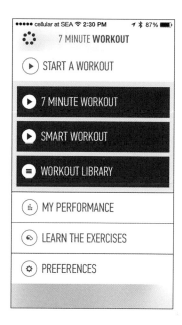

FIGURE 6.13

The Johnson & Johnson Official 7-Minute Workout app offers pre-programmed workouts, a Smart Workout feature, and a customizable Workout Library.

Based on research conducted over decades at the Johnson & Johnson Human Performance Institute, Jordan believes that the key to staying focused and motivated when it comes to working out and staying fit is to have a clearly defined sense of purpose, and achievable and realistic goals.

"Having a purpose and goals can be very powerful and lasting motivators. Think about what matters most to you in your life, and then relate each of your fitness goals to those things that matter to you. For example, what's most important to me is being the best possible dad to my son. In my mind, I truly believe that working out on a regular basis gives me the strength and energy I need to be the best dad possible, especially when I'm spending quality time with my son.

"In terms of short-term motivators, listening to music during your workouts has been proven to work. Make your exercise routine as enjoyable as possible, and if music helps to make it more enjoyable, listen to your favorite music during your workouts. The 7-Minute Workout app works beautifully with the Music app on the iPhone, for example," concluded Jordan.

EXPLORE FITNESS SOLUTIONS FOR WALKERS, JOGGERS, AND RUNNERS

Many general fitness apps, some of which are covered later in this book, offer a wide range of tools that can monitor and track data about your heartbeat, distance traveled, the duration of your workouts, and calories burned during a workout, for example. All this information is useful for someone who is fitness minded and enjoys participating in a variety of activities as part of their overall fitness regimen (see Figure 7.1).

However, if you specifically enjoy walking, jogging, or running, a large selection of more specialized apps are also available from the App Store that work with the iPhone, and in many cases, the Apple Watch as well.

Some of the more popular apps for runners that this chapter introduces you to include Nike+ Running, MapMyRun, RunKeeper, Runtastic Pro, and Couch to 5K. If walking is more your speed, apps such as MapMyWalk, Walkmeter GPS Pedometer, and Sports Tracker (and some of the running apps) can prove to be useful tools.

FIGURE 7.1

Whether you enjoy walking, jogging, running, or hiking, your iPhone and Apple Watch can be a useful tool, particularly when combined with a specialized app.

> ✅ **TIP**   MapMyHike, AllTrails Hiking & Mountain Biking Trails, Ramblr, Gaia GPS—Offline Topo Maps and Hiking Trails, and Geocaching Intro are among the popular apps designed specifically for hikers.

> **❗CAUTION**   While walking, jogging, or running, do not get into the habit of texting or reading emails on your iPhone or Apple Watch. Always pay attention to what's ahead of you. Every day, people are injured by walking into oncoming traffic or tripping over an obstacle in their path, because their eyes were focused on the device's screen and not on their surroundings while they were in motion.

WHAT TO LOOK FOR

Chances are, if want an app to use with your walking, jogging, or running activities, you will only need to choose one primary app to work with.

When choosing the most appropriate app to meet your needs, the first step is to clearly define your fitness goals, and then determine what type of data you want your iPhone (with the Apple Watch or another fitness/activity tracker) to collect and help you analyze.

Next, determine whether you want the app to take advantage of the iPhone's GPS (Location Services) capabilities, so you can keep track of where you walk, jog, or run; plan and log the routes you take; and keep tabs on the type of terrain you cover.

Another key element that some of these apps offer are social tools that enable you to interact with other walkers, runners, and joggers; share your accomplishments; and help motivate one another, even if the other people are not physically with you during your activities.

NOTE This chapter covers apps that you can use when walking, jogging, or running outside. You can also use some of these apps, and others that you'll learn about in Chapter 12, "Getting the Most from General Fitness Apps," indoors with fitness equipment such as a treadmill or elliptical machine.

If you plan to do most of your walking, jogging, or running on a treadmill, for example, ensuring that your app offers the appropriate features and connectivity tools to properly and accurately track this type of activity is important.

After you've clearly determined your goals, choosing the best app to meet your needs is a straightforward process. Based on what you learn here and information you gather from the App Store, select an app with the tools that most closely match your needs, with the best ratings and reviews, and the most affordable price (keeping in mind that one time in-app purchases, or a monthly subscription fee might be required).

TIP Choose an app that offers quick pre-activity set up, enables you to easily view relevant data in real time, and that allows you to navigate around the app quickly and efficiently, especially when you're walking or running.

The app should not distract you or hinder your walking, jogging, or running momentum as a result of your having to constantly tinker with app settings, or navigate your way through multiple menus to display particular information at any given moment.

Ideally, you want the most relevant data clearly displayed on your iPhone and Apple Watch (or fitness/activity tracker's) screen, during your activity.

> **NOTE** Stand-alone Apple Watch apps, available in late 2015, can share data with your iPhone, but don't require your smartphone to remain in close proximity to you or the watch. Thus, while you walk, jog, or run, you could potentially leave your iPhone at home, in your car, or in a locker (or handbag or backpack), and rely only on the Apple Watch to collect and track relevant information.

APPS FOR WALKING

In addition to helping you stay healthy, walking can be a fun social activity if you do it with other people, or it can be something you do alone to think, get away from stressful situations, or to clear your mind.

> **TIP** Walking offers a low-impact and effective method for losing weight, reducing blood pressure, and lowering the risk of heart disease or stroke. It also helps to improve heart and lung health, increases muscle strength, and can help to improve overall balance and endurance.
>
> In fact, research indicates that to achieve the best results from walking, you should strive to take at least 10,000 steps (walk about five miles) per day, which the Apple Watch or another fitness/activity tracker can easily measure.

The great thing about walking is that aside from wearing comfortable shoes and appropriate clothing, and having a bottle of water on hand to stay hydrated, you don't need any specialized equipment (see Figure 7.2).

You can walk anywhere, at your own pace, and you're never confined to following a specific path or route. You can walk repeatedly around a block or running track, explore your community, breathe fresh air as you walk through a local park or along a beach, or follow a designated path, all the while using your iPhone (and Apple Watch or fitness/activity tracker) to monitor your progress and collect relevant data.

This section offers an overview of several specialized iPhone apps for the walking enthusiast, several of which offer compatibility with the Apple Watch.

FIGURE 7.2

Your iPhone and/or Apple Watch can be useful in a number of ways during a walk.

> **NOTE** To find additional apps, launch the App Store app on your Internet-connected iPhone, and in the Search field, type "walking," or "walking tracker." Refer to Chapter 6, "Find and Use Specialized Health Apps," for more information on how to do this.

MAPMYWALK

MapMyFitness (www.mapmyfitness.com) is an app development company that has created a series of iPhone apps for navigating and activity tracking during specific activities. For example, the MapMyWalk app (see Figure 7.3) is specifically for walking enthusiasts, the MapMyRun app is better suited to runners, and the MapMyHike and MapMyRide apps will appeal to hikers and bicyclers, respectively.

Both free and paid ($2.99) versions of the MapMyWalk app are available, although both offer in-app purchases to unlock additional features. The free version of the app displays ads, but the paid version does not. The paid edition also includes an integrated GPS camera feature.

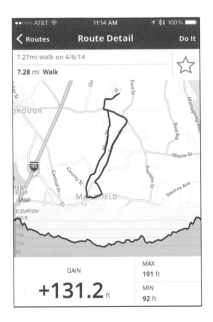

FIGURE 7.3
The MapMyWalk app offers a comprehensive set of tools for walking enthusiasts.

> **TIP**   To fully use the MapMyWalk app, you need a fitness/activity tracker. The app is compatible with virtually all trackers on the market, including those from Fitbit, Jawbone, Garmin, and Withings.
>
> As of mid-2015, the MapMyWalk app did not offer Apple Watch compatibility, although other MapMy apps, including MapMyRun, are Apple Watch compatible. By the time you read this, Apple Watch compatibility for MapMyWalk might also be available.

One of the key features of the MapMyWalk app is that in addition to helping you plan your own route(s) to follow, based on your location, the app can recommend routes in many cities around the world.

The four main components of the app are

■ **Map Your Route:** Keep tabs on exactly where you've been and plan where you're going next. The app contains a database of more than 70 million suggested routes.

- **Track Your Progress:** As you walk, the app tracks all important data it collects from the iPhone and compatible fitness/activity trackers, and enables you to manually enter data if you walk without your smartphone or tracker with you.

- **Maintain a Food Log:** Maintaining your health isn't just about moving and fitness. It also involves staying hydrated and eating a well-balanced and healthy diet. This app lets you easily track what foods you consume, so you can see a more complete picture of your overall health and correlate how diet impacts your energy and capabilities while walking or in other activities.

- **Communicate with Others:** Thanks to social networking and the Internet connectivity of your iPhone, sharing your achievements and communicating with friends, family, and workout buddies provide easy ways to help you stay motivated and focused.

As the MapMyWalk app collects data, like most fitness apps, it displays the important information in real time using easy-to-read charts, text-based displays, and colorful graphs. It automatically tracks, analyzes, and stores all relevant data pertaining to a walk, such as your pace, route, distance traveled, calories burned, elevation, and heart rate (see Figure 7.4).

FIGURE 7.4

Using an easy-to-understand format, MapMyWalk displays relevant information during your walk.

Part of the app's social component includes an online-based service that stores your data online, and enables you to easily communicate with more than 30 million other fitness enthusiasts. To use this optional MVP service, a monthly membership fee applies, but it includes a variety of extra tools for socializing and to help you achieve your fitness goals.

For example, an MVP membership used with the MapMyWalk app includes Challenges, which are virtual competitions you can experience with real-world friends or online friends, and potentially win prizes. You can also create your own Challenges to experience with friends via the app.

Specialized training plans are also offered to MVP members, although this is a tool that runners and cyclists will probably find more useful.

Launching the app for the first time requires you to set up a free online account, or sign in to the MapMyFitness service using a pre-existing account you might have set up when using one of the company's other apps. Tap on the Join Now button to set up a new account, and then follow the on-screen instructions.

> **NOTE** Many fitness apps require you to enter your gender, birthdate, height, and weight. Among other things, the apps use this information to more accurately calculate calories burned during a run or workout.
>
> As your weight changes over time, you might need to manually update this setting in the app you use, unless that app syncs data with the Health app, and you're using a Bluetooth scale to monitor and record your weight fluctuation on a regular basis. In this case, the fitness app automatically retrieves your latest weight data as needed.

After you set up your account, the main app's Dashboard screen appears. From here, tap on the Menu icon (located in the top-left corner of the screen) to access the app's various features (see Figure 7.5). Tap on the Profile icon (also near the top-left corner of the screen) to view your real-time activity graph or edit your profile.

Also from the app's menu, you can easily view your activity feed, plan walking routes, or communicate with friends. Be sure to turn on Location Services on your iPhone (from Settings), and then grant permission for the MapMyWalk app to use this feature so you can take advantage of the mapping and navigation features.

From the app's main Dashboard, your location appears on a map in the main area of the screen (see Figure 7.6). Along the top of the screen are icons for adjusting app-specific features, like Coaching, Music, Live Tracking, Activity Selection, Route Selection, and Gear.

Profile icon —

Menu icon

FIGURE 7.5

The main menu of the MapMyWalk app offers quick access to the majority of the app's features and functions.

FIGURE 7.6

The main Dashboard screen of the MapMyWalk app.

Coaching and Live Tracking are features offered exclusively to paid MVP subscribers. The Music option allows you to select and play music from the MapMyWalk app, as opposed to separately launching the iPhone's Music app.

Tap on the My Gear function to keep track of what walking shoes you wear for each walk, or shop online for new, name-brand sneakers or shoes from the Zappos website.

Tap on the Route icon to quickly find a local route from the app's extensive database, or plan your own custom walking route.

> ☑ **TIP** You can take many types of walks, and the MapMyWalk app enables you to choose a specific walk-related activity to more accurately collect data. Tap on the Activity icon, and then choose among Walk, Stairs, Walk (Treadmill), Dog Walk, or Power Walk.

When you're ready to walk, tap on the Start Workout button. The app then automatically tracks and displays all relevant information, including your exact location, current pace, calories burned, distance traveled, and the duration of your walk.

Music controls appear along the very top of the iPhone's screen. At any time, tap on the Pause Workout button to take a break. At this point, either tap on the Slide to Finish button to conclude your workout and save your data, or tap on the Resume Workout to continue your walk.

> ☑ **TIP** To further customize the app, tap on the gear-shaped Settings icon to access the Settings menu to turn on or off features (such as Voice Feedback), activate the Delayed Start Timer, and pair optional Bluetooth equipment (such as a fitness/activity tracker and/or heart rate monitor) with the iPhone app. From this menu, you can also turn on or off automatic Facebook and Twitter postings, and allow the sharing of collected MapMyWalk data with the iPhone's Health app.

WALKMETER GPS PEDOMETER

The free Walkmeter GPS Pedometer app from Abvio, Inc. (http://abvio.com) offers in-app purchases, and is designed to be a comprehensive tool for people who enjoy walking for health and fitness-related purposes. It works with a wide range of popular fitness/activity trackers, and a Walkmeter GPS Pedometer Apple Watch app is available (see Figure 7.7).

FIGURE 7.7

Walkmeter GPS Pedometer includes a useful Apple Watch app that gathers and displays information that ultimately gets transferred to the iPhone app.

> **NOTE** Also available from Abvio via the App Store are the Runmeter GPS Pedometer, Cyclemeter GPS, and 5K Runnermeter apps, all of which offer a similar user interface and comprehensive set of data-gathering and analysis tools designed for specific types of activities.

A few things set this app apart from others. One is that it is exclusively for walkers. Also, in addition to gathering your walking data, it displays this information in a variety of detailed formats, including colorful charts and graphs that showcase stats, maps, steps, and walk summaries (see Figure 7.8).

Furthermore, all data is stored on the iPhone, with no online-based account required, although you do have the option of sharing data and accomplishments with others via social media.

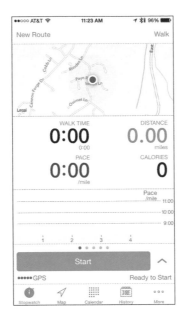

FIGURE 7.8
Walkmeter GPS Pedometer displays information in a variety of ways.

> **NOTE** The Walkmeter GPS Pedometer app allows iCloud data syncing for iPhone and iPad users, so all of your most current data is always accessible, regardless of which iOS mobile device you're using.
>
> For an annual fee of $4.99, you can upgrade to the Elite version of the app, which includes no ads, enhanced Apple Watch functions, integration with the Music app, audible coaching and statistic-related messages, and other features such as the ability to record weather conditions during walks and access to terrain maps (with traffic details).

Another nice feature of this app is that after you install it on your iPhone (or Apple Watch), you can get started using it very quickly. From the app's startup screen, you can custom name a route, choose your activity, start a walk, view a map, or access a calendar that automatically displays your history using the app.

As with most apps, the first time you launch this one, you need to provide basic details about yourself, including your age, gender, height, and weight. However, it can also automatically import this data from the iPhone's Health app.

> ☑ **TIP** If you regularly track your weight via a Bluetooth scale that stores data in the iPhone's Health app (or you manually input weight data into the Health app), be sure to turn on Health app integration when you use the Walkmeter GPS Pedometer app. This allows it to import and take into account your most current weight-related data for each walk.
>
> Also, because the mapping/GPS feature built in to the app uses Google Maps, when prompted, allow the Walkmeter GPS Pedometer app on the iPhone to download and install the official Google app, if it's not already installed.

The app's main Dashboard screen clearly displays all the information you would want to see during a walk, including a map, the duration of your walk, distance traveled, pace, and calories burned, although additional information and other app features are only one tap away.

> ☑ **TIP** Tap on the Walk option in the top-right corner of the screen to quickly select a 7-Minute Workout option, or choose between a Hike, Rest, Walk, Walk for Distance, Walk for Time, or Walk Intervals option.
>
> The Walk Intervals option guides you through your walk, telling you when and where to walk fast, walk at a normal pace, walk slowly, or rest. Take advantage of pre-programmed Walk Interval options, or create your own by tapping on the Edit option related to this feature.

SPORTS TRACKER

The free Sports Tracker app (which offers in-app purchases) provides a comprehensive set of tools for participating in a variety of activities, including walking, jogging, running, or cycling (see Figure 7.9). Using this app, you can track and analyze your performance and share workout data with friends.

As expected, when used with the appropriate equipment, such as a fitness/activity tracker, Sports Tracker tracks all relevant activity data related to the selected activity, including speed, distance traveled, calories burned, heart rate, and altitude. It's also fully compatible with the iPhone's Health app.

By subscribing to the Premium edition of Sports Tracker (a monthly fee applies), you can set weekly, monthly, and annual goals, access many additional route maps, and unlock other motivational tools and features.

FIGURE 7.9
Runners, walkers, joggers, or cyclists, for example, can use Sports Tracker.

Although the look of the screen is different from the MapMyWalk app, for example, the Sports Tracker app does display the same types of real-time information in an easy-to-read and colorful way. Two benefits of the Sports Tracker app are that it is highly customizable, and it enables you to track your progress across multiple activities, not just walking.

> **☑ TIP** Don't forget—thanks to the multitasking capabilities of your iPhone, you can run a specialized app during your walk, jog, run, or hike, but quickly switch between apps as needed.
>
> For example, you might want to answer an incoming call, read or compose a text message, check your email, or enjoy music from your favorite playlist using the Music app, which you'll learn more about in Chapter 13, "Find Music to Keep You Motivated While Active."
>
> To switch to another app while your fitness app is running, quickly press the Home button twice on your iPhone. From the multitasking screen, swipe your finger left or right horizontally to find the app you want to switch to (if it's already running in the background), or choose the Home screen and launch the second app by tapping on its icon. To switch to a second app or access the Home screen, tap on the thumbnail or app icon for it on the multitasking screen.

To later switch back to the fitness app you were working with, again tap on the Home button twice in quick succession, and then tap on the thumbnail or app icon for that fitness app. You'll notice that the fitness app continued to collect data while it ran in the background.

SPECIALIZED APPS FOR RUNNERS AND JOGGERS

Many of the apps specifically for runners work in much the same way as the popular apps for walking enthusiasts, but they collect and analyze data that has a stronger emphasis on pace/speed, heart rate, pulse, calories burned, and distance, for example.

One of the most popular apps in this category is Nike+ Running, although other apps, like MapMyRun, RunKeeper, Runtastic Pro, and Couch to 5K, offer a variety of additional features that runners might find useful. For example, MapMyRun focuses on mapping routes and offers its extensive route database, whereas Couch to 5K serves as a virtual coach and helps a runner build up the speed, endurance, and stamina to successfully complete 5K runs or races.

This section offers an overview of several specialized iPhone apps for running and jogging enthusiasts, several of which offer compatibility with the Apple Watch. To get the most out of any of these apps, use them either with an Apple Watch (when applicable), or a compatible fitness/activity tracker.

NIKE+ RUNNING

Although many fitness-related apps have been created just for the iPhone, or developed for the launch of the Apple Watch, the Nike+ Running app shown in Figure 7.10 was initially designed to be used with the iPhone and Nike FuelBand fitness/activity tracker accessory, but has since been adapted to function flawlessly with Apple Watch (see Figure 7.11).

Designed for ease of use and developed by Nike, this app keeps track of all your runs (or jogs), and records pertinent data. The app also has a well-developed social component via the Nike+ website (which is free to join via the app, or by visiting https://secure-nikeplus.nike.com/plus).

> 🗒 **NOTE** In addition to the popular Nike+ Running app, Nike has released the Nike+ Fuel and Nike+ Training Club apps. You can use the Nike+ Fuel app as a motivational and activity tracking tool for a variety of activities, whereas the Nike+ Training Club app can serve as a feature-packed, virtual personal trainer that tracks a variety of workout and fitness-oriented activities.

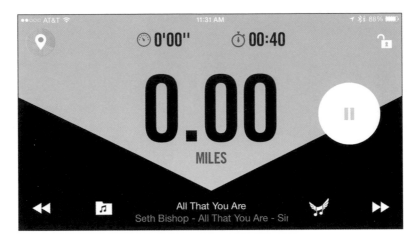

FIGURE 7.10

Shown here on the iPhone, Nike+ Running is a useful app for runners at all skill levels.

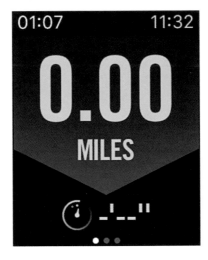

FIGURE 7.11

Nike+ Running works on the Apple Watch.

One thing that sets the Nike+ fitness apps apart from their competition is that these apps focus on the ability for users to earn NikeFuel.

According to Nike's website, "NikeFuel is a simple universal way to measure how much you move, providing you with insights, motivation and opportunities to become a better athlete. NikeFuel measures your whole body movement focusing only on the energy required to do an activity. NikeFuel is calculated the same way for everyone. It doesn't take into account body weight, gender or age."

By analyzing the NikeFuel that's earned, this is one way you can better understand how active you are during any given day, and monitor activity/fitness-related trends across a wide range of activities, over time, or when comparing accomplishments with friends.

The Nike+ Running app offers easy-to-use tools with an intuitive user interface that allows a runner to focus on the activity of running, not on managing the app. That being said, the various features of the app offer a comprehensive toolset, from tracking and analysis, to social interaction, motivation, music control, and route tracking.

After installing and setting up the app, providing basic details about yourself, and then granting permission for the app to access the Health app and various other iPhone features, using the app is a straightforward process. When you're ready to begin a run:

1. Tap the Begin Run button.

2. From the Run Setup screen, shown in Figure 7.12, swipe between the Basic Run, Set Distance, Set Time, or Set Speed options.

3. Tap on the Music option to choose your favorite song(s) or playlists from the Music app.

FIGURE 7.12

The Run Setup screen of the Nike+ Running app on the iPhone.

4. Tap on the Location option to switch between the Indoor or Outdoor options. (Choosing the appropriate option for each run improves data collection accuracy.)

5. Adjust the Orientation you'll be holding or carrying the iPhone (if applicable).

6. Choose which social media services you want to post your run-related accomplishments to by tapping on the Cheers option.

7. Tap on the Run Settings option to customize a variety of other settings. For example, you can adjust the app's Notification options, customize the Run Countdown feature, turn on/off the Auto Voice Feedback feature, and/or turn on/off the Pause Run for Calls feature.

> **TIP** From the Run Settings menu, tap on the Powersongs option and choose from a selection of upbeat songs from your own Music app library that you find particularly inspirational. You can then play back these songs to motivate you at key times during your run either with or instead of the voice feedback that the app can generate.

8. Tap the Start button, and begin running (or jogging). After the 3-2-1 countdown, the app begins playing your selected music and displays real-time information about your progress.

At any time, tap the large Pause button to pause your run. To resume the run, tap on the Resume button, or press and hold the End button to end the run and store and share your data.

The Summary screen then displays details about your distance, average pace, and the amount of NikeFuel earned. Tap on the app's menu icon in the top-left corner of the Summary screen to use the app's other features and functions.

For example, tap on the Activity option to view your run-related history and accomplishments. Tap on the Friends option to communicate and share information with friends via the Nike+ website, or tap on the Challenges option to compete in pre-designed and ever-changing Challenges that are hosted by the Nike+ website. This allows you to compete against other people, display your progress and accomplishments on a leaderboard, and track what your friends are doing.

The Nike+ Coach function transforms the app (when used with the Nike+ website) into a virtual coach that can help you set and achieve personalized fitness goals.

> ☑ **TIP** Nike designed many of the features and functions of the Nike+ Running app to be shared with the Nike+ website. Thus, you'll need to set up a free, online-based account to use this app to its full potential.

MAPMYRUN

The MapMyRun app (www.mapmyrun.com) is much like the MapMyWalk app, but caters to runners and joggers. The layout and design of both apps are extremely similar, but this app offers an Apple Watch component, is compatible with many fitness trackers, and can collect and monitor a wide range of data that goes beyond just stats related to specific runs.

The free version of MapMyRun, shown in Figure 7.13, displays ads while you're using the app. However, unlocking all the app's features requires an MVP membership ($5.99 per month or $29.99 per year). This includes live location tracking, interval training, audio coaching, heart rate analysis, an advertising-free experience while using the app, and additional tools for planning routes, tracking runs, and analyzing progress and accomplishments.

FIGURE 7.13

The MapMyRun app is similar to the MapMyWalk app, but designed specifically for runners.

The Dashboard of the Map My Run app enables you to track workouts, weight, sleep, steps, calories (both intake and burned), and distance, and then analyze this information to get a complete picture of your health, fitness, and progress.

The app also offers a variety of Run Training Plans, as well as tools that you can use to help set, monitor, and ultimately achieve personalized goals through running, while also logging your other workouts and activities.

The key feature that sets this app apart from others is the mapping/GPS tracking function. In addition to displaying maps depicting where you've run, the app offers an extensive database of potential routes and allows you to customize, store, and share your own routes (see Figure 7.14).

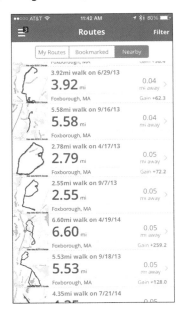

FIGURE 7.14

MapMyRun offers access to a vast database of pre-planned running routes based on your current location.

RUNKEEPER

Another free specialized running app that includes Apple Watch compatibility is RunKeeper (see Figure 7.15). This app enables you to track your runs and all data related to them, but also works with other activities, like bicycling and more traditional training workouts.

FIGURE 7.15

With the help of Apple Watch or a fitness/activity tracker, the RunKeeper app tracks useful information during a run, such as your distance, time, calories burned, speed, and heart rate.

During each run, the app collects, tracks, and displays your distance, time, calories burned, speed, heart rate, and other details in real time, as well as a detailed map. With the RunKeeper app you can create your own route or follow a pre-created route.

Two nice features of this app are the training plan workouts that include audio coaching, as well as the integration with the Music app, so you can enjoy your favorite songs or playlists without leaving the app during a run. Unlike other apps, you can use this one for both running outdoors and on a treadmill or elliptical machine.

The app offers a selection of basic walking and running training plans for beginners, but it also offers virtual coaching elements (developed by Jeff Galloway and other running coaches) to help you prepare for a 10k, half marathon, or full marathon.

To help you stay focused and plan your training, RunKeeper has a built-in training calendar. For people wanting to lose weight or engage in other fitness activities in addition to running, RunKeeper syncs nicely with the Health app, MyFitnessPal, Lose It!, and several other popular apps.

The basic RunKeeper app is free, but is advertiser supported. To unlock additional features and get rid of the ads, a subscription to RunKeeper Elite is available as an in-app purchase for $9.99 per month (or $39.99 per year).

To use this app, you must set up a free online-based account from the app. Beyond providing your name and email address, the app prompts you to classify yourself as a type of athlete. Choices include Athlete, Walker, Cyclist, or Runner. It also asks you to provide your gender, weight, and birthdate.

Using the app's Reminder feature, set up the iPhone to generate reminders to work out each day or several days per week, as recommended by the app (or your personal trainer). When you're ready for a run, tap on the Go Running button on the main screen.

RunKeeper's main screen displays a detailed map that outlines your route and your current location. Tap on the Workout Type option to choose between a Distance Target Run, Time Target Run, Pace Free Run, Interval Run, or Free Run, or choose from a pre-created or custom-created workout, such as a 20-Minute Easy Workout, or a Two-Mile Run with Rest (see Figure 7.16).

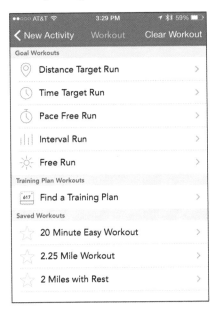

FIGURE 7.16

Tap on the Workout option to select the type of run you'll be doing.

Tap on the Route option to create an outdoor running route, or choose a saved route, and then tap on the Playlist option to select a Music app playlist to listen to during your run without leaving the RunKeeper app. In addition to providing training plans, a RunKeeper Elite subscription also enables your friends to track your progress during a run in real time. This is useful if you're competing in races, working with a remotely located trainer, or participating in charity races, for example.

To help you set and achieve long-term goals, the app offers the My Plan feature, which helps you set a realistic goal with a deadline, and then assists you in devising a daily plan to achieve it. Tap on the Find a Training Plan button to access a detailed daily plan for preparing for a race, learning to run, getting fit, or losing weight.

For runners at all levels, RunKeeper offers a useful set of tools. It is particularly useful when you combine it with an Apple Watch or a compatible fitness/activity tracker to collect and display data during a run.

RUNTASTIC PRO

Runtastic Pro promotes itself as being a full-featured tool for running enthusiasts that comes with a supportive online community (via www.Runtastic.com) that's comprised of fellow fitness enthusiasts. You can use Runtastic Pro to track runs as well as bicycling and strength training (see Figure 7.17).

FIGURE 7.17

Runtastic Pro is another iPhone-based tool for runners.

After installing the app, create a free online-based Runtastic.com account from the app by tapping on the Join Now button. Fill in the on-screen prompts to enter your name, gender, email address, and birthday, and create an account password. Fill in the prompts for your birthday, height, and weight.

You can set up and access all the app's main features by tapping on the Menu icon in the top-left corner of the screen. For example, to view your current and past activity-related data, tap on the Activity, History, or Statistics options, which display information using different formats.

Locate and choose or create your own running route by tapping on the Routes option. The iPhone can figure out your current location and recommend pre-created routes that are nearby. Tap on the Explore Routes option to change locations, switch between routes, or create your own route.

Whether you want to lose a predetermined amount of weight within a specific time period, or gear yourself up for an upcoming 5K race, for example, tap on the Training Plans option to help you set and achieve your goals (see Figure 7.18).

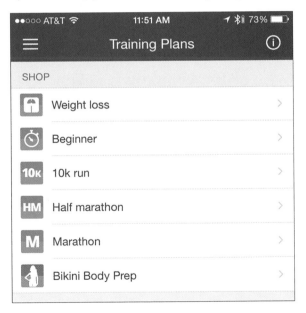

FIGURE 7.18

Use the Training Plans feature of the Runtastic Pro app to help you set and then achieve realistic fitness-oriented goals.

Use the Interval Training mode of the app to create or use pre-created interval training runs that are time or distance based. One interesting feature of the app is called Story Running. For an additional in-app purchase, you can experience a unique form of interval training that involves listening to a motivational story during the run. A variety of different Story Running programs are offered for $0.99 each, although a free sample, called *Wings for Life World Run: Run for Those Who Can't!* is offered.

During an actual run, the display keeps you informed of your distance, duration, and average pace, while displaying your route and current location.

COUCH TO 5K

Couch to 5K ($1.99) from Active Networks, LLC (www.active.com) offers virtual coaching and training tools that are ideal for beginning runners with a specific goal.

If you're willing to commit 20 to 30 minutes per day, three times a week for nine weeks, this app will train a beginner in a non-intimidating way to be able to complete a 5K race (see Figure 7.19).

To accomplish this task, users select a virtual coach (each of whom has a different personality). The coach then offers guidance, challenges, motivation, and precise direction every step of the way. Active.com trainers created the training plans used in this app. In addition to these virtual coaches, the app integrates with the Music app, giving you access to your playlists, which you can listen to during each run.

FIGURE 7.19

This app's virtual coaches offer verbal tips, how-to information, and motivation during your runs.

Couch to 5K offers GPS support to map runs outdoors, but works equally well indoors in use with a treadmill. During each run, while receiving guidance from your virtual coach, the app tracks, displays, and stores relevant data, including your distance and pace.

> **NOTE** A 5K (kilometer) run is equivalent to 3.1 miles. After you "graduate" from using this app, a sister application, called 5K to 10K, is available from Active Network, LLC (www.active.com) via the App Store.

Couch to 5K offers a simple user interface and colorful graphics. From a single screen, you can clearly see a timer, distance traveled, and your current pace. You can also control your music and see the upcoming activity in your current workout (see Figure 7.20).

FIGURE 7.20

As you use this app, various information screens offer guidance and information designed to help you stay motivated.

> ✓ **TIP** Be sure to use this app with (preferably wireless) headphones during each run, because the virtual coach you select speaks to you while you listen to your favorite music.

CHAT WITH AN EXPERT

ANTHONY KNIEREM, MATCHUP CO-FOUNDER, TALKS ABOUT WEARABLE TECHNOLOGY FOR FITNESS TASKS

By combining the power of the iPhone with the world's most popular fitness/activity trackers for step counting, and the motivational capabilities of social media, Matchup Fitness Challenges (www.matchup.io) helps people stay healthy and physically fit by encouraging them to participate in fitness-oriented activities, and share their experiences with others via the Internet.

Anthony Knierem is the co-founder and COO of Matchup, LLC. In this interview, he offers some insight into tapping the power of social media combined with mobile technology to achieve fitness goals.

"I have spent a lot of time working with large corporations helping them focus on employee health and physical engagement. This included helping companies develop and implement healthy workforce initiatives for employees," said Knierem. "While working at this previous job, I helped to gather a tremendous amount of participation-based data, which indicated that people achieved much higher levels of success reaching fitness goals when they worked toward them in conjunction with other people or competing against others."

By creating a social connection that involves peer support and some level of competition between individuals, participants are more apt to stay focused and motivated as they strive toward their fitness goals. This is the premise behind Matchup's proprietary Matchup—Fitness Challenges iPhone app (see Figure 7.21) that you use with a compatible fitness/activity tracker.

"Through the iPhone app, we set specific goals for people on a daily basis. For example, we'll set up a simple challenge for two or more people to compete for having the highest step count, or the least amount of sedentary time in a day," explained Knierem. "We offer a collection of curated challenges, plus allow groups to develop their own challenges, and then through the app and our website, each person can track their activity as they complete."

FIGURE 7.21

The Matchup app shown here on an iPhone displays step-based challenges you can participate in.

Using any fitness tracker, the free Matchup app, and the Matchup website, people can participate in ongoing fitness challenges with friends, coworkers, or individuals they might not even know. The challenges are step-based, community-oriented, and incentive/reward-driven. The Matchup platform is very flexible and scalable, so two or more family members, a group of employees from a small business, or all employees from a large corporation can easily use it.

"We see a lot of couples using Matchup. One person may have an Apple Watch, while their spouse has a Fitbit tracker, for example, but both can participate in the fitness-oriented competition and challenges offered," said Knierem.

Because the app collects ongoing data from each participant, users can track their own accomplishments over time and compare their successes against their competitors.

Knierem added, "I believe that using any type of fitness/activity tracker allows people to collect data and see exactly what they're accomplishing. It provides one of those ah-ha moments when they use a tracker and see how many steps they actually take per day, versus how much time they remain sedentary. This data becomes even more useful when it can be compared against other people, as well as the user's own past performance.

"If someone uses a fitness/activity tracker on her own, she may use it for a few days or a few weeks, and then lose interest. However, we've found that when people compete with other people, they tend to stay interested and motivated."

Compared to other activity/fitness trackers, Knierem believes that Apple Watch is quickly changing the game in a number of different ways. "For example, Apple Watch tracks activity and movement, as well as heart rate. Third-party app developers can use and control the sensors in the device that relate to collecting and analyzing activity-specific actions and range of motion data."

He added, "Not only can the watch track activity, in many cases it can differentiate automatically between the types of activities someone is engaged in. It knows, for example, the difference between walking, running, and climbing stairs. The groundwork has been laid by Apple for third-party developers to utilize the watch to create interesting fitness-related apps and uses, the likes of which we have not seen before."

One area that Knierem sees real potential, in terms of using the iPhone with the Apple Watch for health, diet, and fitness-related tasks, is how various apps are starting to share data with one another to give users a clearer picture of their overall situation.

"The Health app allows the iPhone and Apple Watch to collect a vast amount of data from multiple sources, and then share that data in a very customized way. I think apps and various information providers will soon begin devising more useful ways to pull all of this data together in order for people to take a more targeted approach to their health, fitness, or diet-oriented goals," said Knierem.

IN THIS CHAPTER

- Discover iPhone and Apple Watch apps designed for cyclists
- Learn about optional bike computers that can share data with your iPhone

8

EXPLORE FITNESS STRATEGIES FOR BICYCLERS

By now you know how the iPhone's connectivity features, enabled by Wi-Fi, Bluetooth, and AirPlay technology, let it communicate with a broad range of other technology-based devices, including the Apple Watch. This connectivity allows the iPhone to collect and gather data from other sources, plus share data that's stored in the phone itself. Given that, it's no surprise that cyclists can also benefit from these features (see Figure 8.1).

Small computers that connect to a bicycle are nothing new. These devices measure and display useful information in real time, such as speed, distance traveled, heart rate, temperature, lap times, and potentially GPS navigational data. Many of these bike computers are stand-alone devices.

FIGURE 8.1

For cyclists, the iPhone and Apple Watch can be useful tools, especially when used with a dedicated bike computer.

The latest versions of these bike computers can link wirelessly (via Bluetooth) to an iPhone, allowing the information that's collected to be transferred to the smartphone and imported directly into a wide range of compatible apps. Because cyclists can benefit from having different types of information at their disposal than runners or other fitness enthusiasts, specialized apps have become available specifically for cyclists (see Figure 8.2).

FIGURE 8.2

If you're already using a compatible bike computer, you can wear your iPhone (shown here), mount it on the bike, or even keep it in a pocket, yet still collect important data in real time.

BIKING APPS FOR FITNESS ENTHUSIASTS

As you're about to discover, cyclists can use the iPhone in several extremely handy ways. For example, you can use it as a full-featured GPS navigational tool to help navigate busy streets more easily (and safely), and find your way along designated bike routes or paths. The iPhone (and in some cases the Apple Watch) can also handle much of the functionality you typically find offered by a dedicated bike computer, or share data with an existing bike computer.

This section focuses on a handful of specialized iPhone (and Apple Watch) apps for cyclists, particularly those who enjoy cycling as a fitness-oriented activity or competitive sport.

> **! CAUTION** Many of the specialized apps for cyclists use the iPhone's GPS capabilities. For this feature to work, the iPhone needs to use a significant amount of cellular data usage via a 3G/4G/LTE data connection. Extended use of the iPhone's GPS and Location Services functions also depletes the phone's battery much faster.
>
> Thus, you'll want to begin each ride with a fully charged iPhone battery, and expect that you'll probably need to recharge the phone after a long ride.

CYCLEMETER GPS

Cyclemeter GPS for the iPhone and Apple Watch is a free app with in-app purchase options that's designed to be a full-featured bike and fitness computer that does not require a companion online account to function properly. All data is stored on the iPhone (or can be transferred to a computer or iCloud at the user's discretion). Cyclemeter GPS is also compatible with a variety of popular dedicated bike computers, including the RFLKT+, which you'll learn about later in this chapter.

> **✓ TIP** The Cyclemeter GPS app works best if you mount your iPhone directly onto your bike, so you can easily view it while you ride. Use it instead of or in addition to a dedicated bike computer, depending on what type of data you want to collect.

This app can handle GPS navigation, and is designed from the ground up to cater to the needs of cyclists. For example, not only does the app display information, it can generate 120 different and configurable audible announcements while it's in use, so without looking at a screen, you can obtain real-time information, such as current speed, average speed, fastest speed, calories burned, distance traveled, elevation, and/or heart rate.

If you mount the iPhone onto a bike for easy viewing, the app's main dashboard screen, shown in Figure 8.3, displays pertinent information in a color-coded and easy-to-read format that makes it easy to quickly glance at the screen while riding to obtain important information.

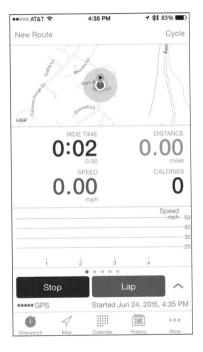

FIGURE 8.3

The dashboard screen of the Cyclemeter GPS app.

Beyond what the main dashboard screen displays, additional information screens are always only one horizontal finger swipe away, and you can configure all the data that appears on each screen to see only the real-time information that you deem relevant.

In addition to displaying information, Cyclemeter GPS gathers and records relevant data you can use for analysis later. (Some of these tools, which include History Dashboards and Historic Key Performance Indicators, Google Maps integration, and Weather Recording, require upgrading to the Elite version of the app.) For navigation, the app offers full integration with Google Maps, so you can view terrain and traffic details on your route (which you can pre-plan).

Another nice feature of this app is that you can display some real-time information, such as speed and heart rate, as colorful graphs. Also, a customizable stopwatch feature automatically detects when the bike starts and stops.

You control the app not only from the iPhone's touch screen, but you can also display and control many of the functions, including the stopwatch, from the Apple Watch. Use of the Apple Watch with this app requires users to upgrade to the ad-free, Elite version.

> **TIP** Thanks to the app's integration with the Music app, from the Cyclemeter GPS app on the iPhone, you can control the music that's played and access pre-created playlists, while simultaneously hearing audible announcements the Cyclemeter GPS app generates.

You can access and customize all the app's features and functions by tapping on one of the five command icons that appear along the bottom of the iPhone app's screen. These include:

- **Stopwatch:** This default option displays the app's main dashboard (which is customizable), and allows you to view a map and real-time information, such as Ride Time, Distance, Speed, and Calories Burned. Tap on the Start button to start the stopwatch feature. You'll then gain access to Lap and Stop buttons. The app automatically records all time-related data.

- **Map:** View a full-screen version of the navigation map, and then customize it by tapping on the gear-shaped Settings icon in the top-right corner.

- **Calendar:** The app enables you to maintain a schedule of upcoming workouts, events, races, or other information that's pertinent to your cycling activities and fitness schedule.

- **History:** Choose from a variety of formats to view all data the app has collected. Several formatting buttons appear along the top of the screen. This feature becomes more useful for analytical purposes, for example, as you continue using the app and collect data over time.

- **More:** Tap on this icon to view a detailed menu of options to customize the app, access additional features, and display information from the app in a variety of different formats.

> **TIP** The first time you use the app, tap on the More icon, and then tap on the Settings option. As prompted, enter details about yourself, such as your gender, birthdate, and weight. If you've upgraded to the Elite version of the app, also enter your Bike and Shoe information (to keep track of your gear), and turn on integration with the iPhone's Health app. You need to turn on or adjust these settings only once, but you can update them at any time from the Settings menu.

The main dashboard screen appears when you tap on the Stopwatch option. However, before you start riding, tap on the Cycle option in the top-right corner of the screen to select the most appropriate mode for your upcoming activity. Options include Cycle (for general bike rides), Cycle for Distance, Cycle for Time, Cycle Intervals, or Mountain Bike.

> **TIP** To customize the dashboard and the information it displays, after launching the app, tap on the Stopwatch option. Tap on the up arrow icon ("∧") to the right of the Start button, and then tap on the Pages option.
>
> To personalize the information and Main Overview screen of the dashboard, tap on the Main Overview option, and then tap on the +/Edit option in the top-right corner. Repeat this process for each of the dashboard pages, and if you choose, create additional pages. Then when you're riding and using the app, you can switch between these page displays by swiping your finger sideways.

Cyclemeter GPS is an advertiser-supported app. Thus, banner ads display on the screen while the app is in use, and periodically, a pop-up window with a short commercial video appears onscreen.

By paying $4.99 per year (via an in-app purchase), you can upgrade to the Elite version of Cyclemeter GPS, which removes the ads and unlocks many additional features, like Apple Watch compatibility, the ability to view terrain maps (via Google Maps), automatically record weather conditions, track biometrics (when you use the appropriate sensors), and log relevant data the iPhone's Health app collects.

> **TIP** You can also use Cyclemeter GPS indoors with a stationary bike, spin bike, bike trainer, treadmill, or other home workout equipment. Just tap on the Stopwatch icon, tap on the up arrow icon ("∧"), and then scroll down and turn on the Indoors option. Be sure to turn this feature off again when you go back to riding a regular bike outside.

MAPMYRIDE+ GPS CYCLING AND ROUTE TRACKING

You've already learned about the MapMyRun and MapMyWalk apps from Chapter 7, "Explore Fitness Solutions for Walkers, Joggers, and Runners." The MapMyFitness company (www.maymyfitness.com) developed both the MapMyRide app (free) and the premium MapMyRide+ app ($2.99). All the apps in this family have a similar user interface, but cater to specific activities.

To fully use the MapMyRide app (shown in Figure 8.4), you must set up a free MapMyFitness online account, which also grants you access to the vast online community of fellow MapMyRide users.

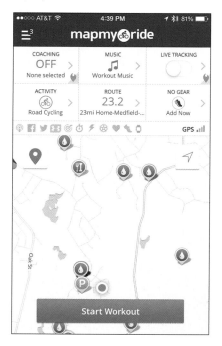

FIGURE 8.4

Use the MapMyRide+ app for navigation, and to collect, track, and analyze fitness-related data of interest to cyclists.

The core functionality of this app is based on planning, tracking, and recording the routes you take while biking. At the same time, the app gathers and tracks a wide range of real-time data, based on what optional equipment (such as an optional bike computer) you have linked to the app.

> **TIP** If you already have a MapMyFitness online account for one of the company's other apps, you can use that same account information with MapMyRide. Just log in to the app with your existing email address and password.

MapMyRide is compatible with more than 400 bike computers, fitness/activity trackers, and other optional data-gathering equipment, and can pull data from these wirelessly connected devices and incorporate it with the real-time navigation information provided by the app. What data is collected and shared with the iPhone is based on which optional bike computer is linked with the app.

As the MapMyRide app gathers data, it can also share it with the iPhone's Health app and other compatible apps, although to use many of the analytical features in the MapMyRide app, you need to upgrade to a paid MVP membership.

> **TIP** One advantage of paying for an MVP membership for the MapMyRide app is that you can participate in Challenges with or against other people from the online-based MapMyFitness community. An MVP membership costs $5.99 per month, or $29.99 per year, and it unlocks a variety of features that you can use for training and live tracking. Virtual mobile coaching is offered as a premium feature, for example.

While you use the MapMyRide app, the main dashboard screen displays a detailed map that shows your current location and can also highlight your intended route (and provide real-time directions to your destinations), and/or it can display where you've been. Details, such as your speed, distance traveled, time, and calories burned, simultaneously appear on the screen.

> **TIP** Perhaps the most popular feature of the MapMyRide app is the vast database of more than 70 million pre-planned routes you can access. Using your iPhone's GPS, the app can detect your current location, and then recommend nearby routes based on your intended goals. You can sort routes by location, length, or level of difficulty, for example.
>
> You can access route information not only from the app, but also from the MapMyRide website (www.mapmyride.com). From either this site or the app, you can also create your own route(s), and/or choose to share them with the online community.

RUNTASTIC ROAD BIKE PRO

Free and paid ($4.99) versions of the Runtastic Road Bike Pro app, shown in Figure 8.5, are available from the App Store. Runtastic developed both app versions as well as the extremely popular Runtastic app for runners (which you learned about in Chapter 7). Designed for cyclists, the Runtastic Road Bike Pro app was created together with road bike experts. It transforms the iPhone into a feature-packed GPS cycling computer.

FIGURE 8.5

The Runtastic Road Bike Pro app serves as a bike computer and navigational tool, while also collecting and tracking fitness-related information about the rider.

Using the iPhone's built-in GPS capabilities, the app can automatically track and record routes traveled, while at the same time collect distance, duration, speed, elevation gain, pace, and calories burned data, and other pertinent real-time information. The app can also gather traffic, weather, wind, and terrain details pertaining to a specified route.

As you would expect, you can custom configure the app's main dashboard to display only the real-time information you're interested in, although the app continues to monitor and record other data in the background.

> **☑ TIP**   Using optional hardware, such as a fitness/activity tracker or a stand-alone heart rate monitor, you can also monitor and record real-time heart rate data during each bike ride.
>
> As of Summer 2015, the app did not yet support Apple Watch, but it does support the Pebble and Pebble Time smartwatches, and a wide range of other popular fitness/activity trackers.

Real-time data always prominently appears on the screen during a ride, but you can also hear a voice coach reciting this information. At the end of a ride, the app offers detailed post-tour analysis. On this report, you'll see information including distance traveled (uphill, on flat terrain, and on downhill terrain), duration of the trip, maximum speed, calories burned, average pace, and average speed.

Like the MapMyRide app, Runtastic Road Bike Pro and its related website (www.runtastic.com) offer an ever-growing database of recommended bike routes. To get the most out of this app, mount your iPhone directly on your bike. You can do this using any optional casing and mount, although Runtastic offers its own Runtastic Bike Case for iPhone ($49.99) for this purpose.

Also available from the Runtastic online store (www.runtastic.com/shop/usa) is a selection of optional sensors that work with the Runtastic Road Bike Pro app for collecting, displaying, and recording real-time data beyond what the iPhone can do on its own. For example, the Runtastic Speed & Cadence Sensor ($59.99) transforms the iPhone into a professional cycling computer that can record speed, cadence, GPS position, distance, altitude, and other data.

You attach this optional sensor directly to your bike, and it can also work with the company's optional Runtastic Heart Rate Combo Monitor (sold separately for $69.99). You wear this Bluetooth-compatible heart rate monitor around your chest, and it shares real-time data with the Runtastic Road Bike Pro app and the iPhone's Health app.

After you set up the Runtastic Road Bike Pro app and get it operational, the on-screen dashboard displays a lot of real-time information, but unlike other apps, much of this data is not color-coded, so you'll need to familiarize yourself with the dashboard layout to be able to understand the information at a quick glance. To access the dashboard, tap on the Session icon at the bottom of the screen.

> **☑ TIP** To customize the Voice Feedback you receive during a ride, from the dashboard, tap on the Voice icon (in the top-right corner of the map). Turn on the Enabled option to activate the Voice Feedback feature, and then use the onscreen controls to adjust the volume, to have the music pause during an announcement, and to choose the voice used.
>
> Under the Include in Feedback heading are a handful of options that allow you to determine exactly what information the Voice Feedback feature will share during a ride. Turn on or off each option's virtual switch to fully customize this feature.

If you're using the free version of the app, banner ads appear near the bottom of the screen between the dashboard display and the app's main command icons. Upgrading to the paid version of the app removes these ads.

The first time you launch the app, be sure to tap on the Settings icon that appears at the bottom of the screen, and then from the Settings menu, tap on each feature to adjust the various options and personalize the app to best meet your needs.

STRAVA RUNNING AND CYCLING

Offering a somewhat slicker-looking dashboard screen than its competition, the free Strava Running and Cycling app for the iPhone is also compatible with the Apple Watch (see Figure 8.6). This app offers many of the same features and functions as the other cycling apps covered in this chapter, in that it allows you to track your rides in real time using your iPhone's GPS capabilities, while also collecting useful data about your trip (such as distance, pace, speed, elevation gained, and calories burned) and biometric data (like your heart rate).

> **☑ TIP** You must use the Strava Running and Cycling app with the Apple Watch, an optional fitness tracker, and/or a dedicated bike computer, for example, to monitor and track your heart rate, power and cadence data, and some other information. You can share all data the app collects (with whatever optional equipment the app is linked with via the iPhone) with the iPhone's Health app and other compatible health and fitness-related apps.

FIGURE 8.6

The Strava Running and Cycling app for the iPhone and Apple Watch is another powerful tool designed for cyclists and runners alike.

The Strava Running and Cycling app has a strong focus on social interaction. You can create a profile for yourself, and then share details about your rides with others via the Internet and participate in competitive challenges. Thus, you need to set up a free online account to use this app. The first time you use the app, if you're a cyclist, be sure to tap on the Cycling option when asked to select your primary sport. This app also offers a comprehensive set of tools for runners.

After the app launches, using it is extremely straightforward. When you're ready to begin recording a ride, tap on the Record icon at the bottom of the screen, tap on the large Record button that then appears near the bottom center of the screen, and start riding.

When you finish the ride, tap on the checkered-flag Finish icon. You can then either save your ride data by tapping on the Save option, or discard the ride data by tapping on the Trash icon.

At any time, tap on the Profile icon to add information to your personal profile, which you can share with the app's online community. Sharing your profile is particularly important if you plan to participate in the organized Challenges (which you can do by tapping on the Challenges icon).

Prior to starting a ride, you can access the Strava website (www.strava.com/routes/new) to create a route to follow, or select from a pre-created route in your area. At any time while you're riding, tap on the Map option (near the top-right corner of the screen) to view a detailed, real-time map.

> **NOTE** To unlock some of the app's more advanced features, you need to upgrade to the Premium version of the app for $5.99 per month or $59.99 per year.

USING THE WAHOO FITNESS RFLKT+ BIKE COMPUTER

Although your iPhone can collect and gather certain types of data on its own, when it comes to cycling, to acquire and track a broader range of data in an accurate way, you'll probably want to connect a dedicated bike computer to your bike. Be sure to select a bike computer that can communicate and share data wirelessly with your iPhone.

Wahoo Fitness offers two dedicated bike computers, the RFLKT ($99.99) and RFLKT+ ($129.99), both of which are available from the company's website (www.wahoofitness.com/devices/rflkt.html). Figure 8.7 shows the RFLKT+. As you can see, it features its own display, is waterproof, and can easily mount to any bicycle.

FIGURE 8.7

The RFLKT+ is a dedicated bike computer that can wirelessly share information with the iPhone.

These computers have their own built-in sensors and GPS capabilities that allow users to collect more comprehensive data (including cycling speed, cadence, and distance data) related to their rides, compared to using the iPhone alone for data collection and tracking purposes.

What's nice about these dedicated bike computers is that they're fully compatible with many popular cycling apps, including Cyclemeter GPS, MapMyRide, Strava Running and Cycling, and the Wahoo company's own Wahoo Fitness app.

> **NOTE** Wahoo Fitness also offers the optional Blue SC Speed and Cadence Sensor ($59.00) and RPM Cadence Sensor ($49.99), which are sold separately, and that enable you to collect and share cycling speed, cadence, and distance data with the iPhone, without using a dedicated bike computer. You can also use the optional TICKR Heart Rate Monitor ($59.99) or TICKR X Workout Tracker with Memory ($99.99) to monitor and gather real-time heart rate data during a ride.

For anyone who is serious about cycling for fitness or competition, using one of the RFLKT dedicated bike computers with a compatible cycling app on the iPhone offers a comprehensive toolset that can collect, display, analyze, store, and potentially share data.

Just as a fitness/activity tracker enhances the iPhone's data collection during your run, workout, or other fitness-oriented activity, using the iPhone with a dedicated bike computer allows your iPhone to track data of particular interest to cyclists.

Other companies that offer powerful bike computers include:

- **Cateye Strada:** www.cateye.com
- **Garmin:** www.garmin.com
- **Sigma Sport:** http://sigmasport.com/us/produkte/bikecomputer
- **Timex:** www.timex.com/sport

You can purchase these bike computers and others like them online, from bike specialty retail stores, and sporting goods stores (like REI).

> **TIP** The RFLKT bike computers are stand-alone devices that can gather and share data, so they have their own display and mount on your bike. However, you can mirror the same displayed information (in full color) on the iPhone's screen. By having two screens mounted on your bike (one from the RFLKT and one from the iPhone) instead of having the same data displayed on both screens, the computer and iPhone can use the same data, but display different information on each screen as it's being collected in real time. You can also just keep the iPhone in a jersey pocket or case, and not actually mount it on the bike.

NAVIGATING SAFELY WITH THE HAMMERHEAD ONE

Released in May 2015, the Hammerhead One ($85.00) is a navigational tool that connects to any bicycle. As you can see from Figure 8.8, it uses GPS information from the iPhone (via a Bluetooth connection), but shows where to go and what turns to make using simple, color-coded LED lights instead of complex maps.

FIGURE 8.8

Instead of displaying complex maps that can distract a cyclist, the Hammerhead One uses colorful LED lights to display navigation information that originates from the iPhone.

Using the proprietary iPhone app exclusively for use with the Hammerhead One device, you can plan a route, and then put your iPhone away in a pocket. The iPhone then communicates with the Hammerhead One wirelessly, and displays navigation information in a simple way that you can use day or night, and in any weather condition. To get to where you're going, you simply follow the lights as you're riding.

Thanks to the active online community that supports the Hammerhead One, a growing number of pre-planned bike routes are available, or you can easily plan your own route by choosing a start and finish location, as well as any waypoints in between.

The iPhone app then serves as a traditional GPS system, displaying a detailed map, with your current location, as well as information about your speed, distance to go, and distance traveled. However, while you're riding, you can place the iPhone in sleep mode and put it in a pocket.

Looking at detailed maps when trying to ride a bike, particularly in a city or on busy roads, can be dangerous. This is where the Hammerhead One is useful. It shows you where to go and warns you of changing terrain and upcoming turns, using colored lights that don't take your focus away from the road ahead or the traffic you're alongside.

NOTE The Hammerhead One provides comprehensive GPS and navigation functionality to cyclists without compromising their safety. This device does not track fitness-related data. It's simply a navigational tool that allows you to preplan a route, and then travel toward that destination without having to look at your iPhone's screen while en route.

Currently, the Hammerhead One is available exclusively from the company's website (http://hammerhead.io). The product was designed by cycling enthusiasts, and ultimately funded thanks to a crowd-funding campaign supported by more than 4,000 cyclists from around the world.

ESTABLISH A MIND/BODY CONNECTION

An important part of maintaining a healthy body is also having a happy and healthy mind. For some people, staying positive, happy, and relaxed as they go through their everyday lives comes naturally. But for many, especially among those who lead stressful lives, staying happy, relaxed, and calm is an ongoing challenge (see Figure 9.1).

Although some people must turn to prescription medications as a necessary fix for their anxiety, stress, and/or depression, others might want to first pursue the medication-free alternatives that are available.

FIGURE 9.1

Working out regularly helps you tone your body and stay physically fit; however, you can also do some things to fine-tune your emotional well-being.

This chapter takes a look at a handful of iPhone and Apple Watch apps—many of which rely on proven research and therapeutic techniques—that help people establish a healthy mind/body connection without the use of medications.

> **NOTE** Research indicates that 40 million people in the U.S. will experience an impairment because of an anxiety condition in 2015, but only four million of those people will receive treatment, and of those, a mere 400,000 will receive proper treatment. Meanwhile, Paxil and Zoloft, both antianxiety medications, continue to be among the top prescribed medications in the United States.
>
> Given that, it's no surprise that one in ten Americans over the age of 12 currently takes a prescribed antidepressant. Each popular antianxiety and antidepressant drug represents a multibillion dollar industry for the pharmaceutical companies. For example, according to WebMD, in 2014 alone, Ambilify (an antidepressant) represented a $7.2 billion business.

> **!CAUTION** Although the iPhone and Apple Watch apps described in this chapter might be able to help you manage anxiety, stress, depression, and other conditions that keep you from living a happy and healthy life, seeking out professional guidance as needed from a doctor, psychiatrist, or a licensed psychologist to help you identify, diagnose, and treat your specific symptoms or problem is essential.
>
> If you're having suicidal thoughts, or think you might hurt yourself or others, call 9-1-1, go to any hospital emergency room, or call the National Suicide Prevention Lifeline at (800) 273-8255. You can also visit www.suicidepreventionlifeline.org using any Internet-connected computer or mobile device.

IMPROVE YOUR MOOD WITH AN APP

For some people, being happy is all about putting themselves in the right state of mind. Learning how to do this is a skill, but after you acquire the right skill set, it's often something that you can do on your own, when needed. Three apps that can teach you the skills needed to help you control your mood and state of mind, particularly when confronted with stress or other emotional challenges, are Happify, Happier, and Calm (the latter of which is covered later in this chapter).

USE THE HAPPIFY APP TO BECOME MORE POSITIVE

Based on more than a decade's worth of research, Happify, shown in Figure 9.2, uses interactive multimedia content, including games and video instruction, to teach life-changing habits associated with reducing stress and leading a happier and healthier life (from a mental health standpoint).

The goals of Happify are to help you conquer negativity, elevate optimism, re-pattern stress, overcome fear, and potentially fix relationship issues. When you first launch the app, it asks you a series of questions relating to yourself, your lifestyle, and your overall happiness. Next, it asks you to set up a free Happify online-based account, which means providing your name and email address and creating an account password.

You then need to choose whether to use the Happify app in Private Mode or Community Mode. Private Mode keeps your profile and all of your information private, whereas Community Mode enables you to interact with other Happify users through an established online community.

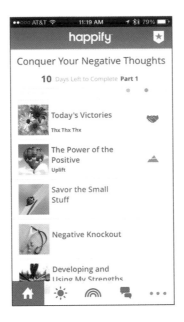

FIGURE 9.2

The Happify app offers a comprehensive toolset to help you adopt a more positive mindset as you work toward overcoming stress, depression, or other mental health issues.

Based on how you respond to the preliminary questionnaire (see Figure 9.3), the app then creates a Recommended Track for you to follow. This includes having you participate in a series of app-based courses, most of which are designed to be completed within one week each, and require a time commitment of only 5 to 15 minutes per day.

FIGURE 9.3

As the Happify app walks you through its preliminary questionnaire, be sure to answer each question honestly so the app can best adapt itself to your needs.

The Happify app also includes the tools needed to create a digital Journal. Using text and photos you take with your device's camera, you're encouraged to create journal entries on a regular basis, and put into practice the skills you acquire from participating in each app-based course.

The Journal part of the app has key categories (see Figure 9.4), including Savor, Thank, Aspire, Give, Empathize, and Recommended, and each walks you through the journal entry creating process by asking you leading questions, or by offering challenges.

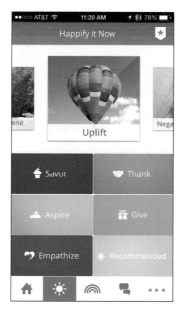

FIGURE 9.4

Happify walks you through the journal creation process and makes logging your thoughts, experiences, and emotions in a secure and private way easy to do.

For example, while creating a journal entry, you might see an instruction like, "Think of something, great or small, that you feel grateful for and describe it in a few words. And add a photo too!" Also, part of each day's learning experience often involves participating in some type of simple game that helps you identify and manage your thoughts or emotions (see Figure 9.5).

As well as being able to do the interactive lessons and maintain a journal using the app, you can access articles and online content (when your iPhone is connected to the Internet) that's directly relevant to what you're currently working on.

FIGURE 9.5

This is one of many constructive, yet simple games built in to the Happify app to get you in touch with your thoughts or feelings faster.

By tapping on the Community icon, you can easily find and interact with other Happify users in real time to share experiences, seek out inspiration, and give or receive support.

Happify provides the initial courses for free; however, available as in-app purchases are an ever-growing selection of Premium courses that offer more specialized and advanced teachings related to specific areas. Each course is created and hosted by a therapist, doctor, or specialist in their field.

Accessing the Premium content directly from the Happify app requires a paid subscription, which ranges in price from $4.99 to $11.99 per month, depending on the number of months you commit to.

Overall, Happify offers extremely well-produced content packaged and presented in a nicely designed and easy-to-use iPhone app.

USE HAPPIER'S COMPREHENSIVE TOOLSET TO ACHIEVE HAPPINESS

Happier is similar to Happify in that it combines how-to videos featuring experts (see Figure 9.6), informative interactive content, and online information into a single iPhone app (that also has an Apple Watch component). In addition to helping you track your mood throughout the day, Happier includes the tools you need to create and maintain a gratitude journal.

FIGURE 9.6

Using Happier involves watching a short video, doing a tiny bit of reading, and engaging in some type of constructive activity.

At the core of this app are a series of interactive courses that teach you skills related to overcoming stress, improving your mood, and changing the way you think about life and the challenges or obstacles you encounter. What's nice is that you can tackle one course at a time, with a minimal daily time commitment, and pick and choose only courses you think will be relevant and helpful to your own life.

Each course is divided into a series of short daily lessons (see Figure 9.7). In addition to a series of free courses in the app, you can purchase premium courses separately (as in-app purchases) that range in price from $4.99 to $24.99. These additional courses teach skills such as meditation, yoga, how to reduce everyday stress, and how to improve your overall attitude.

Like Happify, the Happier app has an online-based community element, and features a colorful, easy-to-navigate interface that makes using each of the app's courses and tools a straightforward process. You use the instructional and interactive elements in the Happier app for just a few minutes each day, so the time commitment is minimal, but the potential benefits of using the app consistently are significant.

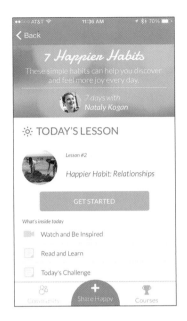

FIGURE 9.7
Each daily lesson takes less than 15 minutes to complete.

GET THERAPY ONLINE VIA AN APP

If you decide that speaking with a psychiatrist or psychologist on a regular basis to help you work through some emotional issues or deal with your anxiety or depression might be advantageous, but you don't have time to meet with someone in person or lack health insurance to cover the high cost, then the less expensive, iPhone-based solutions might help.

Using text messaging and video calling, with the right app, your iPhone can put you in touch with a licensed and certified psychiatrist or psychologist, so you can participate in a live therapy session from virtually anywhere your smartphone has an Internet connection. Depending on the app, an ongoing monthly fee for the service, or a "per session" fee will apply.

> **NOTE** Although these apps work with licensed mental health professionals, few accept health insurance, so the cost of your virtual therapy will be an out-of-pocket expense.

Some of the iPhone apps that allow you to engage in "remote therapy" include the following:

- **Talkspace Therapy:** Communicate with a licensed therapist via text messaging from your iPhone. The service is private and anonymous, and the cost is $29.99 per week to use the one-on-one chat feature.

- **Doctor On Demand:** Engage in a video call with a board-certified physician or doctorate-level psychologist directly from your iPhone. Although this app has no ongoing subscription fees, the cost per "visit" is $40.00.

- **Amwell: Live Doctor Visit:** Available 24/7 with no appointment needed, this app offers instant, live video call connections (see Figure 9.8) with board certified doctors and therapists, as well as nutritionists. One nice feature of this app is that you can choose to give the medical specialist you communicate with access to data stored in your iPhone's Health app, so if you're working with a nutritionist, for example, that person can view details about your diet, food intake, and exercise history. If you consult with a doctor, he or she has the ability to write prescriptions that can be sent directly to your local pharmacy to be filled. This app charges a flat fee of $49.00 per visit.

FIGURE 9.8

Using your iPhone's video call capabilities, use the Amwell: Live Doctor Visit app to speak with a doctor, psychologist, or nutritionist at your convenience.

! CAUTION One drawback to using some of the apps for communicating live with a therapist or doctor is that you can't always speak with the same person if you seek out multiple virtual sessions or visits. Thus, if you're looking for ongoing therapy sessions, choose an app that allows you to pick your therapist, and then schedule recurring appointments with that person.

☑ TIP If you currently work with a therapist, the free Therapy Buddy app for the iPhone allows you to record your therapy appointments, compose a "Helpful Takeaway" for each session, create a homework assignment task list, set an alert reminder for your next appointment, and (in between appointments) maintain a list of topics you want to discuss during your next session.

RELAX WITH THE CALM APP

Many apps can walk you through the process of meditating, for example, but the Calm app shown in Figure 9.9 offers a one-week course for beginners via the iPhone that teaches you the basics of mindful meditation.

FIGURE 9.9

Learn to use meditation to help you control your emotions and stress level using the Calm app. As you listen to each guided (audio) meditation, an animated scene displays on your iPhone's screen.

The Calm app also includes seven guided meditations (each of which you can customize) that last between 2 and 30 minutes each (see Figure 9.10). As the app guides you through these meditations via audio, the iPhone's screen displays beautiful and tranquil nature scenes. The app also includes more than a dozen original music tracks for when you meditate on your own.

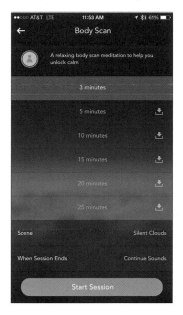

FIGURE 9.10

Choose the focus of the meditation you want to experience, its duration, and the animated scene you want displayed on the iPhone's screen.

In addition to its free content and instruction, the Calm app provides premium content (which you pay for through in-app purchases) that includes a total of 50 guided meditations that have specific focuses, such as improving creativity, energy, confidence, or sleep. Instead of the free *7 Days of Calm* course, premium users can take advantage of the *21 Days of Calm* course, which delves much deeper into teaching you the skills needed for successful meditation.

Subscription options for the premium content cost $9.99 per month, or $49.99 per year.

> **TIP** After you learn the skills required to successfully meditate, you can use the Calm app's built-in music tracks, sound generation tool, and meditation timer anytime and anywhere you want to meditate on your own.

Other apps that teach beginners how to meditate, using live-action video, audio narration, and/or animated graphic content on the iPhone, include

- How To Meditate with Pema Chödrön ($15.99)
- How To Meditate: Discover Different Types of Meditation ($0.99)
- How To Meditate: Learn Meditation & Mindfulness ($0.99)
- How To Meditate: Ultimate Guide ($0.99)
- Meditation & Mind Training: Relax & Reduce Stress ($3.99)
- Meditation Spa (Free, with in-app purchases available)
- OMG. I Can Meditate! (Free, with in-app purchases available)

> **TIP** If you already know the basics of how to meditate, but you want to use your iPhone to experience guided meditations that include music and tranquil sound effects, a bunch of specialized apps are available for this purpose. To find them, enter the word, "Meditation" into the App Store's Search field.
>
> Some of the available apps include Relax Melodies Oriental Meditation, Take A Break!—Guided Meditations for Stress Relief, Simply Being—Guided Meditations for Relaxation, and Stop, Breathe & Think. The majority of these and other guided meditation apps are either paid apps, or have in-app purchases for accessing specific guided meditation programs.

TRY A YOGA APP TO HELP YOU STAY CENTERED

Many people take up yoga as a way to help them stay physically fit and also achieve a mind/body connection. The great thing about yoga is that it requires minimal space and equipment, so even the busiest of people can find time to participate in a yoga session at home, in a hotel room, at a park (shown in Figure 9.11), or at a gym or yoga studio.

Although a number of apps are available for absolute beginners that teach the basics of yoga, you might find it more advantageous to take a few classes or participate in yoga sessions taught by a trained professional first, so you learn how to correctly do the various poses to avoid accidently getting injured. A human instructor can correct your poses based on what he or she sees, but a yoga app on your iPhone can't.

FIGURE 9.11

Thanks to the iPhone and Apple Watch, you can participate in guided yoga sessions or video-based yoga instruction whenever and wherever it's convenient, including at a local park.

> **☑ TIP** To find discounted yoga classes or sessions in your hometown (or almost anywhere in the United States), consider installing the Groupon or LivingSocial app onto your iPhone. These apps pinpoint your current location, and help you discover sales or promotions being offered by local businesses, such as restaurants, day spas, salons, fitness centers/gyms, and yoga studios.
>
> The offers change daily. For example, you can often discover invitations to participate in a free introductory yoga or fitness class, or save up to 75 percent off of multi-class/session bundles.

After you learn the yoga basics, you can use one of a handful of iPhone apps that offer video- and audio-based yoga sessions that feature instructor guidance. All you need to do is watch your iPhone's screen and follow along.

LEARN PILATES WITH AN APP

In addition to the yoga apps you find in the App Store, you can also find apps that teach Pilates.

For example, the Perfect Pilates Body with Andrea Speir app (free with in-app purchase options) uses live-action video, computer animations, and audio narration to teach Pilates to beginners, and also guide more advanced users through customized sessions.

Beginners should tap on the Poses icon at the bottom of the screen to see a photo and description of each pose used in a specific lesson. This helps prepare you to understand and properly do each required pose (see Figure 9.12).

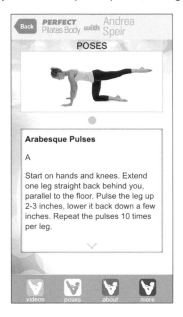

FIGURE 9.12

Before participating in each video-based lesson, use the Poses feature of the app to learn the required individual pose.

The Pilates Body with Andrea Speir app offers 10 different optional sessions (each sold separately for $2.99) that focus on specific areas of the body (see Figure 9.13).

Meanwhile, the Yoga & Pilates with Kristen McGee app (free with in-app purchase options) uses live-action video, audio narration, and other interactive multimedia content to present a series of 10-minute workouts. Specialized classes that cater to specific body areas are available as in-app purchases for $2.99 each.

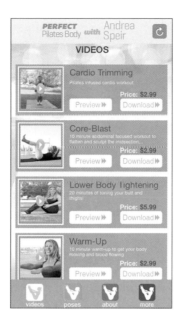

FIGURE 9.13

Each lesson is sold separately as an in-app purchase. After you purchase a lesson, you can watch it as often as you want for no additional charge.

> **✓ TIP**   To find more Pilates apps that offer instruction or guided workout sessions (or both), visit the App Store, and enter **Pilates** in the Search field. You can search for other specialty workout or fitness apps as well.

> **✎ NOTE**   Both the Perfect Pilates Body with Andrea Speir and Yoga & Pilates with Kristen McGee offer self-paced tutorials for learning each pose or move, and then include fully guided, video-based sessions.

JOIN YOGA EXPERT TARA STILES IN GUIDED YOGA SESSIONS

FitStar Yoga (shown in Figure 9.14) uses live-action HD video (featuring Strala Yoga founder Tara Stiles), audio, and multimedia content to provide a yoga teacher whenever and wherever you need one.

FIGURE 9.14

FitStar Yoga is a best-selling yoga app offered for the iPhone and Apple Watch. It's compatible with many popular fitness/activity trackers as well.

This particular app is for people with any body type; offers Beginner, Intermediate, Advanced, and Expert-level instruction; and custom tailors complete yoga sessions to your skill level and past performance.

> **! CAUTION** When you begin using the FitStar Yoga app, choose the appropriate experience level for yourself, and then be very honest when providing feedback about each session. Otherwise, you could wind up attempting poses and exercises that your body isn't ready for, which could result in injury.
>
> FitStar Yoga and apps like it enable you to practice yoga anywhere and anytime it's convenient, but you'll still want to dress in comfortable and appropriate attire. The FitStar Yoga app also recommends using a yoga mat, but this is optional.

> **TIP** The Fitbit and Jawbone UP fitness/activity trackers and apps such as the popular MyFitnessPal app are compatible with the FitStar Yoga app. As a result, the FitStar Yoga app can import data (such as your weight) from compatible apps, and as you complete sessions, export your accomplishments and related stats (such as calories burned during a yoga session) to compatible apps (including the iPhone's Health app) for more streamlined tracking of your overall activity.
>
> The first time you launch the FitStar Yoga app, from the Create Your Profile screen, tap on the Register with Fitbit option. Otherwise, select either the Register option (to create a profile using your email address), or the Register with Facebook option (to create a profile using details from your existing Facebook account).

Part of the account setup process also involves providing the app with your name, and if you choose, including a photo (avatar) within your profile. You can also turn on/off Notifications related to the app. According to FitStar, "Users that receive notifications are over 1.8 times more likely to work out." If you want the app to be able to generate and display Notifications that remind you when to use it, tap on the Okay button. Otherwise, tap on the Ask Later button.

The next step involves participating in a 19-minute yoga session that walks you through a handful of basic yoga poses. This is a video-based program you should actively follow along with. Based on your self-evaluated performance during this sample session, the app can better cater to your skill level in the future.

> **TIP** FitStar Yoga requires continuous Internet access to load content as you're using the app. Although a cellular data connection can work, content loads faster using a Wi-Fi connection.

Prior to starting each session, if you're a Premium (paid) user, you'll be able to customize the duration and intensity of that session when viewing a preview screen for it.

The goal of each customized session is to demonstrate each pose, allow you to follow along at your own pace, and then smoothly transition you into the next pose. At any time, if the app asks you to do a pose that's too difficult, you should tap the icon in the lower-right corner of the screen (see Figure 9.15). When you tap on this icon, it turns red, indicating that you believe the pose is currently too difficult. Based on this feedback, future sessions will automatically better cater to your skill level.

FIGURE 9.15
Paying attention to each pose demonstration and copying it to the best of your ability is important. Unfortunately, there's no human instructor to correct you if you do something wrong.

To pause a session, and/or provide more detailed feedback during a session, tap on the middle of the screen (shown in Figure 9.16). While a session is paused, you can also adjust the music and see a summary of the poses to be included in your current session.

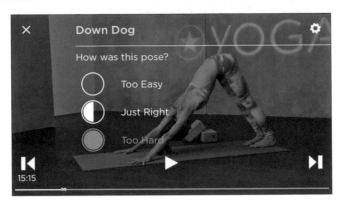

FIGURE 9.16

When you pause the video during a pose, you can rate it as Too Easy, Just Right, or Too Hard with a single tap on the screen.

You can also provide feedback at the end of each session. If you rank poses as being too easy, the app increases the challenge in the future. However, if you rate poses as too difficult, subsequent lessons are simplified, but focus on helping you improve your skill level and flexibility over time.

In addition to following the live-action video on your iPhone, you can also simultaneously display content related to each pose on the Apple Watch (see Figure 9.17). At the time of this writing, this content was still photos demonstrating each pose, but thanks to new programming tools being offered to app developers, this feature will be upgraded to include live-action video on the Apple Watch in late 2015 or early 2016.

Instead of using the iPhone exclusively, the Apple Watch makes your yoga session even more portable. You can view a pose on your Apple Watch's screen and then replicate it as part of your personalized Yoga session.

> **TIP**   Apple Watch users will appreciate the convenience of being able to provide quick feedback related to poses during each session by tapping on the Too Easy, Too Hard, or Just Right icon that appears on the watch face, instead of on the iPhone's screen.

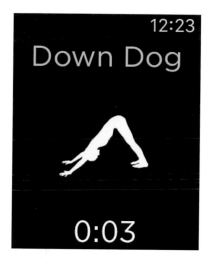

FIGURE 9.17

Instead of looking at your iPhone's screen, you can use an Apple Watch to view a graphic of the pose and a timer indicating how long to hold the pose.

The basic FitStar Yoga app is available for free. A paid subscription to Premium content is available as an in-app purchase. The monthly rate is $7.99, and an annual subscription runs at $39.99. This fee applies to the FitStar Yoga app only, and not other popular FitStar apps, like FitStar Personal Trainer.

In addition to the app's ability to custom-tailor each session based on ongoing feedback you provide, Premium users can also adjust each session's duration and overall intensity, customize the music selection, and track progress.

> **☑ TIP** Instead of watching the HD video on your iPhone's screen while doing yoga at home, you can wirelessly stream FitStar Yoga's video content to your television set for even easier viewing if you have an Apple TV device linked with it.

Out of all the yoga-related apps available for the iPhone and Apple Watch, FitStar Yoga is extremely well designed and comprehensive in terms of the features and content offered. It's also best suited to the broadest range of yoga enthusiast, thanks to its adaptability based on a user's skill level and experience.

> **NOTE** Other yoga apps that offer live-action video instruction and that cater to a broad audience of yoga enthusiasts include Yoga Studio (free with in-app purchases available), Simply Yoga (free with in-app purchases available), and Yoga.com: 300 Poses & Video Classes ($3.99). The Pocket Yoga app (free with in-app purchases available) is also Apple Watch compatible, but features computer-generated animations (as opposed to live-action video) with audio narration that walks users through the yoga poses.

GIVE YOUR BRAIN A HEALTHY WORKOUT

Based on research-driven neuroscience, brain-training apps are comprised of a series of games and challenges that you can play on your iPhone or Apple Watch for just a few minutes each day. Over time, these games can improve your overall brain function.

> **! CAUTION** Although research does exist that shows these "brain game" apps can be beneficial, some medical professionals remain skeptical. If you believe you suffer from memory loss or Alzheimer's, for example, definitely consult with a doctor, and do not rely solely on any of these apps to mitigate the problem.

A variety of apps are available that were inspired by the popular Lumosity.com website (and later the Lumosity iPhone app), such as Fit Brains Trainer, Peak—Brain Training, and Mind Games—Brain Training Games, to help you sharpen your mind over time, improve your memory, enhance your attention span, and increase your ability to concentrate. Keep in mind that these other apps were developed by third-party companies other than Lumosity.

> **NOTE** More than 60 million people worldwide currently use the Lumosity website and/or mobile app. Neuroscientists developed the program. To learn more about the science and research behind this type of app-based brain workout, visit www.lumosity.com.

These games each serve a specific purpose and tap into and improve certain brain functions over time and with repetition. Unlike in some other games found in the App Store, flashy graphics and realistic sound effects are not the focus. These games appeal to adults, are easy to learn, yet difficult to truly master.

> ✅ **TIP** If you decide to start using one of these "brain training" apps, getting into the habit of using it every day for 5 to 15 minutes, as directed by the app, is important for achieving any sort of measurable result over time.

So, in addition to working out your body, or improving your mental state using iPhone and Apple Watch apps, these same mobile technologies, combined with specialized apps, can help you work out your brain.

These tools are suitable for people over the age of 16, and you use them a few minutes every day over an ongoing period. In fact, it could be at least several weeks before you can measure significant improvements, but decades' worth of research shows that these tools do work.

The free Lumosity app (shown in Figure 9.18) works with the iPhone and Apple Watch. The core app includes a handful of games (currently played exclusively on a smartphone or tablet) and tools to get you started. (The Apple Watch is optional, and Lumosity uses it to track scores and improvement, for example.)

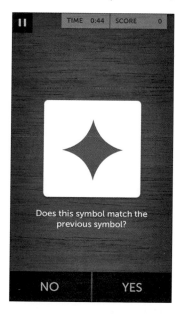

FIGURE 9.18

Lumosity includes a series of fun, but simple games designed to give various aspects of your brain a daily workout.

Ultimately, if you decide to use the app on an ongoing basis, you'll need to pay for a subscription using an in-app purchase ($11.99 per month, or $59.99 per year).

What's nice about Lumosity is that you play each game for just a few minutes per day, and the app has dozens of different games (see Figure 9.19) incorporated into the course, so there's plenty of variety. Each game uses and exercises your brain in a different way, and then tracks your results and improvement over time.

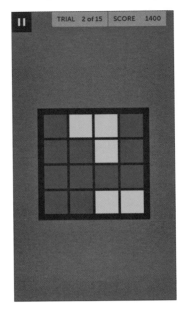

FIGURE 9.19

Lumosity offers dozens of different games to exercise a different aspect of your brain.

> **NOTE**   Similar apps, like Fit Brains Trainer and Peak—Brain Training, allow some of the mind-improvement games to be played on the Apple Watch's screen, in addition to on the iPhone. However, these competing apps don't have the proven track record or established user base that Lumosity has earned.

ACHIEVE YOUR DIETING GOALS

Whether you're big and tall, short and skinny, or anywhere in between, chances are you're not 100 percent satisfied by your current weight and appearance (see Figure 10.1). Unfortunately, in America, an abundance of unhealthy food is readily available to us, and many of our lives involve being sedentary (sitting at a desk and/or in a car commuting) for many hours per day. None of these factors contribute favorably to achieving and maintaining a healthy body.

FIGURE 10.1

After you reach a healthy weight, maintaining it typically requires you to continue eating right and staying active. Simple activities, like walking, jogging, or running, can be extremely beneficial.

People, Americans in particular, are obsessed with diets. In fact, we spend between $20 and $30 billion per year to participate in weight loss programs and buy weight loss products. On one end, as Americans, we're bombarded with advertising from fast food chains, as well as soda and candy companies, for example, that are trying to make us eat poorly, while on the opposite end of the spectrum, companies like Weight Watchers and Jenny Craig spend millions of dollars in advertising in an effort to convince us to diet.

Societal pressures and biases aside, it is undeniable that being overweight adversely affects health. The healthiest diet is the one for which the goal is to lead a more active life through fitness and healthy foods.

> ☑ **TIP** A difference exists between eating healthily and participating in
> a diet. For most people, simply sticking to a healthy diet, avoiding junk food
> and excessive eating, drinking plenty of water, and exercising on a regular basis
> enables them to achieve and maintain a healthy weight.
>
> For those who want to speed up the weight loss process, eat unhealthy foods,
> and/or forego adopting a fitness plan, following a diet might be helpful for weight
> loss. The trick is finding a diet plan that works well for you, that's safe, that will
> help you achieve the desired results, and that encourages you to adopt better hab-
> its, so you can keep the weight from coming back after you lose it.

For those of you looking to eat a well-rounded diet and avoid junk foods, and who are
willing to adopt a healthy lifestyle that involves being active or having some form of
regular fitness routine, with the right app(s) your iPhone and Apple Watch can help
you make this seemingly daunting task more achievable, as discussed in this chapter.

For example, just as the iPhone and Apple Watch can help you monitor your
fitness-related activities, track your workout progress, and then analyze the results,
they can do the same to help you manage your diet. In fact, the Health app that
comes preinstalled on your iPhone offers tools to manage, analyze, and track
nutrition and calorie-related data.

> ☑ **TIP** To help you track what you eat, monitor caloric intake versus calories
> you burn, and help you understand the impact the food and drink you consume
> has on your weight, the App Store offers many calorie counter apps for the iPhone
> and Apple Watch, several of which you'll learn more about in this chapter.

For help with diet or weight-loss plans, the App Store offers literally hundreds of
diet-related apps that you can either use on their own, or as proprietary tools as
part of an established weight loss program from a well-known company such as
Weight Watchers, Jenny Craig, Atkins, Nutrisystem, or South Beach Diet.

> ❗ **CAUTION** Using your iPhone and/or Apple Watch to help you lose
> weight or maintain a healthier diet does not necessarily replace the need to work
> with a trained professional such as a nutritionist and/or a doctor.
>
> Don't get caught up in the promotional hype surrounding any app or diet plan.
> Think of these apps as tools that can help you achieve success as you follow a per-
> sonalized diet or nutrition plan that an expert designed for you.

ACCESS INTERACTIVE COOKBOOKS

If you enjoy preparing your own meals, an interactive cookbook app can be extremely useful. These apps not only help you plan healthy meals and provide a vast collection of recipes, they also often offer video-based cooking tutorials, and enable you to create custom shopping lists.

In addition to comprehensive and general interest interactive cookbook apps, like Must-Have Recipes from Better Homes and Gardens (see Figure 10.2), the Joy of Cooking, and the Betty Crocker Cookbook, available from the App Store, you'll find specialized interactive cookbook apps that can help you follow and maintain a specific type of diet based on your personal dietary needs and/or food allergies.

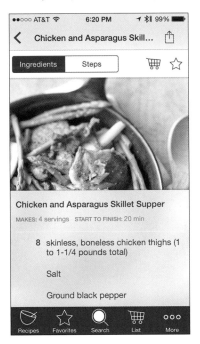

FIGURE 10.2

The Must-Have Recipes from Better Homes and Gardens app offers more than 570 easy-to-follow recipes and 151 how-to cooking videos.

For example, you'll discover sugar-free, low-calorie, gluten-free, vegetarian, vegan, and low-salt cookbook apps, and apps to help you prepare different types of cuisine from around the world.

NOTE Beyond the recipes that come bundled with the Must-Have Recipes from Better Homes and Gardens app, specialty recipe bundles are available as in-app purchases for $0.99. For example, options include 30-Minute Dinners, Healthy Cooking, and Soups & Stews.

TIP To find a cookbook app that will meet your dietary needs, visit the App Store, tap on the Top Charts icon, tap on the Categories option, and then select the Food & Drink option. Alternatively, in the App Store, tap on the Search icon, and in the Search field enter a keyword or search phrase such as "Cookbook," "Gluten-Free Cookbook," or "Healthy Recipes."

GET PERSONALIZED RECIPE RECOMMENDATIONS FROM YUMMLY

Beyond interactive cookbooks, specialized recipe apps, such as Yummly, enable you to choose a food or meal category, or enter exactly what you want to eat, and then the app automatically searches the Internet to find appropriate recipes.

With the Yummly app, you can save your favorite recipes and create a personalized cookbook, and create "smart shopping lists," containing all the ingredients you need to prepare the selected dishes. These lists are automatically sorted, so you'll spend less time searching for items at the supermarket.

NOTE Yummly is a free, advertiser-supported app. So, as you use the app, small banner ads will periodically appear along the bottom of the screen. This app also works with the Apple Watch, so you can find recipes to prepare right from your watch, and then view your custom shopping list on the watch's screen while you're at the supermarket, for example.

When you launch the Yummly app for the first time, it requires you to set up a free account, and then asks you specific information about yourself, including your gender, age, how many people you typically cook for, and the types of cuisine you enjoy. Be sure to indicate any food allergies you have by tapping on icons for common allergies, such as dairy, egg, gluten, peanuts, seafood, or wheat (see Figure 10.3).

FIGURE 10.3

When completing the initial Yummly questionnaire, be sure to provide honest and accurate responses to get the most out of this app.

If you have specific dietary restrictions, the app also prompts you to select from options such as vegetarian or vegan. You can also select foods or ingredients you don't like, and then rank your cooking skills as Beginner, Intermediate, or Advanced.

Taking all the information you provide into account, some sample recipes appear. Pick the ones that have the most appeal (see Figure 10.4) by tapping on the Yum icon. Based on these selections, the app can offer better recommendations in the future.

As you preview each recommended recipe, photos showcase the cuisine, and along the bottom of the screen the number of ingredients, number of calories per serving, and preparation time appear (see Figure 10.5).

FIGURE 10.4

"Like" recipes by tapping on the orange and white Yum icon next to the recipe title; the Yummly app learns your preferences and can offer more personalized meal suggestions.

FIGURE 10.5

A recipe's preview screen shows the number of ingredients, number of calories per serving, and the preparation time.

If you opt to prepare that recipe, tap on the Ingredients icon to display a detailed listing of the items you'll need. By default, each recipe lists what's required to prepare four servings. To change this, tap on the Servings option, and select the number of people you'll be preparing the recipe for. The Ingredients list automatically adjusts. For example, Figure 10.6 shows the ingredients list for the selected recipe based on four servings, so tap on the Servings option, and then select a different number of servings from the menu (see Figure 10.7).

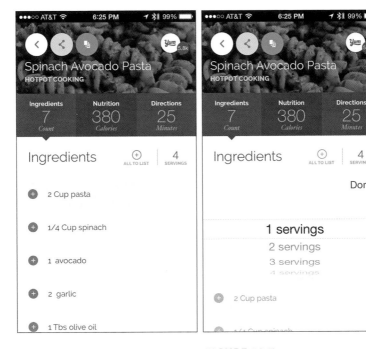

FIGURE 10.6

Initially, the ingredients list is based on preparing four servings of the selected food.

FIGURE 10.7

You don't have to do any math: Enter a different number of servings to prepare (shown here is 1), and the app recalculates the ingredients list automatically.

Then, simply tap on the Add To List option; the app adds the exact ingredient amounts for the servings specified for that recipe to your shopping list.

> **TIP** Use the camera that's built in to the iPhone to scan food product barcodes, or use a menu-driven interactive Shopping List tool to manually create a personalized shopping list or add other items to the list that was automatically created based on the selected recipe(s).

Unlike other cookbook apps, the recipes the Yummly app finds and displays come from many different and independent sources on the Internet. Thus, the format of the step-by-step preparation instructions you're offered varies. In some cases, the steps display using text and photos on your iPhone or Apple Watch's screen. Figure 10.8 shows details about a selected recipe on the watch's screen. In other cases, on the iPhone, you can view video of the recipe being prepared, and have the opportunity to follow along.

TIP To quickly find a recipe with the Apple Watch version of Yummly, tap on the Search Recipe option, and then simply say what you're looking for. Browse through the on-screen recommendations using a swipe motion with your finger, or by turning the Digital Crown on the watch.

FIGURE 10.8

For added convenience, the Yummly app displays recipe information and related shopping lists on your Apple Watch screen.

What's great about the Yummly app is that it only displays recipes that meet your criteria based on information you've initially included in your profile. So, if you stated you're a Beginner who is lactose intolerant, and who doesn't like seafood, for example, then the app only recommends recipes that fit those criteria. Thus, investing the three to five minutes needed to complete the initial questionnaire as accurately as possible when you first begin using the app is important.

> **✓ TIP** At any time, to manually adjust personal profile settings, tap on the Menu icon near the top-left corner of the app's screen, and select the Settings option. Next, tap on the My Account option to adjust certain settings about you and the people you typically cook for, and then tap on the Dietary Preferences option to modify your list of dietary restrictions and/or food allergies.

Unlike a traditional cookbook, or a cookbook app that contains a pre-selected collection of recipes, the Yummly app's focus is on learning about your likes, dislikes, allergies, and dietary restrictions, and then it reaches out to the Internet to find and display appropriate recipes.

> **✓ TIP** Another way the Yummly app makes healthy food preparation easier is through a partnership with Instacart. If you live in a supported city (more than 15 U.S. cities are currently supported) and after you create a custom shopping list in the app, then with a few extra on-screen taps, you can have all the items on your list delivered to your door, typically within an hour. You pay via the credit/debit card you link to your account, which you only need to enter once.

GET THE MOST OUT OF NUTRITION AND CALORIE COUNTER APPS

If your goal is to maintain a healthy diet by eating well, consuming appropriate portions, and avoiding unhealthy junk foods, a variety of apps can help you better understand nutrition, help you plan meals, keep tabs on exactly what you eat, and then help you analyze whether your diet and fitness plan are working well together to help you achieve your overall weight goals.

Calorie counter (also referred to as calorie tracker) apps are widely available from the App Store. Many of these apps use a variety of technologies that are built in to the iPhone (and in some cases the Apple Watch) to help you log everything you eat, and understand the caloric and nutritional information for those foods.

For example, many of these apps include access to vast databases of packaged food and drink items that have barcodes. So, before consuming one of these items, you can use your iPhone's camera to scan its barcode to quickly gather all of its calorie and nutritional information, and import that information into your personal food diary.

Many of these same apps have also pre-analyzed the menus at thousands of popular chain restaurants, so when you're about to order from one of these menus, you can enter the item into the app to access accurate calorie and nutritional data, which can then be instantly imported into your food diary.

These apps also make manually entering specific types of foods and drinks easy as you consume them (or think about consuming them). As a result, by recording details about exactly what you eat and drink each day, your iPhone (and potentially your Apple Watch) can use this information to help you follow a specific diet, or inform you of exactly where you went wrong.

Plus, you can analyze and compare this data to fitness and activity-related data that the iPhone and Apple Watch collects, enabling you to see a much more complete picture of how consumed food and drink, combined with your activity level, heart rate, sleep patterns, and other information, all interrelates.

The goal of iPhone and Apple Watch calorie counters is to make tracking what you eat a quick process that requires no mathematical calculations on your part. For example, if you're trying to adhere to a 2,000-calorie-per-day diet, the app determines how many calories you're consuming based on the food and drinks you select, and can even help recommend healthier alternatives for snacks or upcoming meals that will help you stay within your target calorie count.

> **TIP** Each calorie tracker available for the iPhone and Apple Watch offers a slightly different collection of features. To find these apps, access the App Store and in the Search field, enter "Calorie Counter" or "Calorie Tracker."

TRACK YOUR FOOD WITH MYFITNESSPAL

Calorie Counter & Diet Tracker by MyFitnessPal (shown in Figure 10.9) is one of the most popular tools used by fitness-oriented people to help track their activities. It also helps you accurately and easily track exactly what foods and drinks you consume on a daily basis.

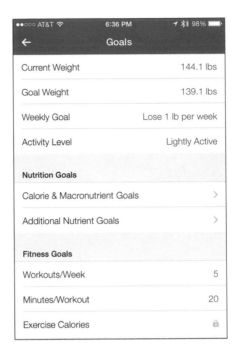

FIGURE 10.9

MyFitnessPal's Calorie Counter & Diet Tracker enables you to not only track calorie intake, but also handle a wide range of other tasks.

> **NOTE** Counting calories manually and documenting exactly what you eat or drink throughout the day can be extremely time consuming and cumbersome. This is a key reason why so many people give up after a short time.
>
> By greatly reducing data entry time and steps, and the need to do any mathematical calculations, the Calorie Counter & Diet Tracker by MyFitnessPal app (and others like it) makes keeping track of what you eat and drink a much less time consuming and less confusing process in your daily routine. Thus, you're more apt to stick with using one of these apps over the long term, and the personalized data that's collected and analyzed on your behalf will help you better understand and achieve your weight loss goals.

This app tracks your daily activity level, has a built-in step tracker, and shares data with the Health app. It's also compatible with virtually every fitness/activity tracker on the market. Using this app for less than five minutes per day will help you better understand and analyze your eating habits, and more easily attain your fitness and weight-related goals.

> ☑ **TIP** By developing a good understanding of exactly where your nutrients and calories are coming from, you can make more intelligent choices about your food consumption. This is all information the app clearly displays for you using text, charts, tables, and graphs.

One of the great things about this app is how easily you can document the food and drinks you consume throughout the day. The app has a built-in and ever-growing database of more than five million foods, so data entry is kept to a minimum, yet you can benefit from the caloric and nutrition information that it acquires about everything you're thinking about consuming or actually consume.

For people who enjoy cooking, this app imports information from recipe apps and recipes from the Internet, again making the data entry aspect of this app very quick and easy.

Using the calorie counter and the app's activity monitor functionality, the app keeps track of the calories you consume and burn off throughout the day. At the same time, the app automatically tracks important nutrient-related data (including fat, protein, carbs, sugar, fiber, and cholesterol) based on the foods and drinks you consume and enter into the app.

Another nice feature of this app is that after you use it a short time, the app learns enough about your activity and eating habits to help you set and achieve realistic diet goals, and it provides information and notifications throughout the day to help you stick to those goals. However, if you're already working with a nutritionist or doctor, you can easily import the plan or goals these professionals provide into the app.

> ☑ **TIP** As with any type of data gathering and analytical app, it only works if you use it consistently and provide it with timely, accurate, and complete information. In other words, if you opt to use a calorie counter/tracker, you must enter in details about all food and drink you consume each and every day. Without all the necessary data, these apps cannot provide helpful or accurate feedback.

When you first use this app, it prompts you to set up a free account and provide information about yourself and your weight/diet-related goals. For example, you'll be asked if your overall goal is to lose, maintain, or gain weight, and if you select either lose or gain weight, the app will ask how many pounds you're hoping to shed or add.

To help you devise an appropriate daily activity and food intake plan, the app then asks questions about your average daily activity, as well as more personal data, like your gender, birthdate, height, and current weight.

Based on the information you initially enter, the app calculates the easiest and safest speed for you to lose (or gain) the desired weight, but also gives you the flexibility to alter this timeframe, assuming you have realistic goals in mind.

After completing the initial questionnaire, which takes about five minutes, the app displays what your daily net calorie goal should be to achieve the desired goal in the pre-defined period (see Figure 10.10).

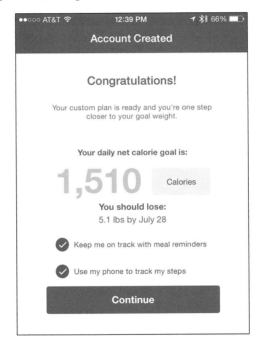

FIGURE 10.10

Let the app help you formulate an intelligent, safe, and realistic plan for achieving your weight loss goals.

Use the Search field to enter food data; just enter a word or phrase that describes what you've eaten (or are about to eat). For example, if you enter "salad," the app displays many different specific salad variations (as well as dressing options), so you can choose the one that most closely applies (see Figure 10.11).

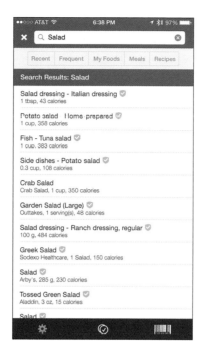

FIGURE 10.11

This app has streamlined the food logging process.

Based on the food/drink type you enter, the app recommends the ideal serving size (relative to your daily goal), and asks you to enter the number of servings you actually consume. Each time you are about to consume another food or drink, tap on the Add (+) icon near the bottom center of the screen, and then tap on the Water or Food icon.

When you select a specific food, complete nutritional information about that food appears (see Figure 10.12). If you decide to consume it, tap on the checkmark icon in the top-right corner of the screen. The nutrition data then imports into the app's food diary.

Tap on the Food icon to Select a Meal (breakfast, lunch, dinner, or snack), and then in the Search field, enter the food type. If you're about to consume a pre-packaged food or drink product, tap on the barcode scan icon to simply scan the product's barcode and eliminate the need for additional manual data entry.

At any time the MyFitnessPal Calorie Counter & Diet Tracker app enables you to view or edit your food diary, view your progress, share details about your activities and/or food consumption with others, set reminders, and handle a wide range of other tasks.

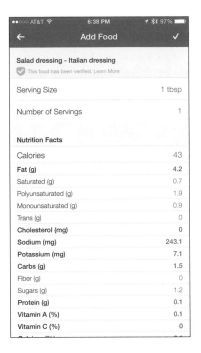

FIGURE 10.12

View a food's nutrition information before you decide to consume it.

📋 **TIP** You can use a calorie counter app to devise and maintain your own diet, or as a tool when following almost any other pre-created diet plan.

📝 **NOTE** Calorie Counter & Diet Tracker by MyFitnessPal is one of the more popular and feature-packed calorie counting apps available from the App Store, but you have many other options.

For example, the LoseIt! app (which you learn about later in this chapter) has calorie counter functionality built in. Other popular apps that offer this type of functionality include My Macros+ Diet, Weight and Calorie Tracker ($2.99); Calorie Counter Pro by MyNetDiary ($3.99); MyPlate Calorie Tracker by Livestrong.com (free with in-app purchase options); Calorie Counter and Diet Tracker by Calorie Count (free with in-app purchase options); and Calorie Counter, Dining Out, Food and Exercise Tracker (free with in-app purchase options).

USE ESTABLISHED DIET PLAN APPS

Many of the best known diet plans, such as Weight Watchers, Jenny Craig, Atkins, Nutrisystem, and South Beach Diet, have been around for decades—much longer than the iPhone, Apple Watch, and other mobile devices have existed. Yet, to help make these well-established diet plans easier to follow on a day-to-day basis, they each offer a proprietary iPhone (and in some cases Apple Watch) app.

❗CAUTION In most cases, if you're not already following one of these popular diet plans (and possibly consuming the meals offered by them), these proprietary apps are not beneficial, because they are tools for people already following a particular diet plan.

TIP If you're following a specific diet plan, enter the name of that diet into the Search field of the App Store to determine whether a proprietary app for that specific plan is available. Otherwise, consider using a more generic calorie counter app to help you manage your diet.

SKIP MEETINGS WITH THE WEIGHT WATCHERS APP

Weight Watchers encourages its subscribers to follow a very specific diet plan, to participate in in-person group meetings, and to interact with a personal Weight Watchers specialist who is trained to keep clients motivated and on track.

NOTE Full use of the free Weight Watchers app requires a paid subscription to Weight Watchers OnlinePlus ($169.00 per year). Other monthly or quarterly subscription plans are offered, however.

Part of the OnlinePlus plan involves using the iPhone app to watch a complete video course (designed to be used over an eight-week period), as well as watch a series of informative three-minute video "bites," and gain access to recipes and customized meal plans. To learn more, visit www.weightwatchers.com.

For people who are too busy to attend in-person meetings, but want to benefit from the Weight Watchers program, the iPhone app allows paid subscribers to interact with a certified coach via text message, any time day or night. These coaches are on hand to offer guidance, motivation, and advice directly from the app (assuming your iPhone has Internet access).

The tools built in to the app also make for easy tracking of your food, weight, and activity on an ongoing basis, and can take advantage of a fitness/activity tracker (from Fitbit or Jawbone) for data gathering. The app also includes many healthy Weight Watchers-approved recipes (one of which is shown in Figure 10.13).

FIGURE 10.13

The Weight Watchers iPhone app offers tools that can supplement your in-person group and one-on-one coach meetings, and help you efficiently log your meals.

Throughout the day, you can use the app for information about foods, restaurants, and recipes, and access tools to help you decide what to eat based on your personal goals. The Cheat Sheets, for example, let you select a food, like pizza, add virtual toppings, and then see the "PointsPlus" value of that food prior to eating it (shown in Figure 10.14).

FIGURE 10.14

Use the app's Cheat Sheets option to try "what if" food scenarios. For example, you can see the impact of eating a slice of plain cheese pizza versus eating a slice of pizza with pepperoni, ham, and/or other toppings.

> **☑ TIP**   Using your iPhone's GPS (Location Services), the Weight Watchers app can tell you when and where the closest meeting is, if you need support beyond the text-based "chat" feature that's built in to the app.

DIET HIGH-TECH WITH THE JENNY CRAIG APP

The goal of the Jenny Craig app is to provide ongoing support when and where you need it, beyond what you receive from your in-person, one-on-one personal consultant. However, to access the tools and features of this app, you must be enrolled in a paid Jenny Craig program.

Among the features of this app include the ability to monitor calories consumed, and view your progress using an "at-a-glance interactive tracker." You can also use the app to plan daily meals and track your fluctuating body measurements.

From the app, you can view (and order) more than 80 Jenny's Cuisine menu items, and locate the closest Jenny Craig Weight Loss Center to wherever you happen to be.

FOLLOW THE NUTRISYSTEM DIET PLAN FROM YOUR IPHONE

Designed exclusively for Nutrisystem customers, the proprietary NuMi app not only helps you monitor your food and drink intake, as well as your activity throughout each day, it also includes a database of more than 250,000 restaurants nationwide, and you can use it to help you choose the best menu options based on your personalized goals. (Your phone's GPS displays all the supported restaurants that are close to you.)

When dining at home, you can scan barcodes for pre-packaged foods, or easily enter the foods you consume. The app also offers on-the-go weight loss advice, and syncs data with many of the popular fitness/activity trackers on the market, so manual data entry is kept to a minimum.

This app is customized based on your particular Nutrisystem plan. The app grants you access to thousands of recipes, and it offers recommendations throughout the day in terms of when to engage in physical activity, and when to eat. This information is tailored to your personal diet plan and goals.

The NuMi app supplements the in-person resources and other tools the Nutrisystem diet plan offers. The app shares data with the Health app, enabling you to more easily gather and organize all fitness/activity, diet, nutrition, and sleep information.

> **NOTE** To learn more about the Nutrisystem diet plan, visit www.nutri-system.com. The Basic plan, which includes prepared meals and snacks, starts at around $10.00 per day. The NuMi iPhone app is only one tool that's available with a Nutrisystem diet plan.

DISCOVER THE LOSEIT! APP

Like MyFitnessPal's Calorie Counter & Diet Tracker, the LoseIt! app for iPhone and Apple Watch is a feature-packed calorie tracker that has a variety of additional features and functions built in that can help people lose weight safely and efficiently. For example, it helps you track detailed information about your weight, body fat, body hydration level, and BMI (see Figure 10.15).

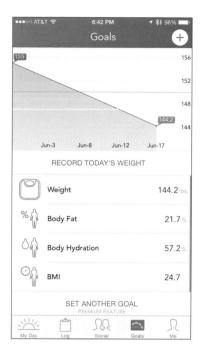

FIGURE 10.15

LoseIt! is one of the most popular weight loss and calorie tracker apps available for the iPhone and Apple Watch.

Thanks to its compatibility with Apple Watch, a variety of other popular fitness/ activity trackers, and the company's own LoseIt! Health-o-Meter Bluetooth scale, the app tracks your activity and weight and helps you easily document the food and drinks you consume each day.

Beyond just being a calorie counter, however, LoseIt! takes all the information and data it gathers on a daily basis, including your weight, body fat, hydration, sleep, exercise/steps (shown in Figure 10.16), and nutrients consumed, combines it with information from the Health app, and then creates a customized diet plan for you to follow that's based on the specific goal and time frame you set.

Based on your responses to the app's initial questionnaire, LoseIt! creates a comprehensive plan to help you lose weight, exercise, maintain a healthy and well-rounded diet, manage your blood pressure, and potentially help you sleep better. The app not only has a vast database of foods, which makes your food diary easy to keep updated, it also accepts barcode scans of packaged food and drink products (via your iPhone's camera).

FIGURE 10.16

Among many other stats, LoseIt! helps you track your daily activity (steps) using just the iPhone, or with the Apple Watch or other fitness/activity tracker.

If you're looking for new ideas about what to eat, the LoseIt! app includes a vast recipe database and tools to help you plan your meals and exercise routines to help you achieve your health goals.

Furthermore, all of LoseIt!'s tools and features appear in a colorful, easy-to-navigate user interface that automates much of the required data collection, and presents information in a straightforward and understandable way.

> **TIP** Lack of motivation or loss of interest is one of the main reasons why people who attempt diets ultimately fail. One tool built in to the LoseIt! app to help overcome this issue is the multi-user challenge. These challenges can be against your real-world friends or family members, or you can participate in them with other people from the online-based LoseIt! community. The challenges are constantly changing, so there are always new ways to keep you engaged and motivated.

Throughout the day, the app offers real-time tips and recommendations based on your activity, weight, nutrition, calorie, and other collected data. For example, if you need to burn off a few calories before dinner, LoseIt! recommends a four-minute workout you can complete almost anywhere. App notifications also remind you when to exercise and log your meals.

The main LoseIt! app is free. However, for $39.99, you can upgrade to LoseIt! Premium via an in-app purchase. Doing this unlocks additional tools that you can use to track and analyze a greater array of health, activity, fitness, and nutrition-related data. For example, the Premium edition of the app includes a Blood Pressure tracker.

CHAT WITH AN EXPERT

LEARN MORE ABOUT LOSEIT! FROM CREATOR CHARLES TEAGUE

Charles Teague is the founder and CEO of LoseIt!, which is a project he's been working on since 2009. The idea for LoseIt! came about after Teague took a look at the very first version of the iPhone, and determined that it could become a powerful tool for weight loss, dieting, and fitness.

"I saw the iPhone as being transformative technology, not just a gadget. I realized the iPhone could really make an impact on the otherwise time-consuming and mundane task of food tracking. There is a large body of clinical research that shows that the most important thing someone can do to start losing weight is to keep careful track of what they eat. Doing this helps people gain insight into the choices they're making, set limits, and become more educated about how food consumption impacts their weight," said Teague. "Food tracking is a great way to build insight into what you're eating, how much you're eating, and why you're eating. For a lot of people, keeping track of their food consumption is a frustrating and annoying experience. Plus, doing this manually requires doing math."

Before using a mobile app to help with food logging became available, it could take 15 minutes or more per day to properly document food intake. According to Teague, "Now, with the help of the iPhone, it takes just seconds per day. The whole food logging process, thanks to the iPhone's touchscreen and other technologies, is now fast, easy, very accurate, and can be done from anywhere. You no longer have to be sitting at your computer. LoseIt! first came out really early in the iPhone's life cycle, and over the years, has been improved as the technology in the phone, and now the Apple Watch, has become more advanced."

When asked to describe LoseIt! in its current incarnation, Teague explained, "It's a stand-alone application that is a weight loss program to help people find a way to make sustainable changes in their lives. One of the biggest mistakes people can make when they think about fitness or losing weight is trying to adopt something that is going to be a quick-fix approach. That kind of approach may work for the very short term, but when you get off the quick-fix diet, the weight you lost will typically be regained quickly."

He added, "A lot of what LoseIt! is designed to do is help users find sustainable ways to lose weight. Based on information the user provides, and that the app collects from the Health app, for example, LoseIt! creates a personalized daily calorie budget. Then, the app tracks activity and exercise, helps people keep track of their food intake, shows people exactly where they're at each day, and then explains where they should be."

LoseIt! helps people answer questions like "Do I need to go to the gym today?" or "Can I have this particular snack right now?" and make intelligent decisions by helping them foresee what the outcome of those decisions will be.

"The app helps people make the right decisions, and adopt very small changes in their life that really add up over time. For example, if there are two different types of sandwiches you like to eat for lunch, the app can help you analyze the calories and nutrition value of each sandwich, and choose the one that has fewer calories, and that can help you achieve your goal faster, without making any significant compromise. If you save 200 calories just by picking the better sandwich, and then over the course of the month repeat this lunch selection five days per week, you'll potentially lose one pound per month just from making this one smart decision," explained Teague.

The other area where LoseIt! excels over competing apps is the tools offered to help people stay interested and on track. "Our app offers a really comprehensive set of social tools that help keep users engaged and motivated. While this app will definitely appeal to people who want to lose weight safely and efficiently, we also have a lot of users who are fitness-minded and who want to incorporate more nutrition-oriented thinking into their overall health and workout routine," said Teague.

> **☑ TIP** The Lose It! app takes advantage of many different built-in iPhone technologies, beyond those used to collect activity data. For example, LoseIt! can work with AirDrop. This feature comes in handy when you're dining with multiple people who are also using the app. If multiple people order the same food, one person can log it into the LoseIt! app via her iPhone, and then wirelessly send that meal data to the other users, so they don't need to log the meal manually as well.
>
> The LoseIt! app also maintains an ever-growing database of restaurants and their menus to make logging food easier when dining out. The iPhone's Location Services can help people find nearby restaurants that the LoseIt! app already supports, so logging a meal into the app becomes even faster and more accurate.
>
> Using the iPhone's camera, you can scan the barcode of pre-packaged food products to enter those foods and drinks into the app's food log. When you scan a packaged food's barcode, all of its nutritional information loads into the app instantly.

One way to achieve success with any diet is to begin with realistic expectations and objectives. "When it comes to dieting, for example, one of the things that mobile technology is really great at is educating you. It can show you how active you are, and what you're eating, and then show you what the relationship is between these two things. For example, you can see that if you use an elliptical machine for 30 minutes and burn 350 calories, all of that hard work will be lost if you then order French fries with lunch," said Teague.

"Ultimately, the person who opts to use any diet app on his or her iPhone or Apple Watch will still need to bring some action, motivation, and willpower to the table. If you want to stay in shape or lose weight, you need to be active, and perhaps go to the gym to work out. You also need to control your eating habits, and make intelligent eating choices. Ultimately, the app can offer you advice, but it's up to you to follow that advice and make the right decisions," added Teague.

> **☑ TIP** Although the LoseIt! app can help people achieve weight loss goals, speaking with a medical professional before starting any type of diet or fitness routine is always best. The LoseIt! app does not flesh out the goal-setting process. Thus, it will work best if you begin using the app with a predetermined and realistic weight-loss goal and deadline in mind.

IN THIS CHAPTER

- Discover iPhone apps that can help you sleep better
- Learn about the cutting-edge S+ Sleep Better device from ResMed
- Get sleep-related advice from world renowned sleep experts

11

MONITOR YOUR SLEEP AND SLEEP BETTER

Three of the most important components needed for maintaining a healthy lifestyle are eating right, exercising, and getting a proper amount of quality sleep. As a result of adverse circumstances, such as a busy work schedule, too many personal commitments, a challenging job, the responsibilities of raising children, financial problems, stress, and other common (but often uncontrollable) life situations, many people have trouble sleeping, suffer from insomnia, or simply don't consistently get enough sleep.

To help remedy this situation, people often turn to prescription medications, over-the-counter sleeping pills, and/or natural remedies (like melatonin). Others try meditation or yoga to help calm their mind before bed, whereas some people who have trouble falling asleep or getting a good night's sleep try watching television, reading, listening to audiobooks or music, or even counting sheep.

Whether you suffer from transient insomnia or chronic insomnia (meaning that you have trouble falling sleep or getting a restful night's sleep either once in a while, or on a frequent basis), iPhone apps and related equipment are available that you can use to help calm your mind, achieve a restful night's sleep, and help you identify and fix the causes of your sleep problems, including diagnosed insomnia. This chapter covers some of these sleep-related apps and devices.

> **NOTE** More than 50 percent of the U.S. population has trouble sleeping, although many of these people don't understand why.
>
> According to BetterSleep.org, "You need different amounts of sleep, depending on your age." People between the ages of 3 and 18 should target 10 hours of sleep per night. People between the ages of 19 and 65 typically require approximately 8 hours of sleep per night, and people over the age of 65 require a minimum of six hours of sleep per night. These numbers can, of course, vary depending on your particular biology.

If you visit the App Store and enter "sleep" in the Search field, you'll discover a handful of sleep-related apps, such as Sleepio, that can handle a variety of tasks, such as:

- Playing relaxing music, tranquil sounds, or white noise to help you calm your mind and fall asleep faster
- Tracking your sleeping patterns and habits
- Walking you through a guided meditation
- Identifying problems with your sleep and sleeping environment, and teaching you how to correct them

Some fitness/activity trackers also have sleep-tracking functionality, so you can track how long it takes you to fall asleep, and how much restful sleep you actually get each night.

The S+ device, from a company called ResMed, is a cutting-edge piece of iPhone-compatible equipment that you'll learn more about shortly. You can use S+ to accurately diagnose the cause of your insomnia or determine why you're not sleeping well, train yourself to adjust your controllable sleep-related habits, and provide personalized sleep tracking data that a doctor can use to diagnose and treat more serious sleep-related medical issues.

> ☑ **TIP** As you learn about the available iPhone-related sleep tools and apps, choose just one and work with it on an ongoing basis until you can determine how effective it is in helping with your sleep disorder. This could take several weeks.
>
> Don't try using multiple tools at once. Also, be sure to follow the directions offered by each sleep tool. Then, if your problems continue, definitely consult with a doctor.

SLEEP BETTER VIA THE SLEEPIO APP AND ONLINE SERVICE

Sleepio, shown in Figure 11.1, is much more than a sleep tracker app for the iPhone. Along with its website at www.sleepio.com (see Figure 11.2), it incorporates several decades' worth of research to provide a comprehensive and affordable Cognitive Behavioral Therapy (CBT) program for treating insomnia and other common sleep disorders.

FIGURE 11.1

Meet "The Prof," the animated (and talking) virtual sleep expert who guides you through the Sleepio program on your iPhone and on the Web.

FIGURE 11.2
To fully benefit from Sleepio, you need to use the online-based tools via the company's website, as well as the proprietary iPhone app.

Sleepio features a 10-day free trial of the complete program, after which a paid subscription plan is required for you to take advantage of the program, which most people can complete in 6 to 10 weeks.

> **NOTE** CBT stands for *Cognitive Behavioral Therapy*. This tool is for training people to use proven techniques that address the mental factors associated with insomnia. These factors can include a "racing mind," as well as stress, negative thoughts, and/or strong emotions. Thanks to Sleepio, you can administer this same CBT program at home via the Internet and an iPhone app, without ever meeting face-to-face with a therapist or doctor.

Short-term subscription pricing for Sleepio is $9.99 per week. However, if you register for 12 weeks, the price drops to $6.66 per week, whereas a one-year subscription to the service costs $2.88 per week. After completing the Sleepio program, 58 percent of participants report a boost in daytime energy and concentration, and 62 percent report fewer awakenings during the night; 54 percent report a reduction in time to fall asleep.

During the first week of using the Sleepio program, you learn about the program's foundations and set personal goals. In week two, you address environmental and lifestyle factors associated with your insomnia or sleep disorder.

Week three of the program focuses on restoring the bed-sleep connection, whereas weeks four and five focus on personalized cognitive training. In week six, you learn how to put together everything you've learned, and discover how to implement your newly acquired knowledge and skills in the future.

After you complete the program, the website and app offer a collection of additional tools and resources and access to an active online community that provides ongoing support.

The Sleepio program uses a dozen distinct tools. Some of these tools are online-based, and others you use directly from the Sleepio iPhone app. Use the tools to

- Take an in-depth sleep test to uncover details about your sleep patterns
- Maintain a sleep diary
- Use a progress tracker
- Listen to pre-recorded relaxation programming
- Create and maintain a "dynamic to-do list"
- Follow a daily, personalized schedule outlined by The Prof (a virtual coach)
- Get daily email reminders to keep you focused and on track
- Use a "Thought Checker" to help you "correct" your thoughts and thinking process
- Interact with others through Sleepio's vast online community
- Use a planner
- Receive a personalized reading list, which includes informative books and articles to help you better understand and manage your situation
- Track and record sleep stats

After you take the initial sleep test online, during the six weeks required to complete the main portion of the Sleepio program, the actual day-to-day time commitment is about one hour per week, which includes about five minutes per day to complete a sleep diary (via the website or iPhone app), and 20 minutes per week to have a virtual online meeting with The Prof.

CHAT WITH AN EXPERT

SLEEPIO'S CREATORS/SLEEP EXPERTS SHARE THEIR SLEEP INSIGHTS

Professor Colin Espie is a world-renowned sleep expert and a Professor of Behavioral Sleep Medicine at the University of Oxford. He has been researching sleep and insomnia for more than 30 years and has published more than 200 scientific papers and five books on the topic.

Peter Hames is co-founder and CEO of Big Health, a digital medicine company. Big Health was created as a result of Hames' personal experience with insomnia, and the difficulty he had obtaining adequate treatment.

Working together, Espie and Hames have developed an online service and iPhone app called Sleepio (www.sleepio.com), which helps to diagnose and fix common sleep disorders and problems. In fact, Sleepio is clinically proven to help users fall asleep 50 percent faster, and spend 60 percent less time awake at night. Sleepio helps to fix common sleep issues by finding and addressing the triggers impacting quality of sleep.

"I developed insomnia a few years ago, which was an incredibly hard thing to deal with, impacting my everyday life," said Hames. "Having studied experimental psychology in university, I knew the evidence behind CBT, and self-diagnosed myself with chronic insomnia.

"After being routinely offered sleeping pills as a solution, I went and got access to a self-help book that was written by Professor Colin Espie, and self-administered a course of CBT. In six weeks, I was better. This led me to asking, are we able to use technology as a way to deliver evidence-based behavioral medicine that mimics the best qualities of drugs?"

Through research, Professor Espie has discovered many causes exist for insomnia and sleep problems. "One of the main causes of insomnia is a combination of poor sleeping patterns and a racing mind. Negative emotions, behaviors, and thoughts all contribute to poor sleep. Additive stress can also trigger the onset of insomnia," he explained.

"There are three overarching categories that help to classify the causes, or the '3Ps of sleep problems,' which are predisposing, precipitating, and perpetuating factors. The predisposing factors increase the likelihood of insomnia, based on family history or anxiety. Changes in lifestyle or a sudden illness are precipitating factors, while perpetuating factors are continual problems that worsen the situation," added Espie.

For people who suffer from sleep-related problems, and who turn to the Sleepio website or iPhone app, Hames offers some useful advice. "First and foremost, Sleepio requires commitment. Sleepio participants need to be engaged with the program. Be prepared to put in the effort and time required to achieve the results."

He added, "A number of our users achieve great success using the program, with the added support from the online-based user community. While we're the experts in science, our users who have been through the program are the experts in the implementation of the techniques and any barriers people may come across. Sleepio users are encouraged to interact with the Sleepio community for sustained and long-term support throughout and after using the core program."

As for how much of a time commitment is required to achieve success using Sleepio, Hames explained, "That's entirely up to you. The program begins with an in-depth sleep questionnaire, which uses a number of standardized clinical measures. This provides us with everything we need to tailor the program to each user.

"Then, once a week, users log on to the website to visit their virtual sleep expert, whom we call 'The Prof.' He guides users through an interactive 20-minute session, and presents tailored CBT techniques to follow, which are personalized to the user's specific problems and progress.

"Between sessions, users record their sleep with an easy-to-use online sleep diary, and put the techniques they learn into practice with the help of online tools that The Prof unlocks for them. Throughout the program users are in control. They can pace the sessions as they wish and are left with a 'toolbox' of techniques to implement as they find most useful."

When asked what sets Sleepio apart from other sleep-related tools available online or for the iPhone, Professor Espie explained, "Sleepio is not just another sleep-tracking app. We take your tracked data and use it to deliver a personalized and uniquely tailored program that is suited to your lifestyle and sleep habits. Beyond just collecting information about your sleep, you get a clinical grade sleep improvement program that's shown to be as effective as face-to-face therapy."

OVERCOME SLEEP ISSUES USING RESMED'S S+ DEVICE

You already know that you can wirelessly link a Bluetooth scale with your iPhone to record your weight on an ongoing basis, and use a specialized app to analyze weight fluctuations over time. This is particularly useful when following a diet, for example.

For people who have trouble sleeping, ResMed (www.keepyoursleep.com) offers a remarkable consumer device that you place by your bed that can automatically track and record all aspects of your sleep without your having to physically wear any type of sleep monitor.

The S+ Sleep Better device ($99.99), shown in Figure 11.3, serves as much more than a basic sleep tracker. When you use it with the proprietary iPhone app, you'll have access to personalized tools to help you sleep better, as well as a smart alarm function. Plus, you'll receive expert advice that's based on decades' worth of sleep-related research.

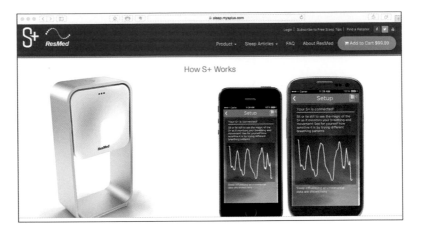

FIGURE 11.3

The ResMed S+ device offers cutting-edge technology. Just position it next to your bed.

The S+ device automatically records, on an ongoing basis, the light, noise, and temperature in your bedroom. As you're preparing to sleep, the device also generates specially designed sounds that synchronize with your breathing, and that gradually slow down to help you fall asleep faster.

The device can also determine when you actually fall asleep, the quality of sleep you're achieving, and then can either wake you up at a designated time, or record when you wake up on your own. It monitors the four stages of your sleep cycle (sleep onset, light sleep, deep sleep, and REM, and when your sleep is interrupted). All of this data recorded over time enables the S+ app to provide you with accurate analysis and sleep-related advice.

> **NOTE** The S+ device works while you're asleep, even if you share your bed with a partner (and/or your pet). The device simply needs to be set up on your side of the bed.

Not only does the app use your own data to formulate personalized strategies to help you fall asleep faster and achieve better quality sleep, it also can anonymously compare your sleep results against averages based on your age, gender, and other information to calculate a personal Sleep Score (see Figure 11.4).

FIGURE 11.4

The S+ app works seamlessly and wirelessly with the S+ device.

Although the S+ is considered a consumer-oriented device instead of a medical device, it uses proprietary technology to acquire extremely accurate data, and uses the Internet and iPhone to analyze that data and provide useful feedback and instruction.

> **NOTE** ResMed's S+ is sold at Apple Stores, Bed Bath & Beyond, and Best Buy, or you can order it directly from the company's website (www.mysplus.com).

CHAT WITH AN EXPERT

LEARN MORE ABOUT THE S+ DEVICE FROM MATT NORTON

Matt Norton is an executive at ResMed with a background in consumer marketing and product development. He's held executive-level positions at companies in several industries and in several countries throughout the world.

ResMed has been around for more than 25 years and is a global leader in sleep medicine and related medical devices. The company was founded in Australia, but is currently headquartered in San Diego, California, and is listed on the New York Stock Exchange.

"ResMed has become one of the most connected medical device companies in the world. Every night, we monitor all aspects of people's sleep, record their data, upload it anonymously to our servers, and then analyze it, so we can provide highly personalized feedback," said Norton.

"Based on several decades' worth of research, we determined there was a consumer need for a device that could help people improve their overall sleep. The S+ is a device for people who have trouble sleeping at least one night per week. They may or may not have already tried taking prescription medications, over-the-counter sleep aides, or natural remedies, such as melatonin. One thing we've learned from our research is that many people who have trouble sleeping have tried several different potential solutions, but they have not been all that effective over time," explained Norton.

Originally, ResMed explored the possibility of using a wearable device to track sleep patterns, but ultimately created the S+ device after determining it would collect more accurate data, without being intrusive. "Providing someone who is having trouble sleeping with just data alone that pertains to their sleep patterns is not enough. People are looking for feedback and directions for how to use that data to take the next steps. The S+ does not just replicate features that are already available on the iPhone, for example, for tracking sleep. It does much more," said Norton.

You put the S+ device next to your bed, and it can wirelessly send data to an iPhone, even if the phone is in another room. According to Norton, "The S+ device gathers the data that's required, but the heavy lifting, so to speak, is done in the cloud via the Internet. We then use the iPhone as the prime mechanism to deliver and present data from the S+ device to the user. We also leverage some of the iPhone's features and Internet connectivity to maximize the S+ device's capabilities. The product is for use by any adult over the age of 18 who suffers from sleep difficulties. What we have seen is that the greater a person's sleep problem, the more of a positive impact the S+ can make."

Many elements go into getting a good night's sleep. Taking a wide range of considerations into account as it collects data, the S+ device calculates a Sleep Score for each user, which fluctuates over time. "A Sleep Score is basically a snapshot of someone's sleep quality level from the previous night. Tracking a Sleep Score over time helps people discern patterns," said Norton. "Based on someone's age and gender, our research shows that the population norm is an average Sleep Score of 78."

When someone starts using the S+ device, the iPhone app walks the user through the account setup process (see Figure 11.5 and Figure 11.6). Then, every night, the app asks the user four questions, which take less than 10 seconds to answer using on-screen sliders. These questions relate to caffeine consumption, alcohol consumption, current stress level, and the amount of exercise someone got that day.

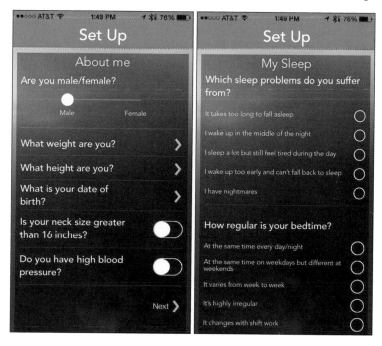

FIGURE 11.5

Initially, the S+ app gathers personal information.

FIGURE 11.6

The Set Up questionnaire involves answering a series of questions about your sleep habits and problems.

"Based on data from the user's profile, answers to these four questions, and the data that the S+ collects each night, we're able to gather a lot of accurate information and provide very useful and easy-to-follow feedback. We're able to determine how someone is sleeping, and pinpoint factors that are preventing good quality sleep," added Norton.

The S+ measures breathing and body movement throughout the night to determine when someone achieves various sleep levels, without making physical contact with them.

"It doesn't matter if you're lying on your back, front, or side, or if there's a partner in the bed with you. The S+ can collect accurate data as long as it's positioned on your side of the bed. Based on this data, we can determine what sleep stage someone is in, how long it took to get there, and how long he or she stayed there," said Norton.

Over time, the S+ iPhone app collects data for inclusion in a personalized sleep report, which you can share with a doctor or medical professional. Norton added, "While many people are familiar with terms related to sleep, like REM sleep, they don't understand the impact these various sleep cycles have on them each night when it comes to things like physical rejuvenation and sustaining and building the body's immune system."

"For someone who works out and is fitness minded, a good night's sleep is critical to the body's recovery. In addition to a workout regimen, virtually all professional athletes also have a professional sleep program designed for them. Getting a good night's sleep allows you to train harder and push yourself harder during your workouts. Understanding sleep patterns and habits can also help someone more easily recover from jet lag, for example."

> **NOTE** According to ResMed's research, 69 percent of consumers see a significant improvement in their sleep after just one week. After the first week of use, users experience an average of 31 minutes of extra sleep per night.

GET ACQUAINTED WITH OTHER SLEEP-RELATED APPS FOR THE IPHONE

Besides the Sleepio and S+ devices, dozens of other sleep-related apps are available from the App Store, most of which are sound generators, basic sleep trackers, or sleep cycle alarm clocks. Some of the Fitbit and Jawbone Up fitness/activity trackers also have a sleep tracker component to them.

> **NOTE** The Sleep Time app (free with in-app purchases available) and premium Sleep Time+ apps ($1.99, with in-app purchases available) can serve as sleep analysis tools, as well as a programmable alarm clock. These apps also offer "soundscapes" that can be played to help users fall asleep faster, as well as integration with the iPhone's Health app.

A sleep tracker documents when you get into bed, how long it takes you to fall asleep, and how much quality sleep you actually get each night. Some of these apps delve deeper, and help you identity the causes of your sleep-related issues, or assist in identifying and correcting environmental factors that might be contributing to your sleep-related problems.

> **TIP** Be sure to refer to Chapter 9, "Establish a Mind/Body Connection," to learn more about apps like Calm and Happify, which can help you adopt a happier, more positive, and less stressful frame of mind, without the use of prescription drugs or professional therapy.

This section offers a small sampling of the apps that can help you in various ways to manage, track, and better understand your sleep-related issues, and/or overcome insomnia.

RELAX MELODIES: SLEEP ZEN SOUNDS & WHITE NOISE

Relax Melodies: Sleep Zen Sounds & White Noise from iLBSoft, shown in Figure 11.7, is a free, advertiser-supported app that offers in-app purchases. Via white noise, calming sounds, and music, the app can help you relax, clear your mind, and fall asleep faster.

FIGURE 11.7

The Relax Melodies app generates sounds and music to help you relax and potentially fall asleep faster.

> **NOTE** White noise, recorded and played at certain volumes and frequencies, sounds like static, but it can help block distractions and calm your mind.

The app comes with 50 built-in sounds and four "brainwave beats" (which include Binaural and Isochronic frequencies that cater to aspects of the brain that go beyond the functions used to listen to music). You can play sounds separately in a continuous loop or on a timer, and you can mix and match the sounds to create a customized "mix" that you personally find soothing. With the timer, you can program when the sounds are played, how long they're played for, and when they automatically fade out and turn off. The alarm clock feature then wakes you up at a pre-programmed time.

One nice feature of this app is its interface. When you launch the app, a selection of sounds appears as icons hanging from virtual strings. Tap on a sound icon, such as River or Rain, to begin playing it. If you want, you can then tap on more sounds to add to your mix, and adjust the sound level of each sound separately using the volume slider for each sound.

To clear your mix and create something new, tap on the Clear icon. Tap on the Pause icon to pause the sound, or tap on the Volume icon to adjust the master volume via an onscreen slider.

> **TIP** Besides sound effects and white noise, the app offers a handful of pre-programmed (and looping) music selections, such as Piano, Lounge, Flute, Orchestral, Melody, and Duduk, that you can mix and match, add to a custom mix, or play separately.

In addition to its pre-programmed sounds, the app offers more sounds via in-app purchases. You can also upgrade the app to unlock more than 106 ambient sounds, 9 guided meditations, and 12 "brainwave beats." You can do this for an annual fee of $29.99, a monthly fee of $4.99, or by acquiring a three-month subscription for $12.99.

Tap on the Clock icon to display the time onscreen, or tap on the Discovery icon to choose from pre-programmed sounds and sound mixes for when you're in a specific mood or situation.

> **TIP** If you have trouble falling asleep or getting a restful night's sleep, tap on the Blog option in the app to access a collection of free articles that focus on sleep, relaxation, stress reduction, and related topics.

! CAUTION Not only can sound and music generation apps like Relax Melodies or White Noise help you fall asleep faster, you can use them during yoga, meditation, while reading, or any time you need to clear your mind and relax. Do not, however, use one of these apps while driving, because they could cause you to fall asleep at the wheel.

SLEEP BETTER: SLEEPING CYCLE TRACKER

Runtastic offers the Sleep Better: Sleeping Cycle Tracker app for free (see Figure 11.8), although it offers an in-app purchase ($1.99) if you want to create custom alarms and access otherwise-locked app features. The free version of the app is advertiser supported; the paid version removes these ads.

FIGURE 11.8

The Sleep Better app is a feature-packed sleep tracker that helps you collect data about your sleeping habits and patterns.

First and foremost, this app can help you track your sleep patterns, monitor your dreams (by serving as a dream journal), and improve your bedtime habits. The app integrates with the iPhone's Health app to record sleep-related data.

Also, based on your recorded sleeping habits, which includes your sleep duration, cycles, and efficiency, the app helps you determine what outside influences might be impacting your sleep patterns, such as the consumption of caffeine or alcohol before bed, your workout routine, ambient noise, your mood, or even the moon phase.

> **TIP** To function properly and gather data while you sleep, the iPhone (while running the app) must be placed on your bed, next to your pillow. You'll probably want to have the iPhone plugged into an external power source. It's also important to understand that there is only so much reliable data such an app can acquire. If you suspect that you have sleep problems, you should consult a specialist.

By understanding your sleep influencers, you might be able to cure your own insomnia and discover strategies from the app that will enable you to fall asleep faster on a consistent basis, without the use of medications. However, if the app doesn't help you overcome your insomnia, the data the app collects will prove useful when you share it with your doctor, therapist, or a sleep expert.

> **TIP** Use the app's integrated Smart Alarm feature to wake you up at the optimal time, which the app calculates based on a variety of personalized factors.

Another feature of the app serves as a dream journal, and enables you to document your dreams using your iPhone, before you forget them. To get the most out of this app, place your iPhone close to your bed, but turn on Do Not Disturb mode, so you won't be distracted by incoming calls or text messages, for example.

> **TIP** To customize the iPhone's Do Not Disturb mode using iOS 8, launch Settings, tap on the Do Not Disturb option, and then turn on/off the Manual and/or Scheduled options. You can also set to let incoming calls from specific callers through, and send others automatically to voice mail.
>
> If you use the Do Not Disturb feature, be sure to turn it off when you're done, or adjust the Scheduled setting to automatically turn off the feature at a pre-determined time each day, or you could wind up missing important calls or messages when you're awake.

The first time you use this app, you need to set up a free, online-based account by tapping on the Join Now button. As with many fitness-related apps, you must enter your full name, gender, email address, and birthday, and create an account password. If you already use the popular Runtastic app, you can use the same account information, and simply log in from the Sleep Better app.

After you launch the app, your pre-set alarm time appears in the screen's main area. To adjust this, tap on the Alarm icon in the top-right corner of the screen. Below the alarm time are six icons. Each icon represents a sleep influencer. Tap on any or all that apply as you're getting ready for bed, and then tap on the Start button.

> **✓ TIP**   When placing the iPhone next to your pillow or close to your bed, keep in mind that the app continues to run, so plug in your iPhone so the battery will be fully charged when you wake up.

Tap the Start button to see the current time. If you wake up in the middle of the night (or in the morning) and want to record details about a dream, tap on the cloud icon in the top-left corner of the screen. Use your iPhone's virtual keyboard to describe your dream in a simple digital diary format.

To quickly turn the iPhone's built-in flashlight on or off, instead of launching Control Center and then tapping on the Flashlight icon, simply tap on the Flashlight icon in the top-right corner of the Sleep Better app's screen (see Figure 11.9).

At the designated time, the app's alarm wakes you up by slowly fading in. If you wake up prior to the alarm, swipe from left to right across the Stop option at the bottom center of the screen. The app records your sleep details and shares them with the Health app.

Along the bottom of the screen are several command icons. Tap on the Diary icon to see information about each night you've tracked your sleep, and review one night at a time. Tap on the Statistics icon to display and analyze saved data recorded over an extended period. Based on the saved information, the app generates customized advice on how you can sleep better. To access this advice, tap on the Insights icon (see Figure 11.10). To control app-related settings, tap on the Settings icon.

FIGURE 11.9

Several options are available while the app monitors your sleep. You can access your Dream Journal or turn on the iPhone's flashlight.

FIGURE 11.10

Tap on the Insights icon to learn more about your Sleep Influencers and how they impact your sleep.

> ☑ **TIP** From the app's Settings menu, be sure to tap on the Apple Health option and turn on the Sleep Analysis virtual switch that grants permission for the Sleep Better app to share data with the Health app.

SLEEP CYCLE ALARM CLOCK

The Sleep Cycle Alarm Clock ($1.99) is one of three sleep-related apps available from Northcube AB. This app, shown in Figure 11.11, is basically an intelligent alarm clock that automatically analyzes your sleep, and then awakens you in a natural way at the designated time. During the night, the app monitors your movement while you're sleeping using the iPhone's built-in accelerometer.

> ✎ **NOTE** When using this or any other sleep-related app through the night, you'll probably want to keep the iPhone plugged into an external power source to ensure battery life throughout the night—when you wake up, the iPhone's battery is fully charged as you begin your day. The downside is that you risk tangling yourself up in the iPhone's USB/power cord while you're asleep if you toss and turn a lot and the phone is positioned close to you.

FIGURE 11.11

The Sleep Cycle Alarm Clock transforms your iPhone into an alarm clock, but one that can help you get a better night's sleep.

Based on the data collected while you're asleep (and if you don't set a pre-determined wake up time) the app can determine the optimal time for you to wake up, and generates an alarm when you're in a light sleep phase.

You can use the app's customizable alarm sounds or the iPhone's Vibrate mode to wake you up. At bedtime, you can set up the iPhone to play sounds or music, and then slowly fade out after the app determines you've fallen asleep.

As the app collects details about your sleeping patterns, it stores the information, shares it with the Health app, and can present it using colorful and easy-to-understand graphs.

> **TIP** If you have the Phillips Hue lighting system set up in your bedroom, the app can control the light(s) and simulate a sunrise when it's time to wake up. You can set this up from the Sleep Cycle Alarm Clock app.

> **NOTE** Two other apps that you can use with the Sleep Cycle Alarm Clock app are Sleep Cycle Heart Rate ($1.99) and Sleep Cycle Power Nap ($1.99), both of which are available from the App Store. To learn more about these apps, visit www.sleepcycle.com.

WHITE NOISE

The White Noise app ($1.99) from TMSOFT is basically a sound-generating app that plays white noise or soothing natural sound effects to help you relax and reduce your stress (see Figure 11.12).

The app itself comes with 40 pre-installed sounds that can loop indefinitely, although you can download additional sounds for free from the White Noise Market website (www.whitenoisemarket.com).

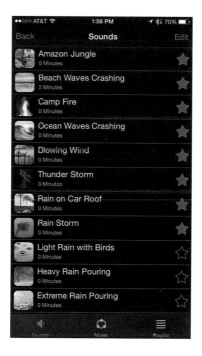

FIGURE 11.12

White Noise is a highly customizable sound-generation tool that can help you relax by playing white noise or natural sounds.

📝 **TIP** Using the app, you can mix and match sounds to create the perfect ambiance for yourself, and just as when playing any audio, you control the volume with an onscreen slider.

Begin by choosing a sound from the app's library, such as Amazon Jungle, Beach Waves Crashing, Camp Fire, Blowing Wind, Rain Storm, Crickets Chirping, Heartbeat, or Thunder Storm. A variety of White Noise sounds also come with the app.

To create a "mixed" sound, launch the app, tap on the + icon at the bottom of the screen, and then select the Create Mix option. From the Create Mix menu, select a sound. A checkmark appears next to the selected sound listing. Next, tap on one or more additional sounds.

After you create your perfect combination of sounds, tap on the Save option. Your sound combination will begin playing in a continuous loop indefinitely, unless you tap on the Timer icon (in the top-right corner of the screen) and set a timer for how long the audio should play.

While the selected sound(s) play on your iPhone, the screen displays a customizable alarm clock. You can display the time and related information in a variety of colors that won't brighten an otherwise dark room and prevent you from falling asleep. By default, a stock photo representing each sound also displays onscreen. Later, when the alarm goes off, it slowly fades in (gets louder) to help ease you awake.

As you're falling asleep, the app can be programmed to slowly fade out the selected sound after a predetermined amount of time. Plus, thanks to AirPlay compatibility, your iPhone can wirelessly play the audio programming via speakers or a television set that's connected to an Apple TV device. You can also control the sounds being played with the Music app controls in the iPhone's Control Center.

> **☑ TIP** To access the Control Center menu, swipe up from the bottom of the screen. In the middle of this menu are Music app controls, which include a Volume Slider, Pause, Play, Fast Forward, and Rewind icon.

> **✎ NOTE** If you want to create your own continuously looped sounds for use with this app, you can unlock a $0.99 Sound Generator via an in-app purchase.

Use the White Noise app to help block outside sounds in your sleep environment, or create a peaceful sound for your mind to focus on in an otherwise quiet environment.

IN THIS CHAPTER

- Discover apps that can help you track all of your activities and workouts
- Learn about apps that go beyond just recording your activity
- Find out how you might benefit from using the Fitmo app to receive personalized fitness coaching

12

GETTING THE MOST FROM GENERAL FITNESS APPS

Many people have an active lifestyle and participate in a variety of different activities as part of their overall fitness routine (see Figure 12.1). This might include working out at the gym several days per week, running on a treadmill at home, or participating in fitness classes (aerobics, spinning, or Zumba, for example) or some type of sport.

FIGURE 12.1

Regardless of what type of fitness activities you participate in, your iPhone and Apple Watch can be handy tools when used with the right apps.

Instead of using separate apps to track each of these activities, and then hoping all the relevant and collected data accurately syncs up and comes together in a meaningful way, you might find that using a single general fitness–oriented activity-tracking app with your iPhone (and potentially your Apple Watch) is more beneficial.

Argus – Pedometer and GPS Activity Tracker, Human – Activity & Calorie Tracker, Nike+ Training, Fitnet Personal Fitness Workouts, and MapMyFitness are all more general workout or fitness-oriented apps that can track activity information and serve as powerful fitness tools, as you'll discover in this chapter.

The Workout app that comes preinstalled on the Apple Watch (refer to Chapter 5, "Use the Activity, Workout, and Other Fitness Apps") is also an example of a more general-oriented fitness app (see Figure 12.2).

One of the most popular general-purpose fitness apps that also has a weight loss focus, MyFitnessPal for the iPhone and Apple Watch, has evolved into the Calorie Counter & Diet Tracker by MyFitnessPal, which you can learn more about in Chapter 10, "Achieve Your Dieting Goals."

TIP Each time you launch the Workout app, the main menu asks what type of activity you plan to participate in, and then the watch tracks your activity and gathers relevant data, and then shares it with the iPhone.

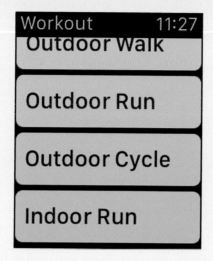

FIGURE 12.2

The Apple Watch's Workout app enables you to track almost any fitness-oriented activity you participate in.

OVERVIEW OF GENERAL FITNESS AND ACTIVITY TRACKER APPS

In addition to the many specialized fitness apps you can use during activities such as aerobics, Zumba, weight lifting, golf, swimming, cross training, running, cycling, or yoga, less specialized apps are available from the App Store that you can use to track your overall daily activity, collect relevant data, and then help you analyze that information.

NOTE To find a specialized app for the specific sport or activity you regularly participate in, use the App Store's Search field. For example, if you're a swimmer, enter the phrase, "swimming training," or if you enjoy Zumba, enter "Zumba" into the Search field.

> ☑️ **TIP** In addition to the third-party, stand-alone apps that can track your physical activity, the proprietary apps for fitness/activity trackers from companies like Fitbit and Jawbone are also useful for monitoring, analyzing, and sharing activity data.

This chapter provides a sampling of more general fitness and activity monitoring apps that you might find useful if you tend to participate in several different fitness activities, as opposed to just one.

Some of these iPhone apps also work with the Apple Watch and/or other popular fitness/activity trackers, and can import data from optional Bluetooth devices, such as a scale, heart rate monitor, or a blood pressure monitor. Many of these apps also can share data with the iPhone's Health app, and some can import data from compatible fitness equipment (like a treadmill or elliptical machine).

ARGUS – PEDOMETER AND GPS ACTIVITY TRACKER

Argus – Pedometer and GPS Activity Tracker is a free iPhone app (that offers in-app purchase options) that also has an Apple Watch app counterpart. This app focuses on counting your steps, regardless of what activities you engage in (see Figure 12.3).

The app serves as a pedometer, can track your fluid intake (water, coffee, tea, and so on), and keep track of where you've been (via the iPhone's GPS). The app automatically calculates your calories burned based on your activity and can display this and other information (such as your daily steps and heart rate data) in a variety of formats (using text-based tables and colorful charts or graphs).

Use this app to set daily goals for steps, sleep time, and hydration, for example, and then automatically monitor all of your activity throughout the day. Whenever you're on-the-go (on foot), Argus tracks your distance traveled, pace, and calorie burn.

As with most fitness-oriented apps, this one requires that you set up a free, online-based account to use it. You do this the first time you launch the app. Beyond the core functionality of the app, if you opt to upgrade to the Premium version ($4.99 per month, or $29.99 per year), the app unlocks the opportunity to participate in Challenges, offers a feature called Audio Coach Guidance, gives you access to additional pre-created Workout Plans (above and beyond what's included in the core app), and if you opt to use the app for sleep monitoring, provides you with Sleep Insight Reports.

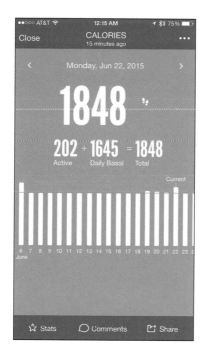

FIGURE 12.3

Use the Argus app to track all of your daily activity, not just your workouts, and display activity data in a variety of easy-to-understand formats.

> **NOTE**   Using just technology built in to the iPhone, the Argus app can serve as a pedometer and track where you've been, and keep track of distance traveled and calories burned. However, the app can collect additional types of data (using the sensors built into the iPhone and Apple Watch, or another fitness/activity tracker, as well as data you manually enter), and then incorporate this information into its analysis.

Argus also offers an interactive, social component that enables you to share your activity information with others in the Argus online community and participate in fitness-oriented challenges with or against other people. These challenges are a fun way to help you stay motivated and active.

The first time you use the app, tap on the Menu icon in the top-left corner of the screen, and select the Settings option. From the Settings page, fill in the fields to create a personal profile. Enter your name, weight, body fat percentage, height, date of birth, and gender.

If you'll be using the app with a compatible Bluetooth scale, turn on this feature so the app can collect data automatically from the scale each time you weigh yourself. To do this, from the Settings menu, tap on the Devices & Apps option, and then tap on the Connect button for your compatible app, device, or equipment.

Also, scroll down the Settings menu to customize specific app settings. For example, turn on the Show Steps on App Icon option to display your current step count for the day as a Badge on the iPhone's Home screen in the top-right corner of the Argus app icon.

Tap on the Me tab along the top of the screen and a unique, easy-to-understand, color-coded, honeycomb-looking interface appears (see Figure 12.4). Each hexagon displays a useful piece of information about yourself, your activity level, or something about your daily fitness. This interface gives you a snapshot view of your daily activity, as well as one-tap tools for logging information or viewing more data. Useful fitness tips, healthy recipes, and local weather information, for example, are also available by tapping on certain hexagons on this screen.

FIGURE 12.4

What sets this app apart is its interactive, honeycomb-looking interface that offers one-tap access to key app features, as well as an at-a-glance view of your daily activity.

Tap on any of the honeycomb hexagons to access additional app features or display more information. For example, if you tap on the Daily Steps hexagon, a more detailed Steps screen appears that includes an hour-by-hour chart showcasing your activity, the time spent that day being active, the number of steps taken, the distance traveled, and the number of calories burned.

> ✅ **TIP** Customize the app's Me screen by assigning color-coded hexagons to display or gather data you want to see. To do this, tap on the plus sign (I) icon in the lower-right corner of the screen (refer to Figure 12.4), and then tap on one of the customizable options (such as Sleep, Status Update, Food, or Heart Rate) to add a honeycomb hexagon for it on the main screen.

The Daily Steps screen is a daily summary of your activity. Tap on the left or right arrow near the top of the screen to view your activity data for previous days. Likewise, if from the main honeycomb screen you tap on the Weight box, a Body Weight screen displays a chart that summarizes your day-to-day weight fluctuation over a one-month period, and provides additional weight-related information in a graphic way.

The Argus app also helps you track your hydration level—how much water, tea and/or coffee you drink per day. When you drink water, for example, simply tap on the Water hexagon on the honeycomb screen to quickly log this fluid intake.

You can access two other elements of this app, Challenges and Workout Plans, from the main screen to help you become more active and stay motivated. Challenges enable you to compete against other people (from the Argus online community) in daily or weekly competitions that involve achieving specific step goals, for example. Each Challenge is slightly different, so there's plenty of variety.

The app's Workout Plans feature enables you to choose and then follow a pre-created workout plan. Each plan includes a personalized schedule, video-based instruction and demonstrations, a virtual coach that offers voice guidance and feedback, and daily summaries of your progress. To set up a Workout Plan, simply tap on the Workout Plans Sign Up box on the main screen. Subscribe to the Premium version of the app to access many more specialized Workout Plans.

After the app collects activity data over an extended period, tap on the Insights tab at the top of the screen to view detailed and colorful charts, easy-to-read tables, and summaries of your activity level, goals, and achievements. If you opt to become active in the Argus online community, tap on the Friends tab at the top of the screen to access newsfeeds from other people and communicate with fellow app users.

Like many of the general fitness-tracking apps, Argus focuses on monitoring your daily movement primarily using a pedometer. Thus, it doesn't matter what types of activity you participate it, because the app continuously tracks your movement. This app is visually interesting, easy to navigate and use, and customizable.

FITNET PERSONAL FITNESS WORKOUTS

The Fitnet app, shown in Figure 12.5, specializes in offering a comprehensive workout routine that you can do almost anywhere, with a minimal time commitment. By combining yoga, strength, and cardio exercise with video-based instruction and virtual coaching, the app helps you experience a well-rounded daily workout in as little as 5 to 10 minutes per day.

> **NOTE** Fitnet is a free app for the iPhone and Apple Watch that offers in-app purchase options that grant access to participate in ongoing fitness challenges.

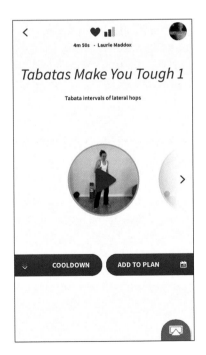

FIGURE 12.5

Use the Fitnet app to guide you through comprehensive workouts without your needing to visit a gym.

In addition to more than 100 video-based workout sessions (hosted by certified fitness trainers), the app offers weekly fitness challenges that you can unlock as in-app purchases. Fitnet also works with the Apple Watch, and to watch the workout videos, you can use AirPlay (via an Apple TV device) to see this content on your HD television set.

Fitnet requires you to select from a library of weekly Workout Plans, each of which can help you achieve a specific goal. The plans are sorted by level of difficulty. After you select a plan, you can add it to the iPhone's Calendar, so you're reminded to participate in each daily session.

As you work out, the app (with the help of an Apple Watch or a fitness/activity tracker) monitors your activity level, steps, and heart rate, and then calculates your calories burned. This is all information that you can share with the iPhone's Health app. The information and data that's collected depends on whether you're using the iPhone app alone, or using it with the Apple Watch or a third-party fitness/activity tracker. To gather the most accurate data automatically during your workouts, use this app with the Apple Watch or an optional fitness/activity tracker.

When you're ready to begin a session, simply tap on the Play icon, and then follow along as you watch the workout videos on your iPhone's screen. These videos are professionally produced and easy to understand. While you work out, your iPhone (and Apple Watch or activity tracker) gathers data, which is ultimately used to help you track your progress.

If you're using an Apple Watch, it displays information pertaining to the workout video you're watching, and works as a remote control that allows you to play, pause, and resume the videos on your iPhone.

> ☑ **TIP**   As you first start using the app, if you're not already in top physical shape, be sure to select one of the easier Workout Plans to follow. By completing the easier Workout Plans first, over a several-week period you'll build up the strength and stamina to tackle the more difficult plans.
>
> Because each workout plan offers a different combination of exercises, this variety might enable you to stay motivated and interested in pursuing your fitness goals over the long term.

Fitnet is ideal for beginners who want to become more physically active and participate in an organized fitness routine, without making a serious time commitment or having to join a gym.

> **TIP**   One unique feature of the Fitnet app is that while you're watching a workout video and following along with it, your iPhone's front-facing camera can record you working out. The app analyzes your movement and synchronicity with the trainer in the video and provides you with real-time feedback. Fitnet refers to this feature as the world's first "biometric webcam" for the iPhone. You can also forward the recorded video to a Fitnet personal trainer for evaluation. An additional fee applies for this consultation service.

HUMAN – ACTIVITY & CALORIE TRACKER

The Human – Activity & Calorie Tracker is a free app (with in-app purchases offered) that's also compatible with the Apple Watch. Ideal for beginners, the focus of this fitness app, shown in Figure 12.6, is to get you to move for at least 30 minutes per day. The app automatically tracks your activity throughout the day, whether you're walking, running, cycling, participating in a fitness class, or a working out at the gym.

FIGURE 12.6

The goal of the Human app is to encourage you to move and be active for at least 30 minutes per day.

Throughout the day, the Human app continuously measures your active minutes, distance covered, and calories burned, and collects other data if you use the app with the Apple Watch or another fitness/activity tracker.

> **NOTE** To gather accurate data throughout each day, you must either carry your iPhone with you at all times, or wear the Apple Watch (or a compatible fitness/activity tracker).

You can set up the app to remind you throughout the day to stand up and be active, so that you can achieve your daily activity goal. At any time from the app, you can see an "at-a-glance" summary of your progress.

In addition to tracking your movement, the app encourages you to be active with other people (real-life friends).

> **TIP** The Human app, and others like it, uses several different technologies built in to the iPhone. The first time you use the app, you need to grant permission for the app to access your iPhone's Location Services (GPS) and motion tracking capabilities. So the app can display reminders throughout the day, turn on the Notifications function. Also be sure to grant permission for the Human app to share data with the iPhone's Health app.

After you set up a profile in the app and register for a free online-based account, the app begins tracking your activity. You can view activity data from the app's main dashboard, or exit out of the app by pressing the Home button, and then go about your day. The app continues tracking your activity in the background.

> **! CAUTION** The Human app needs to run in the background throughout the day. After you launch the app, press the Home button to exit out of it, leaving it running in the background. Do not shut down the app by double-pressing the Home button to access multitasking mode, and then swiping up to shut down the app.
>
> If you need to reset your iPhone for any reason, simply relaunch the Human app so it can resume tracking your activity.

The Human app is not designed to transform your body, help you lose a lot of weight, or assist you in building muscle. It's simply a tool created to help you lead a healthier overall lifestyle by motivating you to move and be active for at least 30 minutes per day. What's nice is that you can spread out your daily activity throughout your day in short increments. You receive activity credit for doing basic activities such as walking your dog or taking the stairs instead of an escalator or elevator.

> **TIP** From the Settings menu in the app, be sure to adjust your Daily Goal. For example, you can start out at 30 minutes per day, but after a few weeks, extend this goal to 60, 90, or 120 minutes. To access the Settings menu, tap on the Profile icon at the bottom of the screen, and then tap on the gear-shaped Settings icon in the top-right corner of the screen. Next, tap on the Daily Goal option to adjust it.
>
> Also turn on and adjust the Nudge If Inactive option, so the app will remind you to be active throughout the day and help you achieve your daily activity goal. When you set this option to Never, the app issues no reminders.

MAPMYFITNESS

Other chapters in this book offer tips for using the MapMyRun, MapMyWalk, and MapMyRide apps (each available separately from the App Store). MapMyFitness is a more general-purpose activity monitoring app that not only tracks your daily activity, but also keeps track of where you've been and enables you to select a pre-planned route to follow when participating in a walk, run, or bike ride, for example.

MapMyFitness, shown in Figure 12.7, is available as a free or paid ($2.99) app. An additional in-app purchase option for subscribing to the premium MVP service is offered for $5.99 per month or $29.00 per year. The free version of the app displays banner ads, whereas the paid version offers an ad-free experience.

Unlike the other more specialized Map My… apps, this one allows you to track activity for more than 600 different types of workouts and activities, from walking or running, to cycling, yoga, gym workouts, or cross training. You're free to do whatever fitness activities you want, and this app tracks and analyzes the results of the activity.

Although as of Summer 2015 MapMyFitness did not yet support the Apple Watch, it is compatible with many of the other popular fitness/activity trackers and optional Bluetooth health and fitness-related devices on the market. When you use any of these devices with the MapMyFitness app, it can collect a broader range of data.

FIGURE 12.7
The MapMyFitness app's user interface is similar to that of the other apps in the MapMy... series.

CONNECTING TO FITNESS EQUIPMENT
MapMyFitness is compatible with ANT+ devices, including compatible home gym equipment and workout equipment found at many gyms and fitness centers (see Figure 12.8).

To learn more about how this industry-standard wireless communications protocol allows your iPhone to import data from other equipment and devices, such as an ANT+ compatible treadmill or elliptical machine, for example, visit www.thisisant.com/consumer/ant-101/what-is-ant.

From this website, you can access an interactive database of all fitness equipment and devices that are ANT+ compatible and that can share data with the MapMyFitness app and your iPhone.

These days, most gym equipment is ANT+ compatible or has its own proprietary app that allows workout data to be transferred from the equipment's own onboard computer to your iPhone via a Bluetooth or Wi-Fi connection.

This is true for the popular Peloton Cycle (www.pelotoncycle.com), NordicTrack equipment that supports the iFit feature (www.nordictrack.com/fitness/en/NordicTrack/iFit), and several pieces of home fitness equipment from Bowflex (www.bowflex.com), such as the Bowflex Max Trainer.

FIGURE 12.8

Many pieces of home fitness equipment can wirelessly transmit workout data from their own onboard computer to a compatible app on the iPhone.

NOTE   Wahoo Fitness and Garmin Fit are two other free, fitness-oriented iPhone apps for activity and workout tracking that can collect data from ANT+ compatible gym equipment like treadmills, elliptical machines, and exercise bikes.

Depending on your chosen activity, the MapMyFitness app automatically collects relevant data and stats, like pace, route, distance, time, heart rate, and calories burned.

Like the other apps in the MapMy… collection, this one has a strong focus on route planning and tracking where you've been. This feature is particularly useful during outdoor walks, runs, bike rides, or other similar activities, but less useful during traditional workouts, fitness classes, or in-home exercise routines, for example.

The app's other features, however, are more useful, regardless of the activity being tracked. If you're already using one of the other MapMy… apps, use the same MapMyFitness.com account login information and password. After you create your free account, you can freely participate in the active MapMyFitness.com online community, and share details about your achievements online.

> **NOTE** The MapMyFitness app uses the same user interface as the other MapMy… apps and gives you online access to a vast database of walking, running, or bike routes. By unlocking the paid MVP features, you can take advantage of the app's virtual coaching tools and other more advanced features.

NIKE+ TRAINING CLUB

The Nike+ Running app for the iPhone and Apple Watch has been a pioneer when it comes to using mobile technology as a fitness tool. If your fitness activities extend beyond running and are more exercise or workout oriented, the Nike+ Training Club app will probably be better suited to your needs. This free app offers a guided collection of exercises and workout routines that display on your iPhone in live-action video (see Figure 12.9).

FIGURE 12.9

The Nike+ Training Club app features more than 100 professionally produced video workouts that are easy to follow.

Many of the more than 100 video-based workout routines available via this app are hosted by celebrity athletes and Nike Master Trainers. Beyond just providing workout videos to watch and follow along with, the app focuses on motivating you and serving as a virtual fitness coach that's available to you whenever and wherever you can work out.

Whether you're looking to tone up, lose weight, or enhance your strength, for example, the individual workouts offered by Nike+ Training Club can help you achieve specific goals. However, by grouping these workouts together into organized four-week programs, this single app can help you more systematically achieve your goals.

> **NOTE** Like the other Nike+ apps for the iPhone, Nike+ Training Club tracks your activity and allows you to earn NikeFuel. According to Nike, NikeFuel is, "a simple universal way to measure how much you move, providing you with insights, motivation and opportunities to become a better athlete…NikeFuel measures your whole body movement focusing only on the energy required to do an activity. NikeFuel is calculated the same way for everyone. It doesn't take into account body weight, gender or age."

Nike+ Training Club is for people at all fitness levels, enabling users to design a fitness and workout routine that fits into their schedule and that's for the home, outside, or at a gym. The app includes tools for gathering, tracking, and analyzing activity data, and for sharing the workout experience with others.

After you create a free online-based account, the Nike+ Training Club encourages you to select an initial workout based on a goal. Goal options include Get Lean, Get Toned, Get Strong, or Get Focused. Next, select an Experience Level.

> **TIP** Choose the Beginner level if you work out less than four or five times per month, or you're just starting to pursue a more fitness-oriented lifestyle. Select the Intermediate level if you already work out between two and three times per week. Only select the Advanced level if you typically work out three to five times per week and are ready for more physically demanding workouts.

Based on your overall goal and activity level, the app recommends various workouts, which range in length from 15 to 60 minutes each. After you select a workout, the iPhone downloads it from the Internet. The workout's description lists its focus, duration, approximately how many calories you'll burn, how much NikeFuel you'll earn, and whether special equipment is required, such as a resistance band.

One nice feature of the app is that while you're watching the workout videos, you can select your own music to play in the background. From any workout's description screen, tap on the musical note icon, and then select a pre-created Playlist from the iPhone's Music app, select an Album that's stored on your iPhone, or choose songs from the Music app's library.

Tap on the Customize icon to see an exercise-by-exercise list (see Figure 12.10) and how much time will be spent on each exercise during the selected workout. If you choose, from this screen, tap on the Edit icon to adjust this list and modify the workout by moving, adding, or removing exercises, or altering the amount of time you'll spend on one or more of the listed exercises during that workout.

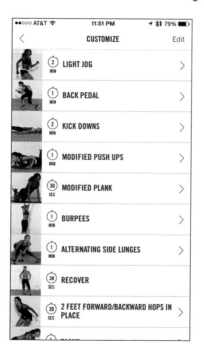

FIGURE 12.10

You can view an overview of each workout, and then customize it.

After the workout loads into your iPhone, either watch the video on your iPhone's screen, or use the iPhone's AirPlay feature (with an Apple TV device) to view the video on your television set. When you're ready to begin, tap on the Do Workout button, followed by the Play button.

Now, follow along with the fitness trainer. At any time, tap on the Pause icon to take a break. To end the workout early, tap on the End Workout button. Because a real-life personal trainer isn't on-hand to help you, pay careful attention to the onscreen trainer during new exercise demonstrations.

> **❗CAUTION** When using any fitness app or watching any fitness video, perform each exercise correctly to avoid potential injury. The Nike+ Training Club app offers detailed instructions, photos, and video demonstrations for each exercise.
>
> However, if you're a beginner, consider supplementing what you learn from the app with in-person sessions with a personal trainer or fitness coach. By working with a trainer at a local gym, for example, you can learn the basics, and ensure you're performing exercises correctly. You can then use an app to work out at your convenience, and know you're doing the moves correctly.

Out of all the general fitness apps available from the App Store, the Nike+ Training Club app is one of the very best. It offers you a comprehensive workout plan, top-notch instruction, flexibility, plenty of variety, and the ability to work out when and where it's convenient, without your having to visit a gym.

> **☑ TIP** During a workout, if you're instructed to do an exercise that you've never done or are not familiar with, or you're not sure you're doing it correctly, pause the video and tap on the Information icon near the lower-right corner of the screen. A series of photos with informative captions explains how to correctly do that particular exercise in greater detail (see Figure 12.11).
>
> After scrolling through the photos and reading the instructions, tap on the Video icon to view a short video of the exercise being done correctly. When you're ready to resume the workout, tap on the "<" icon in the top-left corner of the screen, and then tap on the Resume Workout button.

FIGURE 12.11

For every exercise featured in the app, you can access step-by-step text, photos, and video-based instructions for how to perform it correctly.

FITMO GOES BEYOND OFFERING JUST A VIRTUAL TRAINER

The majority of fitness-related apps available for the iPhone take the knowledge, experience, and philosophies of real-life trainers and fitness experts and use this information to create a virtual coach or trainer who typically offers guidance in the app. Although this guidance might be based on the app's analysis of your performance data, it is not based on a human trainer or coach actually seeing or monitoring your activities.

By using more of the technologies offered by the Internet and iPhone, including text messaging and video call capabilities, some fitness apps provide innovative ways to enable human trainers and fitness experts to interact with people using specific apps. Of course, using one of these apps is more costly than one that relies solely on a virtual coach or instructor, but this alternative is much less costly than hiring a personal trainer at a local gym, for example.

What's great about apps that merge interactive technology with human trainers or coaches is that the data the iPhone (and Apple Watch) collects while you work out on your own can easily be shared with the human coach, so he or she can see exactly what activities you do, without physically being next to you during your workouts.

The Fitmo app for the iPhone provides the knowledge, experience, and benefits of a personal trainer during your workout. What sets this app apart from other general fitness apps is that this one connects you to a handpicked personal trainer who is matched up with you based on your experience level and your goals.

The personal trainer you're linked up with helps you more clearly define your goals, and then develops a personalized plan to help you achieve them. The Fitmo app tracks all of your workout activities and relevant data is sent to your trainer, who stays in contact with you via text message and video chats.

Using an app like Fitmo, you can work out when and where it's convenient, follow a fitness plan that was created specifically for you by a professional trainer, and have access to that human trainer who will hold you accountable, help to keep you motivated, and make sure you're doing everything correctly.

Fitmo, for example, is ideal for fitness enthusiasts at all levels who are too busy to join or visit a gym on a regular basis, or who travel often and find themselves needing to work out at different times of the day or night in various locations.

> **✔ TIP** The Fitmo app helps you set your fitness-oriented goals, and then matches you with a handpicked personal trainer. Based on your level of commitment and budget, you select the level of the trainer's involvement. You then receive a personalized plan, which the app guides you through. Results from your workouts are transmitted to your trainer, who then provides feedback.

Prior to being matched up with a trainer, you must answer basic questions about your goals (see Figure 12.12). Your primary goal can include maintaining a healthy diet, building strength, losing weight, running, enhancing your flexibility, or it can be something more specific or personalized. If you need help choosing a goal, tap on the Need Help? option to initiate a text message–based conversation with a fitness expert.

FIGURE 12.12

Answer the goal-related questions posed to you by the app as honestly as possible, to ensure you're matched up with the most appropriate trainer.

Based on the overall goal you select, the app asks you additional questions to help you more clearly define that goal. Then, based on the responses you provide, the app asks you to choose a subscription level, which determines how much access you'll have to your personal trainer each month.

For less than $10.00 per month, one plan includes one monthly video call with your trainer, as well as a personalized training program. For about $50.00 per month (prices vary based on the trainer), in addition to one video call per month and the personalized training program, you can communicate daily with your trainer through unlimited text messaging.

Starting in 2016, the app will also offer an option to hire your personal trainer for in-person training sessions (at a per-hour rate the trainer sets), in addition to the monthly video call and ongoing text messaging. Apple Watch integration is also in the works.

> **NOTE** The initial consultation with the handpicked trainer is free. You can do this either via video call or text message.

CHAT WITH AN EXPERT

LEARN MORE ABOUT THE FITMO APP FROM ONE OF ITS CREATORS

Paul Musters is an executive at Fitmo and one of the people responsible for the creation of the Fitmo app. One reason this app was developed was because the founders of the company saw how difficult it is for some people to get started working out, and then stay focused and motivated.

Prior to joining Fitmo, Musters was a professional triathlete. After sustaining a shoulder injury that prevented him from competing in future triathlons, he pursued a career as a fitness trainer. His focus was on helping clients prepare for marathons and triathlons. After several years working as a personal trainer, he wound up meeting the founder of Fitmo and joining the company.

"Everyone knows that it's good to work out and be physically fit, but far fewer people take the steps required to get started," said Musters. "It's very hard for an iPhone app alone to be able to provide someone with enough truly personalized information and feedback. Plus, after a while, those reminders or motivational messages the generic fitness app generates tend to be ignored. It's much harder to ignore messages and reminders from a human trainer, who is there to hold you accountable."

One goal of Fitmo is to give more people affordable access to personal trainers. "An in-person appointment with a personal trainer can easily cost between $80.00 and $100.00 per hour, and to see real results, you'll need to meet with that trainer regularly over an extended period. Many people who could benefit from working with a personal trainer can't afford this. Thanks to Fitmo, someone can have access to a personal trainer for an entire month, for less than the cost of one in-person, one-on-one session."

Obviously, when you work with a Fitmo trainer, he or she is not standing next to you and watching you work out, and cannot provide feedback on the spot. The advantage, however, is that you can get your questions answered, receive personal guidance, and receive a personalized fitness plan at an affordable price.

Fitmo works with a constantly growing team of more than 100 personal trainers, each of whom has a specialty. Based on the questions posed by the app, the Fitmo company can match up people with the most appropriate trainer. "If someone tells the app she wants to train to run a marathon, we'll team that person up with a coach with experience training marathon runners," said Musters. "Our goal is to combine technology with human interaction to pair up people with the most appropriate trainer possible, to ensure their success."

The Fitmo app provides the tools needed to participate in video calls and text message–based conversations (see Figure 12.13). In other words, the user doesn't have to use FaceTime, Skype, or the Messages app.

"We encourage the first interaction someone has with their trainer to be via a video call. This allows for a personal relationship to be developed. Then, after this initial video call, the trainer will create a personal fitness plan and schedule, which becomes accessible to the user from the Fitmo app," said Musters.

FIGURE 12.13

After you're paired up with a personal trainer, your introduction and free consultation can be via a video call or chat.

Each personalized workout plan includes a detailed schedule and workout videos for the user to watch and follow along with. These videos are either produced or handpicked by the trainer, based on the user's goals and fitness level. As workouts are completed, information is sent to the trainer, who can then provide feedback or motivation in the form of text messages.

"Participants are constantly encouraged to provide feedback to their trainer, so the workouts and schedule can be tweaked as needed, if something is too easy or too difficult, for example," said Musters. "While Fitmo can be used to help people become more physically fit in general, we found that our app and service works best if the client has a specific goal they're trying to achieve, within a particular time period. For example, they want to lose 20 pounds in time for the summer, or they want to prepare for a marathon or triathlon to be held on a certain date.

"Our trainers make sure each client's goals are realistic and attainable. One of the common mistakes we see people make is that they set unrealistic goals or unrealistic time frames in which to achieve those goals, and then they become frustrated, and ultimately lose focus or interest. Our trainers work with clients to understand the reason for the goal. I believe that the reason why someone wants to achieve a fitness goal is often more important than the goal itself when it comes to motivation."

Thanks to the iPhone and Apple Watch, fitness-minded people now have access to extremely powerful tools to help them collect data. The problem, according to Musters, is that people can now collect too much data, or data that they don't know what to do with.

"People need to understand how to collect and track data, but more importantly, they need to understand what this data means and how it can help them. This is one area where working with a personal trainer can be useful. The trainer, who understands the data, can help decipher it for the user," explained Musters.

One piece of advice that Musters offers when working out while wearing the Apple Watch or another device with a display is that the athlete doesn't always need to focus on the real-time data as it's being collected. Instead, athletes should focus on enjoying the activity, knowing that their Apple Watch or fitness tracker is collecting data. They can often wait until the end of their workout to review that data.

When Musters works out on his own, he personally uses the Strava Running and Cycling app (which you can learn more about in Chapter 8, "Explore Fitness Strategies for Bicyclers.")

He explained, "I like the way this app tracks data, and I also like the social aspect it offers. With Strava, you can compete against other people and compare your stats and accomplishments with your friends. Another app that I use often is called Inner Balance. This more specialized app measures heart function during workouts using a proprietary sensor that clips to your earlobe to measure your heart rhythm."

One of the biggest misconceptions people have about working out, according to Musters, is that it always has to be difficult. "After setting a goal for yourself that you are passionate about, and that you have a strong motivation to achieve, find ways to make your workouts or fitness activities enjoyable and fun," said Musters.

FIND MUSIC TO KEEP YOU MOTIVATED WHILE ACTIVE

An extensive amount of research indicates that music can be an extremely powerful motivational tool during a workout or intense physical activity (see Figure 13.1). Putting the research aside, when you're running, working out, or being physically active, if you're listening to one of your favorite up-tempo songs, chances are you'll feel a bit more motivated and energetic.

FIGURE 13.1

Listening to upbeat music while you work out is proven to have a variety of benefits.

> **TIP** Just as you can use slow-tempo music to help relax your mind and put you to sleep, up-tempo music can help your brain harness your energy and focus it on your activity. The trick is to choose appropriate music that you truly enjoy and that inspires you. Many popular music streaming services have curated playlists geared specifically to motivate you during fitness activities.

Everyone's musical taste is different. Thus, choose a music genre and selection of songs that you personally enjoy and relate to, and that upon hearing, make you want to push harder. People often associate their favorite songs with events or moments in their lives. As a result, when you listen to songs that your mind associates with winning, success, power, or achievement, for example, your body will react accordingly, and you can more easily muster the strength, determination, and physical energy needed to complete the fitness-related task at hand.

Research published by numerous sources over the past decade has identified five ways in which music can influence preparation and competitive performances. For each of these five areas, the positive impact that listening to the right music can have is explained here:

- **Dissociation:** Music can distract the mind from sensations of fatigue.
- **Arousal Regulation:** Music can stimulate the emotional and psychological arousal of the mind, and work as a stimulant.
- **Synchronization:** Music can help an athlete synchronize repetitive behaviors to generate increased levels of output during activities like running, rowing, cycling.
- **Acquisition of Motor Skills:** Music can enhance someone's motor skills and help to improve coordination, particularly in situations where stylistic movements are important.
- **Attainment of Flow** (or getting in "the zone"): Music helps someone more easily reach a mental state of flow, get into "the zone," or reach a state of hyperfocus. This is a mental or psychological state in which athletes are totally focused on the task at hand, time seems to disappear, and they become less focused on fatigue or even pain, as they become completely absorbed in what they're doing. They also lose a sense of reflective self-consciousness, which can be detrimental to achieving success.

These positive impacts are the reasons why gyms pump loud and upbeat music through the speakers, and always play high-intensity music during aerobics, Zumba, or spinning classes, for example. By creating your own custom playlists to enjoy during solo activities, you can just as easily benefit from the positive impact music can have on your workout or physical performance.

MAKE YOUR MUSIC READILY ACCESSIBLE

If you're working out or doing a fitness-oriented activity in your home, for example, connecting your iPhone to speakers or your television set (either using appropriate cables, a Bluetooth wireless connection, or an AirPlay wireless connection) enables you to blast your music so that the sound surrounds you.

When you're working out outside, at a gym, or elsewhere, you'll still want to experience your own music, played loudly, but you'll need to use headphones or earbuds to keep the listening experience private.

The Apple EarPods that came with your iPhone or that you can also purchase separately ($29.00; http://store.apple.com/us/product/MD827LL/A/apple-earpods-with-remote-and-mic#) are cable-based earbuds that you place in your ears and that you connect to your iPhone via a short cable (see Figure 13.2). Many similar earbud and headphone models are available, but any of these can potentially hinder your physical activity due to their often annoying (and often too short) cable.

The EarPods cord connects to the iPhone

FIGURE 13.2

Earbuds, like Apple's EarPods, or headphones with a cable can hinder your movement during a workout or physically intense activity.

Thus, thanks to Bluetooth technology, both earbuds (which you can insert into your ears) and headphones (which you wear over your ears) are also now available in wireless models, so you can be up to around 30 feet from your iPhone, yet still hear your music and control your playlists via the iPhone's Music app. Figure 13.3 shows traditional wireless, over-the-ear headphones. These particular headphones are from Jabra.

The Beats PowerBeats2 Wireless In-Ear Headphones ($199.95, www.beatsbydre. com) appear in photos throughout this book, because they're one of the most popular options for active people. These wireless headphones come in a variety of colors, fit snugly in your ears, and enable you to do a wide range of activities without them falling out.

They are available from consumer electronics stores, but plenty of other companies, including JBL, Jabra, Plantronics, and Sony, also offer wireless headphones or earbuds that are suitable for athletes and active individuals because they are lightweight, fit snugly in or over your ears, offer superior sound quality, and in some cases, are waterproof (so that you can use them while swimming, for example).

FIGURE 13.3

You wear these Jabra wireless headphones over the ear.

> **TIP** Based on the type of activities you plan to do, choose a speaker, ear-buds, or headphone solution that enables you to experience high-quality sound, drown out ambient noise, and provides easy access and control over your music while you participate in that activity. Chances are that a wireless solution will be more comfortable and convenient than having to be physically connected to your iPhone via a cable.

> **TIP** If you're an Apple Watch user, you can remotely control the Music app on your iPhone directly from the watch.

CHOOSE YOUR MUSIC

Whether you work out for a few minutes or several hours per day, you'll want to compile a personal digital music library that consists of music that's suitable to listen to during these activities. You'll ultimately pinpoint a handful of songs that you love and that generate the best results for you. However, you also want suitable music to help you warm up, cool down, and keep you motivated and energized throughout your chosen activity.

To create a soundtrack for your workouts, think about the music genres, artists, or bands that make you want to move, that inspire you, or that help to quickly put you in the right frame of mind for the activity you plan to do. The genre of the music you choose (rock, pop, techno, or even show tunes) doesn't matter, as long as the tempo of the songs you choose is upbeat, and the music selection helps you get and stay "in the zone" during your workouts.

There are many music streaming services to choose from, such as Apple Music, Pandora, and Spotify. There are also apps that allow you to stream live radio broadcasts via your iPhone. Using the Music app that comes preinstalled with your iPhone, you can manage the digital music you own and that you have stored within your smartphone, plus access the Apple Music service and iTunes Radio. This chapter focuses mainly on using the Music app, iTunes Radio, and Apple Music. At the end of the chapter, you learn about some alternative options available to you.

FIND AND PURCHASE MUSIC FROM THE ITUNES STORE

Apple's online-based iTunes Store, shown in Figure 13.4, offers one of the largest collections of digital music in the world, making it an ideal source for music for iPhone and Apple Watch users. From here, you can find, preview, purchase, and download individual songs or entire albums.

NOTE Information about the iTunes Store app in this chapter relates to the iOS 8.4 version of the app released in June 2015. In late 2015, Apple plans to release iOS 9. Thus, additional features, the layout of screens, and/or the appearance of icons might be different if you have a newer (or older) version of the iOS installed on your smartphone.

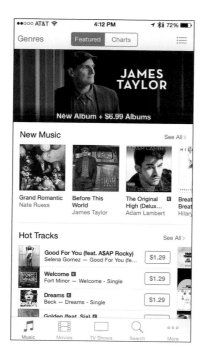

FIGURE 13.4

You can access the iTunes Store directly from your Internet-connected iPhone, as well as from an iPad or any computer that has the iTunes software installed.

Each time you purchase music content from the iTunes Store, that content is downloaded and stored on the mobile device or computer it was purchased from. However, that same content is also added (for free) to your online-based Apple iCloud account. Thus, it instantly becomes accessible from all of your computers and mobile devices that link to that same iCloud account, so you don't have to purchase multiple copies of that song or album.

> **NOTE** Apple's streaming music service called Apple Music, while integrated with iTunes and the Music app, is a distinct service from the music purchases described here. To learn more about Apple Music, see "Discover the New Apple Music Service," later in this chapter.

You use the iTunes Store app that comes preinstalled on your iPhone, as well as the iTunes software that comes preinstalled on all Macs (and that you can download and install for free onto Windows-based PCs) to browse and purchase music from the iTunes Store.

After you set up a single account using your Apple ID and password, you pay for all music and content from iTunes using the credit/debit card that's linked to your account. Thus, you do not have to manually re-enter payment information for each purchase.

> ☑ **TIP** Instead of paying for iTunes Store content using a debit/credit card, prepaid iTunes Gift Cards are available from Apple Stores, Apple.com, convenience stores, bookstores, gas stations, pharmacies, supermarkets, and many other retailers nationwide. These gift cards come in many different denominations, and you can quickly redeem them via the iTunes Store app or software to purchase content.
>
> You can also purchase iTunes Gift Cards online for yourself or give as a gift via email (http://store.apple.com/us/accessories/giftcards).

The iTunes Store app comes preinstalled on your iPhone and requires an Internet connection to use. For purchasing music, a cellular or Wi-Fi connection works fine. However, for purchasing other types of content, such as video (TV shows, music videos, or movies), you must use a Wi-Fi Internet connection.

To browse the online-based iTunes Store to find and purchase music, launch the iTunes Store app from the Home screen. Tap on the Music icon in the bottom-left corner of the screen (see Figure 13.5). If you know exactly what you're looking for, tap on the Search icon at the bottom-right corner of the screen.

After you tap on the Music icon you have a variety of ways to find music. Near the top-center of the screen, tap on the Featured tab to view listings for new and popular songs and albums that Apple recommends, and that are showcased in the iTunes Store's Featured section.

> ☑ **TIP** After tapping on the Music icon and Featured tab, if you scroll down to the bottom of the screen, you'll see a Quick Links heading. Below this heading are a variety of other options (shown in Figure 13.6).
>
> For example, to access content you've previously purchased from the iTunes Store, but that's not currently stored on the device you're using, tap on the Purchased option. To redeem an iTunes Gift Card, tap on the Redeem button. To send someone an iTunes Store Gift Card via email, tap on the Send Gift button, or to manage your Apple ID account, tap on the Apple ID button (which also displays your Apple ID username).

FIGURE 13.5

To browse the iTunes Store for music, tap on the Music icon, or use the Search feature if you know what you're looking for.

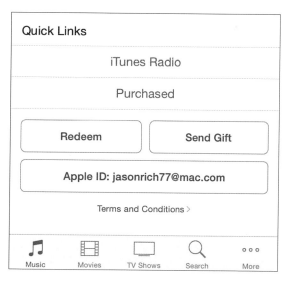

FIGURE 13.6

Manage your Apple ID account, redeem iTunes Gift Cards, or handle other features using options offered under the Quick Links heading.

VIEW ITUNES CHARTS TO SEE WHAT'S POPULAR

To view a listing of Top Charts and discover what's popular, tap on the Charts tab at the top-center of the screen. Then, if you're looking to see a Chart showcasing the most popular songs, look under the Songs heading, and to the right of that heading, tap on the See All option (see Figure 13.7). To see a chart listing the most popular Albums, look under the Albums heading, and tap on the See All option to the right of that heading.

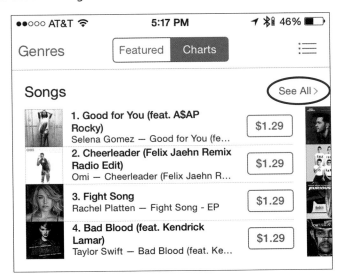

FIGURE 13.7
View all songs in a particular chart by tapping on the See All option.

> **TIP**   Another option when browsing the iTunes Store for music is to tap on the Music icon, and then tap on the Genres option in the top-left corner of the screen. From the Genres menu, tap on the type of music you're interested in. More than two dozen genre options are offered, including a Fitness & Workout genre, which offers an eclectic listing of popular songs to enjoy while working out.
>
> After choosing a specific music genre, tap on the Charts tab to view a "Best Sellers" chart for songs or albums in that particular genre. For example, select the Fitness & Workout genre, tap on the Charts tab, and then tap on the See All option next to the Songs heading to view a comprehensive listing of the most popular songs being purchased from the iTunes Store in the Fitness & Workout genre (see Figure 13.8). In other words, you can see the most popular songs other people are working out to.

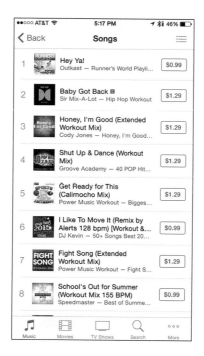

FIGURE 13.8
View a chart of the best-selling songs (or albums) from a particular music genre. Shown here is the Fitness & Workout Songs chart.

USE THE ITUNES SEARCH FIELD

To find a specific song, album, or music from a particular artist or band, tap on the Search icon, and in the Search field, enter what you're looking for. This can be an exact song title, a portion of a song title, an artist/group's name, or any other keyword or search phrase that will help you find what you're looking for.

After filling in the Search field and tapping on the Search key (on the iPhone's virtual keyboard), relevant song and album listings appear on the smartphone's screen. Tap on a listing to view more details about that song.

> **TIP** If you hear a song playing (on the radio, or over the speaker system at your gym, for example), and you want to know the name of the song, who it's performed by, and have the option to quickly purchase the song from the iTunes Store, then while the song is playing, activate Siri by pressing and holding down the Home button on your iPhone for one to two seconds, and when you hear the Siri prompt, say, "What song is this?" (You can also do this using the Apple Watch.)
>
> Siri listens to a few seconds of the song and then displays information about that song in the form of an iTunes Store listing.

PREVIEW SONGS BEFORE MAKING A PURCHASE

Any time you're viewing a music listing in the iTunes Store, tap on that listing to see more details about that song and the album it's from. Tap on the album's price button to purchase that entire album, or tap on the song's price button to purchase and download just that song.

To preview a song before purchasing and downloading it, tap on the song's title (not the Price icon). A portion of the selected song will stream from the Internet to your iPhone, and a preview of the song will start playing. If you like the song, tap on the Price icon to purchase it (shown in Figure 13.9).

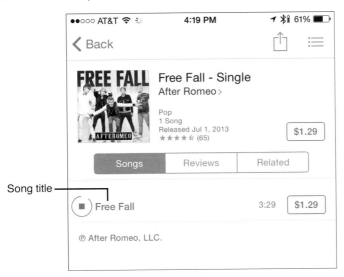

FIGURE 13.9

Tap on a song listing's title to hear a preview of the song.

> ☑ **TIP**   If you subscribe to the Apple Music service (described later in this chapter), you can access the iTunes Store's entire music library, which is comprised of more than 30 million songs, and stream any of those songs via the Internet to your iPhone (or almost any other Internet-enabled mobile device, Mac or PC).
>
> Apple Music enables you to listen to any music, and then if you choose, purchase your absolute favorite songs or albums so you can store that music on your iPhone, for example, and have it available to you anytime later, whether or not an Internet connection is available. Using Apple Music, it's also possible to store music you don't own within your mobile device for offline listening. This is done using the Make Available Offline option, which is a command that's accessible from the More menu while you're listing to music.

From an album or song's detailed description screen, tap on the Reviews tab to view the star-based rating and text-based reviews of the music. Tap on the Related tab to see similar listings for music from the same artist or similar bands or artists.

PURCHASE MUSIC FROM THE ITUNES STORE

When you're ready to purchase a song or music from the iTunes Store, tap on its Price button. The Price button lists the price of that content.

As soon as you tap on the Price button, it transforms into a Buy Song or Buy Album icon (see Figure 13.10). Tap on this icon to confirm your purchase. Enter your Apple ID password, or if you have an iPhone that's equipped with a Touch ID sensor, place your finger on the sensor to finalize the purchase.

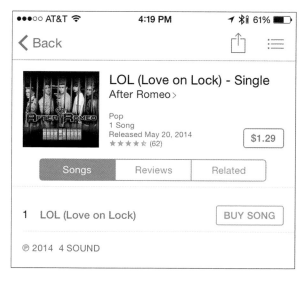

FIGURE 13.10

Tap on the Buy Song button to confirm your purchase decision.

The song/album you've purchased then automatically downloads to and is stored on your iPhone. In less than one minute (per song), it will then be available to play using the iPhone's Music app.

> **NOTE** If a Price button for a song or album says the word "Free," as opposed to listing a price, then the iTunes Store is offering the content at no charge. You still need to acquire that music and download it, using the same steps outlined in this section.
>
> As you browse music in the iTunes Store, when you see a Price icon with the word "Play," you have already purchased the song and it is currently stored on your iPhone.

> ☑ **TIP** To see how much internal storage space your digital music library is using on your iPhone, launch Settings, tap on the General option, tap on the Usage option, and then tap on the Manage Storage option. Tap on the listing for the Music app icon (or for any other music app you use, such as Spotify). A listing of all music stored on your device (and how much storage space these files use) appears. Tap on an individual listing to view more storage-related information.
>
> To delete songs and free up storage space, from the Music listing, tap on the Edit button, and then tap on the minus sign icon for each song you want to delete from your iPhone. Remember, you can always reload the previously purchased music from iCloud for free.

> ☑ **TIP** From the iTunes Store, you can purchase one or more songs from a particular album, or purchase the entire album outright. However, if you purchase one or more songs, when you view the album's listing either with the iTunes Store app or the Music app, the Complete My Album option displays.
>
> The Complete My Album option enables you to purchase the remaining (yet un-owned) songs from that album at a pro-rated price. In other words, you don't have to repurchase songs you've already bought separately to later get the entire album.

USE OTHER OPTIONS TO PURCHASE MUSIC

In addition to purchasing music from Apple's iTunes Store, which is accessible using the iTunes Store app on an iPhone or iPad, or the iTunes software on a Mac or PC, you have other options for purchasing music in digital format.

For example, there's the Amazon Digital Music Store (www.Amazon.com). Music acquired from the Amazon Music Store, however, requires the free Amazon Music app (https://itunes.apple.com/us/app/amazon-cloud-player/id510855668) on your iPhone; that is, unless you subscribe to the iTunes Music Match service that you can add to your iCloud account for $24.95 per year. With that service, you can load any music you have stored on your computer, whether purchased as a download or physical media, to your cloud-based music library. To learn more about this service, visit www.apple.com/itunes/itunes-match.

CONTROL YOUR MUSIC WITH THE MUSIC APP

In June 2015, Apple released iOS 8.4 for the iPhone, which included a totally redesigned version of the Music app, which is now chock-full of new features and functions, including access to the new Apple Music service.

> **NOTE** Apple describes the new Music app as being a "complete eco-system around music," and by the time you're done reading this chapter, you'll understand why.

The Music app continues to serve multiple purposes for experiencing music content. For example, it enables you to play purchased songs or albums stored on your iPhone. You can also use the app to create, manage, and play back custom song playlists that you create or acquire.

Plus, when your iPhone has a continuous Internet connection, you can launch the free iTunes Radio feature to stream music from the Internet, listen to the Beats 1 global radio station, and take advantage of the Music app's new Connect feature.

DISCOVER THE NEW APPLE MUSIC SERVICE

Also in June 2015, Apple launched a new music service called Apple Music. Although a free, three-month trial subscription to the service is available, individual users ultimately need to pay $9.99 per month for an ongoing subscription (or $15 a month for a family subscription that supports up to six users). Apple Music is accessible on the iPhone using iOS 8.4 or iOS 9. (It's also available from the iPad and Apple Watch, as well as PCs and Macs.)

Apple Music allows users to stream (not download) any music that's available from the iTunes Store on an on-demand and unlimited basis. In addition, music from independent bands, artists, and musicians is available.

> **NOTE** Music content you experience via Apple Music is streamed from the Internet, not purchased and stored on the device or computer you're using. One benefit to the on-demand aspect of the listening experience is that you can incorporate songs into playlists, even if you don't own them.

Apple Music also allows users to access curated playlists compiled by others, and listen to the live Beats 1 Internet radio station that can be heard globally. In addition, Apple Music allows fans to interact with their favorite artists and music groups in new and innovative ways through a feature that's built in to the new Music app called Connect.

Another useful feature of Apple Music is that you can quickly select one or more artists, songs, albums, or music genres that you love, and the service will recommend other music that's similar, based on your personal tastes. This is a great tool for discovering new, up-and-coming artists and bands, or for previewing new music from some of your favorite artists or bands.

 NOTE To learn more about Apple Music, visit www.apple.com/music.

USE THE MUSIC APP ON YOUR IPHONE

The Music app gives you total control over your music listening experience for music stored on your iPhone, and when listening to iTunes Radio and music from the iTunes Store that's streamed from the Internet.

NOTE This quick tutorial is based on the iOS 8.4 version of the Music app. Details and screens might vary based on the version of iOS on your device.

When you launch the Music app from the Home screen on your iPhone, along the bottom of the screen five new icons display: For You, New, Radio, Connect, and My Music (shown in Figure 13.11). From these icons you manage and experience music.

Here's a rundown of what each icon is used for:

- **For You:** Based on past music purchases, your music listening habits using the Music app, and information about your musical tastes that you provide to the app, the Music app recommends music you might be interested in, and provides collections of curated playlists.

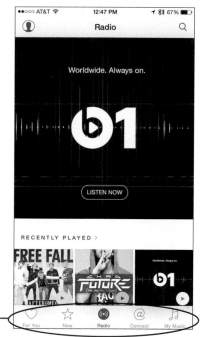

The Music app's new command icons

FIGURE 13.11

The Music app offers a new selection of icons displayed at the bottom of the screen. The Radio icon is selected here.

> ☑ **TIP**   When viewing the For You section of the Music app, tap on any music selection or listing to stream that music (if you subscribe to Apple Music). Tap on the song's More icon to add the selected (and playing) song to the My Music section of the app, or make it available for offline playing. This feature requires that you turn on the iCloud Music Library feature from Settings. To do this, launch Settings, tap on the Music option, and then turn on the iCloud Music Library feature.

■ **New:** Discover newly released music from well-known recording artists and bands, as well as music from independent and up-and-coming artists and bands. This includes new singles, new albums, spotlights on new artists, and curated music selections.

TIP If you're seeking recommendations for motivational, upbeat music to go along with your workouts, for example, after tapping on the New icon, scroll down to the Activities option, and select the Running or Working Out option (see Figure 13.12) to discover new music recommendations that will fit perfectly with your planned activity.

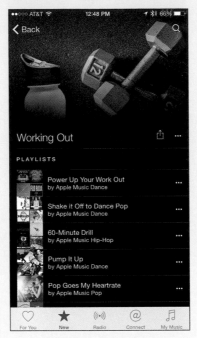

FIGURE 13.12

Discover new music to listen to during specific activities, like working out.

▪ **Radio:** In addition to giving you access to the free iTunes Radio service that allows you to create custom radio stations based on your music preferences, or listen to pre-created streaming stations, you can also tap on the Listen Now button for Beats 1 to tune into this 24/7 global broadcast. Using this feature requires a continuous Internet connection.

TIP Using iTunes Radio, to listen to a pre-created radio station, launch the Music app, tap on the Radio icon, and then scroll down to the Featured Stations listing. Tap on a listing to play that station, or scroll down further for a more extensive listing of stations based on genre.

Any time you're listening to any music with the Music app, to quickly create a custom iTunes Radio station based around that music selection, tap on the More icon (...) from the mini-player or Now Playing controls, and then tap on the Start Station menu option (see Figure 13.13).

FIGURE 13.13

Use the Start Station command when listening to any music with the Music app to create a custom iTunes Radio station based on that selection.

NOTE Based on the song, album, artist, or music genre you choose, iTunes Radio creates a custom radio station for you. Unless you're a paid Apple Music or iTunes Match subscriber, however, the programming will include commercials.

Keep in mind that you do not control the song selections or song order. You can, however, skip to the next song at any time, and for songs you like, tap on the heart-shaped "like" button, so iTunes Radio can better learn your music preferences.

- **Connect:** The Music app now offers an interactive online community where any artist or band can communicate directly with its fans by publishing music, videos, photos, or other content. A growing number of popular, as well as up-and-coming, artists and bands use this interactive online forum in much the same way as they would use a Facebook page or Twitter feed to communicate with their fans. In addition to the content that the artist/band uploads, Connect offers direct access to the selected artist's music.

> **☑ TIP** If you want to see the content uploaded by your favorite artists using the Music app's Connect feature, you first need to follow that artist. To follow artists/bands, navigate to the artist's page and tap the Follow button.
>
> To manage your list of followed artists, tap on the Connect icon and then tap on the See Who You're Following option. From here you can unfollow artists and find other artists or curators to follow. Tap on the Done option to save your changes.

■ **My Music:** From here you can manage all the music stored in your library. To use the My Music functionality portion of the app, no Internet connection is required, unless you want to listen to music that's stored in your iCloud account, but not on your smartphone. After tapping on the My Music option, tap on the Library tab at the top of the screen to find and play individual songs or albums, or tap on the Playlists tab to listen to or manage your playlists.

> **☑ TIP** Any time music is selected or playing via the Music app, near the bottom of the screen, just above the five command icons, a new mini-player displays that enables you to play or pause the music, or quickly access the app's Now Playing screen, which gives you more options than ever before for controlling the music playing on your iPhone.

MANAGE YOUR MUSIC FROM THE MUSIC APP

You can access, manage, and enjoy music stored on your iPhone either one song at a time, or by creating and listening to custom playlists. You do this by tapping on the My Music icon at the bottom of the Music app's screen.

For example, tap on the Library tab near the top center of the screen to see music you've recently acquired, under the Recently Added heading. You also can sort the music on your smartphone alphabetically by song title, artist, album, genre, or one of several other ways (shown in Figure 13.14). To do this, tap on the Songs pull-down menu and decide how you want your music sorted and displayed (shown in Figure 13.15).

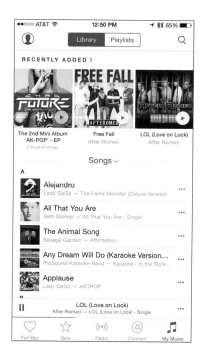

FIGURE 13.14

Manage the music stored on your iPhone by tapping on the My Music icon, followed by the Library tab.

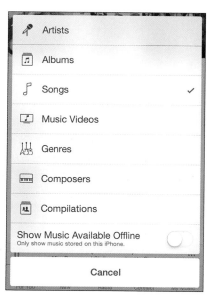

FIGURE 13.15

Sort and display the music stored on your iPhone in a variety of ways.

Also from the My Music screen, tap on the Playlists tab near the top center of the screen to access the in-app tools for creating, managing, accessing, and playing custom playlists.

CONTROL YOUR MUSIC USING THE MINI-PLAYER CONTROLS

Whenever music is playing via the Music app, and the app is currently open, the mini-player controls appear near the bottom of the screen, above the five command buttons (see Figure 13.16).

New mini-player controls

FIGURE 13.16

The mini-player controls display the name of the music, a time slider, a Play/Pause button, and a More icon.

To use the mini-player controls, tap on the Play/Pause button to start or stop the currently selected music, or tap on the More icon to display a menu that offers the following options:

- **Start Station:** Create a custom iTunes Radio station based on the currently playing music selection, whether it's a song stored on your iPhone, or any music streaming via the Apple Music service, for example.

- **Show in iTunes Store:** Immediately launch the iTunes Store app to view a listing for the currently playing music. From here, you can purchase the song (if applicable), purchase the album the song is part of, or see listings for other music from that artist/band.

- **Share Song:** Share your musical taste with others by sharing details about the song you're currently listening to. Tap on the Share Song option to display the familiar Share menu. You now have the option to send details about the music directly from the Music app via AirPlay, Messages, Mail, Twitter, Facebook, or Facebook Messenger, for example.

- **Remove from this Playlist:** If the currently playing song is part of a playlist you're listening to, tap on this option to remove the song from that playlist permanently. (If the song is stored on your iPhone, it remains accessible, but it will no longer be part of the currently selected playlist.)

- **Add to a Playlist:** If you want to add the currently playing song to one of your already-created playlists, tap on this option, and then select the playlist from the displayed listing.

> ☑ **TIP**   From the mini-player, to instantly switch to the Now Playing screen (see the next section), place your finger on the mini-player controls and swipe up.
>
> To then close the Now Playing screen and return to the mini-player controls and the Music app screen you were previously viewing, tap on the down-arrow icon in the top-left corner of the Now Playing screen.

CONTROL YOUR MUSIC FROM THE NOW PLAYING SCREEN

Whenever music is playing via the Music app, when you access the Now Playing screen, the album/artist artwork appears on the top half of the screen (see Figure 13.17).

FIGURE 13.17

The Now Playing screen displays information about the currently playing music.

Immediately below the album/artist artwork is the time slider. Place your finger on this slider to fast forward or rewind the song. To the left of the slider is a clock that displays how much of the song has played. To the right of the slider is a clock that displays how much of the song is remaining.

The song's title appears below the time slider, and below that are music control icons, which include:

- **Like:** Tap on this icon to "like" the currently playing song. This helps the Music app better learn your music preferences, which then helps it make more accurate music recommendations, and create more personalized programming when you use iTunes Radio, for example.

- **Rewind:** Tap this icon to switch to the previously played song. Press and hold down this icon to rewind the song.

- **Play/Pause:** When the music is playing, press the Pause icon to pause the music. When the music is paused, press the Play icon to restart the music from where you last left off.

- **Fast Forward:** Tap this icon to jump to the next song, or press and hold down this icon to fast forward the song.

- **Up Next:** View a listing of songs stored on your iPhone from the current playlist, or from the iTunes Radio programming lineup you're listing to. To switch to a different song, tap on its listing.

Located below the music control icons on the Now Playing screen is the volume slider; use your finger to move this slider left or right to decrease or increase the volume. You can also use the volume control buttons on the side of your iPhone and/or the volume control buttons on your earphones or headphones.

> **TIP** Yet another volume control slider is in the Control Center. Place your finger at the bottom of the iPhone's screen and swipe up to access the Control Center menu.

Four additional icons appear along the bottom of the Now Playing screen. From left to right, they are as follows:

- **Share:** Tap on this icon to access the Share menu and share details about the song with other people, or access the Remove from this Playlist option (if applicable).

- **Shuffle:** Shuffle the order in which you hear the currently selected playlist or music selections.

- **Repeat:** Tap on this icon to continuously repeat the currently selected song.

- **More:** Tap on this icon to reveal a menu that offers the following options: Start Station, Show in iTunes Store, Share Song, Add to a Playlist, and Delete.

> **NOTE** When your iPhone has Internet access, you can stream and listen to any songs stored in your iCloud account but not currently stored on your iPhone, without first downloading that content to the smartphone. These songs (or albums) have an iCloud icon to the right of their listings.

MAKE WORKOUTS FUN USING PLAYLISTS AND THE MUSIC APP

You use playlists with the Music app to create a custom selection of songs. If you're an Apple Music subscriber, you have access to a host of professionally curated playlists and the ability to create them using any music that's part of the iTunes Store music collection. However, if you're not an Apple Music subscriber, the music that you can add to playlists is limited to music stored on your iPhone (or the mobile device or computer).

> **NOTE** Using the Music app, you can create or access an unlimited number of playlists, so you can have separate playlists for different types of workouts or activities, for example. Each playlist becomes quickly accessible via the Music app on your iPhone, iPad, and/or Apple Watch, when you use the iTunes software on your Mac or PC.

Even though you must create playlists with the Music app, many specialized fitness-related apps enable you to access and play back your pre-created playlists, as well as songs stored on your iPhone directly from that app, without your needing to launch the Music app separately, or even access the Control Center.

Thanks to iCloud, when you create a playlist on your computer, for example, it almost instantly syncs between your iPhone and all other computers and iOS mobile devices that are linked to your iCloud account, so all of your playlists are always accessible when and where you want them.

Furthermore, if you're an Apple Music subscriber, an ever-changing and growing selection of curated playlists is accessible to you via the Music app.

> **TIP** Playing a playlist comprised of music stored on your iPhone requires no Internet connection. However, streaming music from your iCloud account or via the Apple Music service requires a continuous Internet connection.

CREATE A PLAYLIST USING THE IOS 8.4 (OR LATER) VERSION OF THE MUSIC APP

If you're using the iOS 8.4 (or later) version of the Music app, follow these steps to create and save a custom playlist using the Music app on your iPhone:

1. Launch the Music app on your iPhone.

2. Tap on the My Music icon in the bottom-right corner of the screen.

3. Tap on the Playlists tab near the top center of the screen (see Figure 13.18).

FIGURE 13.18

Tap on the Playlists tab at the top of the My Music screen to create, manage, or play a playlist stored in the Music app.

4. To the right of the All Playlists option, tap on the New option.

5. Using the iPhone's virtual keyboard, enter a custom title for the playlist, such as **Workout Music** (see Figure 13.19).

6. In the Add Description field, type a short description of the playlist. For example, type **Music to listen to at the gym**.

7. Tap on the Photo icon to import any image that you want to associate with that playlist. You can either take a photo using the iPhone's camera, or select a photo that's already stored on the iPhone.

FIGURE 13.19

Fill in the Add Title and Add Description fields, and select an optional photo or graphic for your playlist.

8. Tap on the Add Songs option.

9. From the Add Music screen, choose an option based on how you want your music selections displayed. Options include Artists, Albums, Songs, and so on (see Figure 13.20).

10. If you select Songs, for example, all the songs currently stored on your iPhone, or that are accessible via your iCloud account, will display in alphabetical order (see Figure 13.21). Each song has an Add icon to the right of its listing. Tap on this plus sign–shaped Add icon to add the song to your playlist.

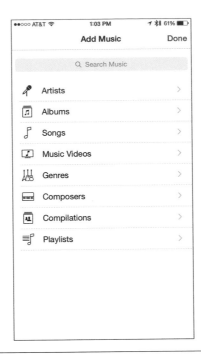

FIGURE 13.20
Select how you want the music stored on your iPhone to display.

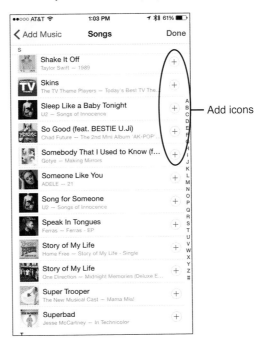

FIGURE 13.21
Tap on the Add icon for each song you want to add to your playlist.

> **NOTE** If you select Artists or Albums, for example, then after tapping on the Add Music option, a list of artists whose music you have stored on your iPhone or a list of albums (or partial albums) appears. Tap on a listing to view individual song titles, and then tap on the Add icon for each song you want to add.

11. Tap on the Done option when you've finished compiling the list of songs you want to add to your playlist.

12. A summary screen for your playlist appears (see Figure 13.22). To the right of each song listing you will see a Move icon. Place your finger on any of these icons, and then drag it up or down to rearrange the order of the songs.

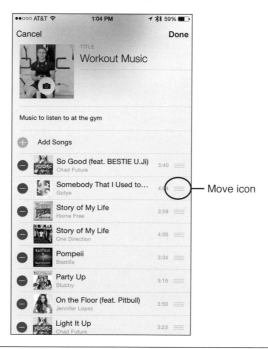

FIGURE 13.22

After the list of songs for a playlist has been compiled, use the Move icon for any song to move it around and change the order of the playlist.

13. Tap on the Done option to save your newly created playlist.

14. The new playlist appears below the All Playlists heading any time you tap on the My Music icon, and then tap the Playlists tab (see Figure 13.23).

FIGURE 13.23
Access or manage a playlist by tapping on its listing below the All Playlists heading.

15. Tap on the playlist listing under the All Playlists heading to access that playlist.

16. Tap on any song listing in the playlist to play it.

> ☑ **TIP**   To edit the contents of a playlist from the playlist screen while a playlist is playing, tap on the Edit option. Alternatively, while a song from a playlist is playing, access the Now Playing screen, and then tap on the More icon to remove the currently playing song from the currently selected playlist.
>
> To delete a playlist, tap on the My Music icon, tap the Playlists tab, and then tap on the More icon for the playlist title below the All Playlists option. From the More menu, tap on the Delete option, and then when prompted, confirm your decision by tapping on the Delete Playlist button.

TIP Regardless of what you're doing on your iPhone, you can play a playlist, or any song, by activating Siri and issuing a command like, "Play [*insert playlist title*] playlist." You can also ask Siri to play a particular song, or music from a specific artist, for example.

CREATE A PLAYLIST USING THE IOS 8.4 (OR OLDER) VERSION OF THE MUSIC APP

If you have not yet upgraded to iOS 8.4 (or iOS 9), follow these steps to create and save a custom playlist using the Music app on your iPhone:

1. Launch the Music app on your iPhone.

2. Tap on the Playlists option at the bottom of the screen.

3. Tap on the New Playlist (+) option. You might need to place your finger near the center of the screen and swipe down to display this option (see Figure 13.24).

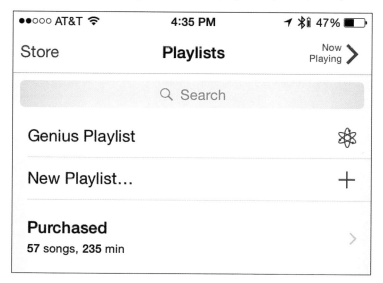

FIGURE 13.24

Tap on the New Playlist option to create a playlist from scratch.

4. From the New Playlist pop-up box, enter a custom title for the playlist you want to create (see Figure 13.25). For example, a playlist name might be, "Workout Music," "Running Music," "Aerobics Music," or "Meditation Music." Tap on the Save button to continue.

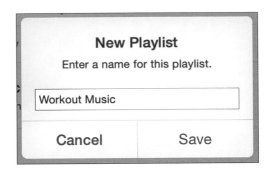

FIGURE 13.25

Create a custom and descriptive name for your playlist.

5. Under the Playlists screen in the Music app, your newly created playlist appears, but it contains no songs. Tap on the Done option (in the top-right corner of the screen) to continue.

6. From the Playlists screen, the message, "Add songs to "[*insert Playlist name*]"" appears at the top of the screen. Tap on the Songs icon at the bottom of the screen.

7. From the Songs screen (see Figure 13.26), one at a time, tap on the Add (+) icon for each song listing for the songs you want to add to that playlist. You can add as many songs to the playlist as you want. Tap on the Done option when you've added all the desired songs.

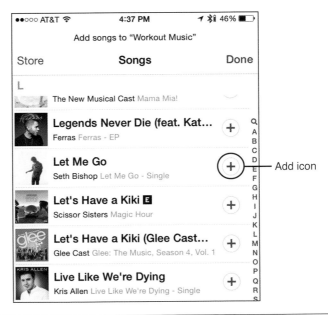

FIGURE 13.26

One at a time, select songs to include in your playlist by tapping on the Add (+) icon for each desired song listing.

8. The playlist title, along with the selected songs for that playlist, appears next. The order in which you selected the songs is the order in which they appear in the playlist, and in which they're ultimately played.

> **TIP** To manually rearrange the order of the songs in a playlist, from the Playlist's screen in the Music app, tap on the Edit option. Place your finger on the Move icon for a song listing, and then drag it up or down. Repeat this with various songs until the order of the displayed songs is to your liking, then tap on Done.
>
> To delete a song from the playlist, tap on the minus sign icon to the left of a song.

9. The playlist is now ready for your enjoyment (see Figure 13.27). Tap on the first song listed in the playlist to play it. Tap on the Shuffle option to randomly play the songs from the selected playlist.

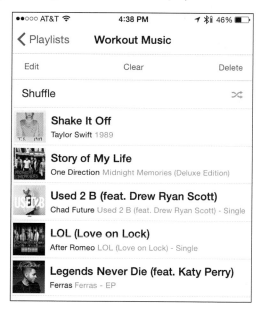

FIGURE 13.27
Once created, tap on any song in the playlist to play it.

10. After a playlist begins playing, exit out of the Music app, and that playlist will continue playing.

> **✓ TIP** To learn more about using iOS 9 on your iPhone, be sure to pick up a copy of *iPad and iPhone Tips and Tricks: 5th Edition* (Que) by Jason R. Rich, available in late 2015.

CONTROL THE MUSIC APP USING THE IPHONE'S CONTROL CENTER

After music is playing via the Music app, you can control the playback of that music in several ways. For example, many headphones and earbuds, including those packaged with your iPhone, have controller buttons that replicate the Rewind, Pause/Play, and Fast Forward buttons you see in the Music app (as well as the volume control slider).

However, regardless of what you're doing on your iPhone, you can control music playing using the Music app controls that appear in the Control Center. To access the Control Center, place your finger near the bottom of the iPhone's screen and swipe up.

In the Control Center (see Figure 13.28), the Music app controls include a time slider, details about the song that's playing, the Rewind, Play/Pause, and Fast Forward icons, and a volume slider. If you're listening to iTunes Radio, the Rewind icon is replaced by the star-shaped icon for liking the currently playing music.

FIGURE 13.28

You can access the Control Center regardless of what app is running on your iPhone. From settings, you can also grant permission to access the Control Center directly from the Lock screen.

CUSTOMIZE THE ITUNES STORE AND MUSIC APPS ON YOUR IPHONE

To customize some of the functions and features for the iTunes Store and Music apps, launch Settings on your iPhone, and from the main Settings menu, scroll down to either the iTunes & App Store option, or Music option, and tap it. After adjusting the relevant settings, go back and tap on the other menu option.

When you tap on the iTunes & App Store option, under the Show All heading, turn on the option to see all music you own, regardless of whether that music is currently stored on your iPhone. When this switch is turned off, only music that's actually stored on the smartphone (not that is accessible from your iCloud account) appears.

Under the Automatic Downloads option, turn on the Music option if you want songs you purchase on other computers or mobile devices that are linked to the same iCloud account as your iPhone to automatically download to your iPhone. If this feature is turned off, you always have the option of manually downloading that music.

> ☑ **TIP** If you have a pre-set cellular data monthly usage allocation, turn off Use Cellular Data option. This prevents your phone from using iTunes Radio or automatically downloading content from the iTunes Store using a cellular (3G/4G/LTE) connection, which quickly uses up your monthly data allocation. These features work fine, however, any time your iPhone has a Wi-Fi connection.

Tap on the Music option and turn on/off each customizable option, or when applicable, tap on the option to select options from a submenu.

USE THE MUSIC APP ON YOUR APPLE WATCH

If you're an Apple Watch user, you already know that until late 2015, any Apple Watch app must also have an iPhone component to it. This is true for the Music app, which also comes preinstalled on the Apple Watch.

To launch the Music app from the Apple Watch, press the Digital Crown once to reveal the watch's Home screen, and then tap on the Music app icon to launch the app (see Figure 13.29).

Music app icon

FIGURE 13.29

From the Apple Watch's Home screen, tap on the Music app icon to launch the app.

The main menu of the Music app on the Apple Watch includes buttons for Now Playing, Artists, Albums, Songs, and Playlist (shown in Figure 13.30). Tap on the Now Playing button to remotely control the music originating from the iPhone. Use the music control icons on the watch to remotely control the music being played (shown in Figure 13.31).

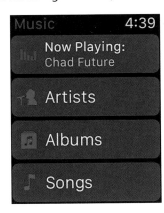

FIGURE 13.30

Just like on the iPhone, the Apple Watch can sort your music by Artists, Albums, Songs, etc.

FIGURE 13.31

Remotely control the music playing via the Music app running on the iPhone from the Apple Watch.

These music controls include a Rewind, Pause/Play, and Fast Forward icon, along with a volume slider and details about the song currently being played.

> **TIP** Tap on the Artist, Albums, or Songs button to view an alphabetical listing of songs stored on your iPhone, sorted by artist name, album title, or song title, respectively.
>
> To access a list of the playlists you've created using the Music app on your iPhone, and remotely play a playlist, tap on the Playlist button, tap on the listing for one of your saved playlists, and then tap on a song listing to play that playlist. Then, tap on a song to view the music control icons.

STREAM MUSIC VIA THE INTERNET

iTunes Radio offers a free music streaming service that's operated by Apple. This service does not allow you to create custom playlists, but it does allow you to create custom iTunes Radio Stations that will play music that the service believes you'll enjoy.

By subscribing to the new Apple Music service (see "Discover the Apple Music Service," earlier in this chapter), you can create and stream any music you want: either individual songs, entire albums, or custom playlists, pulling from almost any music the iTunes Store offers. (Some artists and bands have opted to keep Apple from streaming their music via Apple Music or iTunes Radio, even when it is available for purchase from the iTunes Store.)

You can also enjoy many other free and subscription-based streaming music services from your iPhone (and often control from your Apple Watch). To use one of these services, like Pandora, GooglePlay, Last.fm, Amazon Cloud Player, or Spotify, for example, you'll need to download and install the iPhone app for that service, set up an account, and if applicable, pay for a subscription.

In addition, virtually every radio network and local radio station in the world, as well as Sirius/XM Satellite Radio, now have proprietary apps that enable you to stream live programming from the Internet directly to your iPhone. An AM, FM, or satellite radio receiver is not required, but a continuous Internet connection for your iPhone is needed.

TIP   The free iHeartRadio app, for example, allows you to stream live radio (music) programming from many of the most popular radio stations in the United States. You can also create customized radio stations, based on your favorite music genre, artist, or favorite song(s) using this app.

Meanwhile, some streaming music services, like Spotify, offer pre-created playlists designed to be listened to while engaged in fitness-oriented activities. It's also possible to share playlists with other Spotify users, or receive music recommendations based on your personal tastes. In addition, Spotify has a dynamic playlist feature for fitness that adjusts its playlists based on the intensity of your activity.

Index

V

W

Y-Z

Other Books
YOU MIGHT LIKE!

ISBN: 9780789753553

ISBN: 978078975312X

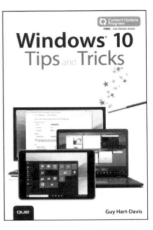

ISBN: 9780789755653

SAVE 35%
Use discount code **APPLE**

Visit **quepublishing.com**
to learn more!

ALWAYS LEARNING   PEARSON

More Best-Selling **My** Books!

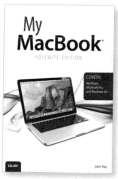

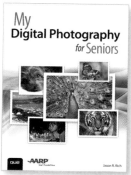

Learning to use your smartphone, tablet, camera, game, or software has never been easier with the full-color My Series. You'll find simple, step-by-step instructions from our team of experienced authors. The organized, task-based format allows you to quickly and easily find exactly what you want to achieve.

Visit quepublishing.com/mybooks to learn more.